An Introduction to Journalism

An Introduction to Journalism

A Survey of the Fourth Estate in All Its Forms

Second Edition

F. Fraser Bond, *Professor Emeritus*
Department of Journalism
New York University

The Macmillan Company   New York

To John Richard Nichols

Other Books by **F. Fraser Bond**

Mr. Miller of "The Times"
Breaking into Print
Give Yourself Background
You Can Write
How to Write and Sell Nonfiction

Preface

The aim of this book is to serve as an introduction, at once comprehensive and compact, to the whole field of contemporary American journalism. Accordingly, it takes account of all those agencies through which news and views, either separately or hand in hand, reach the general public—our present-day vast system of mass communication.

When a book comes out in a new and revised edition, two questions inevitably spring to mind: "What's new?" and "What's revised?" In the case of *An Introduction to Journalism*, second edition, the whole emphasis is new. Where formerly first attention went to the print media, the present edition is now geared to meet the needs of students of mass communications generally. Because of the growing importance of industrial and business journalism, not only in its own right but as a field for student employment, a new chapter on this subject has been added. Where formerly advertising and public relations shared attention under a joint heading, each now has a new and separate chapter.

And as for revision? So many technical developments have come to the scene in the past few years relating to the mass media that practically every chapter has had to be at least partially rewritten. Some examples of the widespread effects of new technology are: the impact of television and radio on sports writing, the growing development and increasing use of "run of press" color in news pictures, and the use of videotape on TV news shows, miraculously to diminish the time lag between the news happening and its pictorial representation.

In preparing this text for the use of students in general beginning courses the author has used his own experience in teaching such courses at Columbia University and at New York University as a guide in shaping the content of each chapter. This volume differs somewhat from earlier surveys in both organization and range, and has been written to serve as a textbook either for a whole year's course or for the work of one intensive term.

F. Fraser Bond

vii

Acknowledgment

The author is deeply indebted to the authors, editors, publishers, news services, and other agencies for the kind and ready assistance given him in the preparation of this book.

He particularly wishes to thank the McGraw-Hill Book Company for permitting him to incorporate some material from a former textbook, *Breaking Into Print*, which is now out of print; *Fortune* Magazine for the use of its exposition of printing processes; Joseph G. Herzberg and Holt, Rinehart, and Winston, Inc., for permitting the inclusion of several quotations from *Late City Edition*; Merton T. Akers, United Press Associations, for the use of his bulletin on copyreading; and Prentice-Hall, Inc., for permission to quote from *Effective Public Relations* 2nd edition, by Scott M. Cutlip and Allen H. Center.

The author is grateful to *Editor and Publisher*, the Associated Press, the New York *Herald Tribune* and the New York *Daily News* not only for the fine photographic illustrations but for the time, interest, and courtesy expended in their selection.

He wishes also sincerely to thank the following individuals, agencies, and publications for permitting him to use the material for which they hold the copyright: Dean Kenneth G. Bartlett, Syracuse University; Dean Wilbur Schramm, University of Illinois; former Governor Charles A. Sprague of the *Oregon Statesman*, and Mr. Westbrook Pegler, Messrs. Schwab & Beatty, Incorporated, The Associated Press, United Press International, Advertising Research Foundation, Inc., *The Atlantic Monthly*, *The American Mercury*, the *Saturday Review*, *The Writer*, *Journalism Quarterly*, *The Quill*, *Industrial Marketing*, and the New York *Times*, the New York *Herald Tribune*, the New York *World-Telegram and Sun* the Milwaukee *Journal*, the Richmond *Times-Dispatch*, the Charlotte *Observer*, the Louisville *Courier Journal* and the Des Moines *Register*.

Contents

An Introduction to Journalism

1
The Nature of Journalism

Journalism Defined—The Duties of Journalism—Its Purposes—
Criticisms of Journalism—Consumers of Journalism—Journalism
and Literature—Journalism as a Career

Today the term *journalism* embraces all the forms in which and through which the news and the comments on the news reach the public. All that happens in the world, if such happenings hold interest for the public, and all the thought, action, and ideas which these happenings stimulate become the basic material for the journalist.

Definitions differ as the point of view differs which shapes them. To the cynic journalism is merely a trade; to the idealist it shines as a responsibility and a privilege.

Said Leslie Stephens: "Journalism consists of writing for pay on matters of which you are ignorant."

Says Eric Hodgins of *Time* magazine: "Journalism is the conveying of information from here to there with accuracy, insight and dispatch, and in such a manner that the truth is served, and the rightness of things is made slowly, even if not immediately, more evident."

Both concepts of journalism flourish under guarantees of freedom, whether such guarantees are deserved or not. The one philosophy holds: "Give the public what it wants," the other: "Give the public the truth it must have."

This freedom which journalism in all its forms now enjoys has been painfully won. In the early days, Authority, both civil and ecclesiastical, had a way of

1

clamping down on all announcements of fact and opinion which did not coincide with Authority's wishes, for Authority feared the biblical pronouncement: "The truth shall make you free."

Where men cannot without fear convey their thoughts to one another, no other liberty is secure. That is why the First Amendment to the Constitution of the United States states that "Congress shall make no law . . . abridging the freedom . . . of the press," and that is why the constitution of every American state contains a similar or more elaborate statement. That is why the United Nations has established a Freedom of Information Subcommission to its Commission on Human Rights.

A free press must be free from any compulsions, governmental or social. As Milton pointed out in his great plea for freedom to publish, it is impossible to determine whose judgment shall decide what is good and worthy for the public to read. Only public support can be accepted as a safe criterion; the unworthy publications will find few readers who derive benefit from them and will soon cease to exist.

Freedom of speech and of the press are not ends in themselves. They merely enable people to express freely their thoughts on events so as to bring forth the best possible decision out of all shades of opinion—it is not merely "freedom from" but "freedom for." A person may cause evil not only by his actions but by his inactions. As Andrew Hamilton said back in 1735 at the trial of the printer and publisher, Peter Zenger, ". . . I beg leave to lay it down as a rule that the *suppression* of evidence ought to be taken for the *strongest* evidence."

The battle for freedom of thought and expression knows no armistice; the fight to safeguard it is a continuing warfare so long as forces opposed to such freedom exist in the world. No editor, no commentator, no author can accept freedom of expression with complacency. Practically all countries now entangled in the web of controlled information were once free from it and had the feeling, "It can't happen here."

Even war does not abolish the freedom of the press; it merely restricts it. When a nation's security is at stake, the general safety demands the suspension of some civil liberties and the curbing of others.

In wartime, this freedom does not protect the right to publish material that would undermine the public morale, encourage men to refuse to fight or give information to the enemy.

In peacetime and in wartime there are, of course, some freedoms which the press has never had—the freedom, for example, to be libelous or obscene.

The Duties of Journalism

Accepting as it does the guarantees of freedom, journalism accepts also the obligation to deserve them. Self-respecting journalism in all its forms strives constantly to meet this obligation—to fulfill its duties to society.

The press must be independent. To be independent it must stand on its own feet, earning a profit without subsidies. It cannot serve the public which supports it if it is a tail to anyone's kite.

John Thadeus Delane, the great editor of *The Times* of London from 1841 to 1877, eloquently set forth this principle in the following words:

To perform its duties with entire independence and consequently with the utmost public advantage, the press can enter into no close or binding alliance with the statesmen of the day, nor can it surrender its permanent interest to the convenience of the ephemeral power of any government. The first duty of the press is to obtain the earliest and most correct intelligence of the events of the time, and instantly by disclosing them, to make them the common property of the nation. *The press lives by disclosures.* Whatever passes into its keeping becomes a part of the knowledge and history of our time. The duty of the press is to speak; of the statesmen to be silent. Governments must treat other governments with external respect, however black their origin or foul their deeds; but happily the press is under no such trammels. . . .

The duty of the journalist is the same as that of the historian—to seek out truth, above all things, and to present to his readers not such things as statecraft would wish them to know, but the truth as near as he can attain it.

The press must be fair. Most individuals regard fairness as a virtue which they strive to achieve. Journalism sets fairness up as an ideal. The better writers and the better papers seek to avoid deliberate and intentional partiality. It is now a widespread practice to permit opposing sides to state their own cases. The ideal of fairness is achieved by journalism which avoids error, bias, prejudice and false color.

The glory of democracy, as many working journalists have pointed out, is that it is the one type of government which provides for the continuing rights of a minority not in power. Fair journalism is peculiarly the medium for the expression of these minorities because it is not under government control.

The press must be accurate. The effort for impartial accuracy is one of the measures of journalistic character, whatever the medium. To broadcast true and objective fact shines as the ideal in journalistic attainment. Of course, the accuracy of the daily press has a time element, as the late Louis Wiley, former business manager of the New York *Times*, once pointed out:

The news editor prints the most reliable story he can obtain of the event, bearing in mind that the presses must be running at a certain time, and that the witnesses who give the reporters the alleged facts are just human after all. If the newspaper were to wait until the final truth had been ascertained, the world might still be in ignorance of historical events of centuries past, for historians have not yet been able to agree on what was the precise truth.

The press must be honest. Good character is not easily acquired or maintained without a daily struggle. No business is subjected to such a multiplicity of changing contacts with the public, such shifting problems calling for immediate decisions as journalism. But the simple elements of character in journalistic media remain fixed. They are honesty in news and advertising.

The press must be responsible. As Grove Patterson of the Toledo *Blade* has observed, "a free press is vastly more than a meal ticket for publishers." It enjoys this freedom because it is a semi-public institution. As such the press owes a duty to the community which it serves and which supports it. Disposing in his will of the San Francisco *Chronicle* which he founded, M. H. DeYoung said: "A great newspaper should be concerned with the accomplishment of great ends for the benefit of the public, rather than be designed simply and solely as a gainer of money for the benefit of the stockholders of the corporation." With that declaration he created a trust, directing that his paper continue as during his lifetime "without being influenced, hampered, or controlled by any hostile interest, in carrying out its work for the benefit of the city of San Francisco and the state of California."

The press must be decent. The duty to be decent concerns not only decency in the language and pictures which journalism uses, for the law sees to that, but in the way it goes about obtaining its news. As critics of newspapers have pointed out, there are situations occurring in human life into which no newspaper can decently justify intrusion. The better journalists impose upon their work as they impose upon themselves the censorship of good taste.

The Purposes of Journalism

Journalism has four main reasons for being: to inform, to interpret, to guide, to entertain. It performs other important functions, such as the circulation of advertising and the dissemination of a vast mass of information and comment that hardly come under the general concept of news.

To broadcast news is the first concern of journalism. As the American Society of Newspaper Editors has put it: "It is the primary function of newspapers to communicate to the human race what its members do, feel, and think."

It is for this, the news function, that journalism enjoys the protection of the federal and state constitutions. Society extends protection because of the responsibility of the press for communicating the news. As James Russel Wiggins, former editor of the St. Paul *Pioneer Press* and St. Paul *Dispatch* and later managing editor of the Washington *Post*, has pointed out:

These rights and privileges are warranted because civilization as we understand it could not exist if there were no facilities for the dissemination of news. Without the news, individuals in society would lack that sense of identity but for which the creation of formal and informal law are not possible. . . .

Newspapers that do not acknowledge the public importance of the news are engaged in a trade where printed words take the place of prunes.

H. G. Wells once said the Roman Empire could not endure because there were no newspapers—no methods of apprising the outlying peoples of the behavior of the center.

Today, journalism's first purpose and responsibility is to make certain the people shall know. This responsibility calls for complete objectivity in the news.

The need for interpreting and explaining the news in our day and age is readily apparent. Life has become so complex and its interests so manifold that even the specialists become baffled in their own fields of knowledge. The ordinary mortal caught in a maze of economics, science or invention needs to be led by the hand through its intricacies. Accordingly, present-day journalism sees to it that, along with its announcement of a fact, event, or theory, the reader or listener also gets explanation, background material, interpretation, and diagrams. These are all aimed at helping an individual to achieve a better understanding of the significance of what he reads or hears. In line with the growing trend toward specialization, the best journalism employs men and women who have an adequate background of knowledge in their particular fields to provide the average person with these explanations. A great part of today's journalistic writing takes the form of this useful and often able exposition.

From earliest days journalism has sought to influence mankind. Journalism endeavors to sway the minds of men through the printed word, cartoons, and pictures as they appear in newspapers, magazines, pamphlets, and books and through the spoken word over the air. To these ends it uses all the nuances of argument and all the devices of propaganda. News is "the raw material of opinion," and opinion may be indicated without a word of comment being uttered—by the way in which the news itself is announced, either prominently or inconspicuously. Avowedly the newspaper strives to influence its readers through its articles of opinion, its editorials, its cartoons, its signed "columns." Avowedly the radio seeks to influence through its commentators, interviews, and many speakers who advocate varying points of views, and television impresses its viewers and listeners through its panels and documentaries and its interviews.

Side by side with its more serious roles as a purveyor of information, interpreter, and molder of opinion, journalism puts increasing emphasis on its function as an entertainer. This aspect has historical precedent. The troubadour of old, who brought tidings from castle keep to castle keep, was welcomed not only for the news he gave of the seigneur on the next hill, but for his ability to sing, dance and play the lute.

The newspaper and the magazine appeal to the fun-loving public by playing up the amusing aspects of everyday life in "human interest" stories, by printing humorous anecdotes and stories and by finding space for an increasing array of entertainment features which include such popular favorites as "cute sayings of children," crossword puzzles, and comic strips. Journalism over the radio and on the screen has its comedians and its comedy shows, its "quiz programs" and its funny stories.

Criticisms of Journalism

Journalism, in the opinion of many, sometimes falls short of the prize of its high calling. Critics of journalism in all its forms abound and have abounded through the centuries. They range from the man in the street to members of the craft itself. Indeed, many of journalism's severest critics have been its closest friends. The wise editor never ignores a criticism. Because the newspaper is among the oldest and most popular forms of journalism, most of the adverse comments are aimed against the press, but radio, television, book publishing, and filmdom frequently make vulnerable targets too.

Here are some of the chief accusations:

   1. That the press is inaccurate. This criticism is summed up

in the phrase, "You can't believe what you see in the papers." This damning statement may refer either to the publication of "fake news," to deliberate misstatement, or to unintentional error. Fake news covers stories like the famous "Moon Hoax" which the New York *Sun* perpetrated in 1835 when it published a series of pseudo-scientific articles purporting to relate the astronomical discoveries of Sir John Herschel at the Cape of Good Hope. They told of the construction of a giant telescope and of the details of the lunar geography which its lenses disclosed, and finally of the actual existence of life on the moon—*vespertillio homo* or men bats—and of their odd behavior "which would ill comport with our terrestrial notions of decorum." Actually these stories had no basis in fact but were the imaginative creation of a *Sun* reporter, one Richard Adams Locke. Fake news also covers stories like the rumors of the Market Rigger, whose business it is to cause prices in Wall Street to rise and fall suddenly in order that he or his associates may profit, and the fabrications of the professional propagandist. The phrase "deliberate misstatement" defines itself. Unintentional errors are a professional hazard and each day across the country the press exhibits a considerable list of common offenders. These errors occur in copy, heads, and advertisements and are roughly divisible into four groups: errors of ambiguity, errors of make-up, errors of typography, and miscellaneous errors, the last being mainly reportorial.

2. **That the ownership of newspapers, radio and television stations, and motion picture studios is too limited and is shrinking; that this state of affairs may enslave our freedom of expression.** This criticism cites such facts as these: ten states have no cities with competing daily papers; only 117 cities have competing dailies (in Canada only ten); fourteen companies with eighteen papers control a quarter of our daily circulation. The reader can list many reasons to show how a monopolistic situation hampers journalism.

3. **That the press gives too much space to crime.** Newspapers are probably more often reproached for reporting crime news too fully than for reporting it inadequately. It has been contended that crime news increases crime by inviting imitation; that it injures

innocent relatives of law violators; that it offends good taste. Fair critics admit, however, that news of crime holds interest for all classes of readers, and that it frequently aids in the apprehension of criminals. Contrary to popular theory, crime news averages less than 3 per cent of the news content of leading serious papers.

4. That the press too often publishes the trivial for the sake of sensation, to the neglect of the significant. It is true that some newspapers devote a disproportionate amount of space to ephemeral items. It is true that some magazines, books, motion pictures, and radio and television shows similarly exploit the trivial. It is possible, however, for intelligent and thoughtful people in most cities to buy a newspaper, a magazine, and a book of real value, to patronize a worth-while film, and to tune in a radio or television program of some merit.

5. That the press too often publishes only the surface of events, neglecting to dig underneath for causes. Because of this, some critics contend, the people do not get the information which they need regarding social, economic, and political conditions to enable them to vote intelligently. In too many instances this criticism is fully justified. However, the better journalism in newspapers, magazines, and on the air aims not only to report but to interpret. In this way journalism aims to provide the public with the perspective necessary to place facts in their relative sequence in time and in importance.

6. That certain journals and journalists manipulate the news to serve their own ends. On this point, Grove Patterson, delivering the eighteenth Don R. Mellett Memorial Address, had this to say:

There is no crime committed in the field of journalism, not even super-lurid sensationalism, not even general inaccuracy, that is more subversive of the principle of the free press, more indefensible, than the crime of slanting the news to meet a publisher's policy. . . . The departure from objective writing in the news columns not only makes a tragic mockery of a free press, but creates a vicious weapon in the hands of journalistic gangsters.

7. That the press is sentimental. All journalistic media—the press, the movies, the radio, and television—share in varying degrees in this condemnation. Their common vice, according to the late Sir Willmott Lewis, is sentimentalism, "which is to sentiment what religiosity is to religion or legalism is to law." Sentimentalism, according to Leslie Stephens, "is emotion for its own sake."

8. That the press is averse to publishing facts which seem not to be in agreement with expressed editorial opinions. This practice is not today characteristic of the reputable press, though it may have been so sometimes in the past. At present no fair-minded or intelligent newspaper would think of excluding from its columns views which did not agree with its own. On the contrary, all views are welcomed as part of the public discussion which ought to be encouraged. As the New York *Times* remarked editorially:

Newspapers are not at all disturbed or fretted by the opinions of people who differ from them. If the critics are responsible and have anything to say worthwhile, they are given the privileges of print, in pursuance of the duty of an honest newspaper to print all the relevant facts for which it can find room.

9. That the press publishes "defamatory" statements, made under Congressional immunity, without additional information to aid readers in evaluating the charges. Constructive critics of the press, such as Professor Zechariah Chafee, Jr., formerly of the Harvard Law School, have decried the constant repetition of defamatory statements about American citizens by newspapers which suspect with good reason that these statements are largely untrue. Facts, Professor Chafee contends, should be given meaning by newspapers:

Sometimes a fact is accurately printed and yet it leaves an altogether incorrect impression on the reader unless its significance is evaluated at the time it is printed.

The Consumers of Journalism

Journalism, through the printed page, on the screen, and over the air, reaches a vast multitude, and this mutitude gains in numbers yearly as popular education brings the illiterate minority into the ranks of the semiliterate majority. The writer and commentator knows that his audience comprises what the prayer book describes as "all sorts and conditions of men." He knows that what he writes or says reaches that limited group which Arnold Toynbee calls the "creative minority"—the minority of the public that is fully informed, capable of understanding, able to divorce fact from opinion, and ready to debate issues; and the writer knows also that what he writes or says reaches that vast population which has little knowledge and no true conception of government or the lessons of history, a population which fails to differentiate between news and opinion and lets itself be swayed by pressure groups, demagogues, and propagandists.

While surveys are seldom definitive, they have a real value as indicators in a general sense. Here is an approximate breakdown of the American reading public. Discounting overlappings, it can be assumed that some fifty-five million Americans buy daily and weekly newspapers; forty million buy magazines; thirty million read books drawn from the public libraries; between three and four million rent their books, and some five hundred thousand to a million buy them.

This public consists of the small minority of discriminating readers whose taste is already established, plus the vast number whose appetite for reading has been whetted by elementary education but whose taste is still untrained.

As education spreads, public taste improves, and the writer of today can look toward the future with optimism, confident that his audience will be far bigger and of far higher caliber. He finds his optimism strengthened by a report such as that made by Francis Cornell of the United States Office of Education in the *Authors' League Bulletin*. Mr. Cornell breaks down the kind of reading people are willing to do into "very difficult" or graduate level (which he defines as the *Scientific Monthly* type of audience), "difficult" (*Yale Review*), "fairly difficult" or high-school level (*Harper's*), "average" or junior high school (*Reader's Digest*), "fairly easy" or seventh grade (*Liberty*) and "easy" or sixth grade level (*True Story*). By 1960, says Dr. Cornell, the *Scientific Monthly* level of audience will have more than doubled, to perhaps an eighth of the adult population; the *Yale Review* will seem easy enough reading to 25 per cent of us; *Harper's* will be perfectly understandable to more than half of us.

Arrived at 1960, Wilbur E. Elston of the *Minneapolis Star & Tribune* would seem to bear out the earlier forecast when he wrote:

Newspapers will have to publish more news of interest to educated people simply because a larger share of the population will be well-educated. There will have to be greater emphasis on national and international news of a serious nature simply because our shrinking world makes foreign news into local news.

Journalism and Literature

No clear line of demarcation exists between what we call literature and what we call journalism. The general reader finds himself puzzled as to which is which. He encounters the work of leading contemporary writers in his newspapers and in his magazines and calls it journalism; some months later he finds the same material encased between the covers of books and calls it literature. Nor do definitions help him much. "Literature," said George Santayana, "consists of turning events into ideas." The better newspaper and the better magazine contributors all try to follow this line. The whimsical James M. Barrie decided that journalism was that form of writing which honors a man after he has given it up. He had in mind the vast army of literary men who started as writers for periodicals and then turned to "literature." We make no distinction with regard to manner and style. Sometimes the best writing of an age is done for newspapers and magazines. We can make little distinction with regard to matter although it seems clear that there is a plain difference between newspaper articles and literary, historical, and philosophical writings. The basic difference would seem to point toward the writer's *purpose*. The author expresses his own thoughts and experiences; the journalist expresses those of the community. Literature can be timeless; journalism must be timely.

The roster of good newspapermen who have helped to make good literature is a long one. The list in England of the last two centuries is impressive. It begins with Daniel Defoe, Joseph Addison, Richard Steele, and Jonathan Swift. It takes in Charles Dickens and William Makepeace Thackeray. It includes Rudyard Kipling, James M. Barrie, Arnold Bennett, John Galsworthy, G. K. Chesterton, St. John Ervine, H. G. Wells, George Bernard Shaw, and Rebecca West.

In the United States a parallel list can well begin with Alexander Hamilton and take in such names as William Cullen Bryant, Harriet Beecher Stowe, Mark Twain, Eugene Field and modern writers like Ernest Hemingway and John Steinbeck.

From these partial lists it should become immediately apparent what the practice of regular journalism may do toward endowing literature with the highly desirable stylistic qualities of clarity and "punch."

With the English it is far less the custom than with Americans to abandon journalism in order to devote oneself to literature. Even when they have created good literature and made good money, English authors do not abandon journalism. Commenting on this fact, the late Simeon Strunsky once suggested that "it would be an excellent thing for American literature, on its formal side at least, if authors were sent back for a thorough post-graduate course under a good copy desk and city editor. There would be a good deal less of the 'beautiful' writing for which our admiration is so continually being invited."

Careers in Journalism

Journalism as a lifework makes a strong appeal to a wide variety of people possessed of a wide variety of talents. Today, with the whole system of mass communications expanding rapidly, journalism can make use of this diversity of persons and this diversity of skills, for in its comprehensiveness journalism includes not only the fields of the newspaper and the magazine, but those of the trade journal, the house organ, and the specialized review. It covers much of the writing work behind radio and television programs, and it lends its procedures to the allied callings of advertising and public relations.

Journalism shares with the theatre the magnet-like power to

attract many young people who feel they will find their chief reward in the work itself. This fascination results in creating a supply of eager applicants far greater than the demand. For years, because of this situation, the starting pay in both journalism and the theatre was low. Today, thanks to the American Newspaper Guild and to Actors Equity Association, this situation has improved and a fair minimum wage has been established for recruits in both callings.

Apart from any false glamour with which Hollywood and exuberant fiction occasionally seek to endow the craft, journalism does exert a genuine appeal due largely to the interest, variety, and even excitement which many phases of the work offer. However, the eager neophyte must bear in mind that keen competition for the best jobs is always the rule, and also that the great majority of men and women in journalisic fields are still overworked and underpaid when compared to workers in other professions and in business. Even so, these workers know in their hearts that journalism is the career for them, and they frequently feel that they have rewards beyond mere money in the satisfaction and stimulation which they find in their jobs and in the opportunities which their work often gives to help along a good cause or in some other way to bring lasting benefit to their community and to their fellow men.

For the benefit of students and others who are considering journalism as a lifework, here is a list of the main fields, with each one considered from the standpoints of the training required, immediate prospects of employment, chances of advancement, financial rewards obtainable, and some hint of the general attitude of the public at large toward the calling.

WORK ON NEWSPAPERS

Training. Both the editorial and business departments of the newspaper have career opportunities for men and women, and each department has its own training requirements. For the editorial or writing end of the paper, employers prefer an applicant equipped with a good educational background. A college degree, while not insisted on, naturally helps here, particularly if the degree implies substantial work in history and economics. Many colleges and universities now give degrees in journalism, and newspaper editors have come to respect this professional training.

Men and women seeking employment on the business end of a paper should have behind them practical experience in business or sound academic training in business and commerce courses which the leading educational institutions across the land now offer.

Immediate prospect. Jobs are always hard to get on the great metropolitan papers. Better chances for employment generally exist on the papers in small towns adjacent to the major cities or on small city dailies. The beginner who starts on a small city paper has the advantage of a wider training through the opportunity such a paper offers him, to try his hand at a variety of assignments. There is a tendency on metropolitan papers to keep a man on the same beat or in the same department in order to make him a specialist in one particular line.

Advancement. Advancement on a paper rewards ability and enterprise. In the business end of journalism such advancement leads to executive positions in the paper's business departments and even further. Publishers and owners of radio and television companies are primarily business men and not journalists and have close contact with the more capable personnel of the business side of their enterprises. Men and women with administrative talent are in line for executive positions. Workers on the editorial side, after a success in the local reporting field, may go to Washington or abroad as correspondents or achieve editorial jobs on the paper itself. Important positions are those of department editors and that of managing editor or editor-in-chief. Popular newspaper writers have joined the well-paid tribe of syndicated columnists. More frequently trained men and women have left the newspaper for the field of public relations.

Financial rewards. Because of the oversupply of individuals eager for newspaper work, beginning pay is traditionally low, but it depends somewhat on the size of the paper giving employment and also on the section of the country in which such employment is obtained.

The existence of the American Newspaper Guild has had its

impact on salaries, duties, and fringe benefits everywhere. The Guild's contract with a metropolitan paper sets starting pay at $86.50 a week. This must be treated largely as a nominal figure, however, for in actual practice very few reporters "start" on metropolitan papers; they come into the field on the strength of experience gained elsewhere. Actually there is no "average." The amount ranges all the way from the *Wall Street Journal's* reported $100 a week for a few young graduates to the country weekly which pays what it feels it can afford. However, like other callings newspaper work rewards success. For top ranking reporters, editors, and correspondents, the pay is high.

Community regard. The public at large realizes the importance of newspapers to society and has had from time to time a high respect for individual editors. Accordingly it regards journalism and journalists favorably, but prestige goes to the individual on the basis of his character and work and the extent of his contribution to the community.

THE MAGAZINE FIELD

Next to the newspaper, the magazine in all its branches and types opens up a wide field of employment and, particularly on its editorial side, offers influential careers to individuals possessed of editorial facility. As with the newspaper, the good magazine editor does not create copy but frequently manages to transfigure it through his critical revisions and suggestions. This editorial faculty is buttressed by sound judgment, but like other faculties is cultivated by experience and training. The magazine field stretches all the way from popular general magazines with circulations in millions; women's magazines; equally prosperous newcomers in the large circulation field such as the news weeklies *Newsweek* and *Time*, the picture weeklies such as *Life* and *Look*, and the widely circulated digests; on into the publications of religious denominations, the specialized technical journals, the thousands of house organs, and the "little" magazines with their somewhat precious literary and artistic standards. All have departments parallel to daily journalism, though the journalistic applicant naturally turns toward the editorial department.

Training. Knowledge of what the public wants to read in terms of what the public is willing to buy is what the successful editor must have. Courses that lead to this knowledge, psychology, history, sociology, and the like all have their part in the editor's background. Along with this knowledge must exist a critical faculty—an awareness of the standards of good prose and of the stimulations to interest which good writing possesses. Work on the editorial end of student publications, campus papers, magazines, and year books occasionally indicates to students that they have a taste for editing and perhaps some ability in that line. Some schools and departments of journalism give special training programs with careers in magazine work as their objective.

The most that these courses can do is to give the student a rather broad and general understanding of the business as a whole, so that he won't be completely lost when he gets his first magazine job. Actually, most magazine editors prefer on-the-job training. Here the new employee must expect to perform many routine jobs at first. Magazine editing and other chores connected with the periodical require very careful work which cannot be learned overnight.

Immediate prospects. Although the cities of the eastern seaboard —Boston, Philadelphia, New York—claim a concentration of magazine output, there is hardly a section of the country without magazine publication. The field holds many opportunities for women who have skills as researchers, editorial assistants, and editors. Women sometimes get a foothold on magazines through first accepting secretarial jobs on a publication. The secretarial type of opening with stenography as its required skill is a valuable one which many applicants, particularly male applicants, frequently overlook.

Present opportunities on magazines are much better than on newspapers or on any other of the communications media, simply because there are so many more magazines. Most of these opportunities lie in the trade magazine field where there always seem to be numerous jobs. These are good from the experience standpoint and provide valuable knowledge that can always be used on a general magazine. The jobs are relatively few as one goes up the scale to the big slick-paper consumer magazines. At all levels of the business jobs are more numerous for women than for men. Women's jobs on the big women's magazines tend to be very good while those on news magazines, for example, are for the most part very routine and "dead end." Jobs on small magazines offer the greatest variety and the most responsibility, though they are not ordinarily well paid.

Advancement. Advancement on magazines is inclined to be much faster than on newspapers because the personnel turnover is greater. Magazine staffs have a high rate of turnover which means less security along with more opportunity. The magazine business is highly competitive, but because of the numerical advantage in jobs and the turnover just mentioned, the chances for advancement are good.

In the growing field of industrial publications there appears to be greater job security than with the consumer magazine group.

Financial rewards. Many magazines have attractive salary scales. Although beginning pay may be relatively low, the rewards for ability are high. A hard working staff writer may make as much as $20,000 a year. Executive jobs pay from $15,000 to over $100,000.

Community regard. There is a great deal of prestige attached to magazine jobs, especially if the magazine is well known. The glamour of working for the *Saturday Evening Post* or *The New Yorker* or any other famous publication is ego-satisfying compensation for the nerve-racking impacts which these highly regarded jobs sometimes make on the general well-being of the persons holding them.

CAREERS IN RADIO AND TELEVISION

Training. Here, as in most phases of journalism, background as well as specialized training is essential. While no employer in this field insists on a college diploma, the rounded education which a college degree implies is all important, and college-trained applicants are preferred. As for specialized training, most network radio news departments adhere to the theory that at least five years of newspaper experience is imperative. Local stations, however, frequently take

journalism students trained in radio courses. In practice, other elements in the applicant's qualifications enter into the picture, and as a general rule perhaps no more than 50 per cent of the radio and TV news personnel have had extensive newspaper experience either on large or on small papers. In fact, many successful radio newsmen now working for the networks obtained their journalistic experience on small-town papers. Anyone who can write for a newspaper can also write for radio and television. In radio, of course, strict attention is given to the sound of the script. Radio men at work move their lips while they type, actually sounding out the verbal expressions which they put down.

Immediate prospects. Broadcasting revenue both in radio and in television comes from the advertisers. Accordingly, the prospects in both media coincide with the prevailing economic health of the country. In prosperous times the openings naturally exceed those in periods when the advertiser tightens his belt and his pocketbook. With television now well established, the chances for employment in this expanding medium are bright. Many companies operate both radio and TV stations; some tend to play down one or the other.

Advancement. As in other departments of journalism, creative ability counts. A flair for turning out interesting and voice-worthy copy naturally enhances the writer's value and increases his income. It must be borne in mind that the radio and TV writer is by no means limited to news writing. He can turn his hand to continuities, and if he has the requisite skill, he can get into the production aspect of the business. Writers from time to time emerge as program directors. In each case their fund of general knowledge has given them the preference over applicants who boast merely training in direction. Station executives are on the lookout constantly for new and fresh ideas. It is hardly surprising then that members of the writing craft can supply them.

Financial rewards. Salaries are generally higher than those in the newspaper field. In the case of local stations, pay is regulated by the amount of business done by the station. In the case of networks, newswriters are represented by the National Association of Broadcast Technicians and Engineers. The Radio Writers Guild, a section of

the Authors League of America, represents newsmen of the Columbia Broadcasting System.

Because both radio and television have a closer affiliation with show business than with journalism, the show business personalities receive higher rewards than the merely journalistic ones. For instance, the newscaster who reads the script ranks as "talent" and his income far exceeds the income of the man or woman who wrote the actual words. Accordingly the versatile newsmen who both write and read the scripts for their own news shows receive the highest rewards in the news field, with salaries sometimes reaching $100,000. They are members of the American Federation of Television and Radio Artists.

For the creative writer in both media, the rewards are high, and writers of dramatic and documentary shows get, in addition, either audible or visual credit for their work.

Community regard. Although there is a certain aura of glamor attendant to employment in radio and television, owing to the identification of these media with the entertainment world, journalistic employees in radio and television, notably newswriters, must anticipate much the same anonymity held by most writers on newspapers. In radio there are no by-lines; television, however, does occasionally grant a visual credit line to the newswriter during the course of a telecast.

CAREERS IN ADVERTISING

Advertising, which pays the bill for journalistic endeavors in the mass media, is a field that attracts many recruits. As a rule it offers interesting outlets for creative effort, for originality, and for business ability. On the whole it pays its workers handsomely when compared to newspaper standards. The field gives plenty of scope to both men and women, and as the vast continent is publicity minded to an acute degree, there is hardly a town of even minor importance which does not offer openings in one or another of advertising's branches. Accordingly, men and women find careers for themselves in the advertising departments of newspapers and magazines large and small, in commercial advertising agencies, and in the advertising departments of stores, other business firms, and manufacturers.

Training. Cultural background with its wide range of knowledge and interests stands out as a prerequisite here as elsewhere in journalism, and most employers favor the college-trained applicant. In fact, the high-powered agencies throughout the country make it a practice to cull the colleges for what they call "copy cubs"—men and women who seem to them possessed of executive potential as well as writing ability. However, it must never be forgotten that advertising is essentially person-to-person selling, and that department store experience with its training in individual approach to a customer ranks high. In fact, the training programs of many agencies keep the young advertiser for a week at least actually selling the product he is to advertise in order that he may acquaint himself with and understand the public who may buy it. Advertising agencies and the advertising departments of large firms give their trainees a thorough preparatory course, putting them through phases of agency operation and making them familiar with the production and merchandising of the products before they let them try their hand at copywriting or layout work. Similar preparation is given students by the many universities which contain schools or departments of business and commerce.

Immediate prospects. Linked so closely as it is with the country's economic picture, the advertising business prospers best when times are good. It still prospers, though not so markedly, when times are bad. Accordingly, openings usually exist in normal years for the applicant with aptitude and a fair education.

Advancement. Advertising constantly seeks new ideas and new trends and is quick to reward those individuals who possess a flair as idea men. In fact, an agency or department breakdown divides between the people who go out and get the business and the people who provide the ideas. Advancement follows as talent develops along creative lines, such as copywriting or art work, along research lines, in space buying, or in the production of radio and television programs. Top positions are those of copy chief, account executive, and director of a department such as radio or television.

Financial rewards. Salaries in most branches of advertising are relatively high. A "copy cub" might start at $300 a month and by the time he becomes a junior copy writer he will at least have doubled that amount. In agencies, copy chiefs, account executives, and department heads are well paid. For example, the director of radio or television for a medium size agency would receive $12,000 to $15,000 annually and in a large agency up to double that amount. A vice-president's salary would start at $20,000.

Community regard. In advertising the community regard largely depends on the individual. The public has read books like *The Hucksters* and seen movie versions of advertisers' penthouse parties and the effect lingers in its mind. No special prestige goes to advertising as such, but the individual connected with this calling can, unhampered or unaided by tradition, make his own mark.

CAREERS IN PUBLIC RELATIONS

Because of the great growth of the whole field of public relations during and since World War II and the inevitability of future expansion, public relations work offers interesting, useful, and lucrative employment to men and women whose qualifications satisfy its specific requirements. In operation it brings into play skills and techniques which journalism has long used in stimulating public interest and in molding public opinion.

Although among the newer callings allied to journalism, public relations is new chiefly in the way it integrates the scientific methods and procedures borrowed from the social sciences as well as from journalism. Accordingly, this field has a special attraction for individuals who are experts in these skills or who feel that they have aptitudes for them.

Training. Although a broad and sound academic background stands out as an obvious prerequisite, preparation for public relations work does not rely on formal education alone. The qualifications which the work calls for are personality qualifications. The men and women who succeed in this field need outgoing, attractive, and persuasive personalities. None of these traits develops easily from a textbook formula. Any training which gives the individual experience in dealing with people—selling, teaching, public speaking, reporting, acting—makes a valuable contribution to a person's qualifications for public relations work. When the Opinions Research Corporation made a survey of public relations executives to find out what these men look for in job applicants, the replies showed that 22 per cent of those interviewed considered a college education of prime importance; 38 per cent rated news experience or training as the chief essential; 22 per cent voted for common sense, intelligence, and good judgment and an equal number stressed the possession of an attractive personality and of an ability to get along with people as the main prerequisites.

Some 120 universities and colleges now offer courses in public relations, and the best of these courses tend to stress a broad background in the social sciences and in business. In addition, specialized courses deal with such subjects as mass communications, public opinion, audience analysis, and social movements.

Immediate prospects. While the openings for beginners are not so numerous as they were immediately after World War II, the qualified applicant usually manages to get placed. As in the case of an advertising agency, the public relations firm will require an apprentice period of training. In addition, openings can be found in the smaller-staffed public relations departments of social service agencies, educational, religious and philanthropic institutions, and in individual business firms. Many individuals get valuable experience while attached to the public relations departments of the armed services. Openings, too, are found for public relations work with local, state, and federal governmental departments across the land. Apprentice jobs for beginners might include writing for house publications, or work as handyman for an account man in a counseling firm or as an assistant in the research department. In instances where there is a very small staff, the beginner, like the young reporter on a small paper, gets a broad training because he gets the opportunity to handle a variety of jobs.

Advancement. Advancement in this field depends on how fast a beginner can grow in ability and capacity to carry responsibility. If he quickly develops the knack of getting along with and influencing people, a working knowledge of the structure and functioning of organizations, skill in policy making, or a flair for the presentation of his client's case in writing or in speaking, his rapid advancement is assured.

Financial rewards. As in advertising, the salaries earned in public relations far surpass those which the successful newspaperman ever achieves or dreams of. The apprentice starts quite low, say at $225 to $325 a month, but as he grows in stature with his firm or department, the increases in his income can come quite fast. At the top of the ladder, public relations counselors and staff directors earn as much as $75,000 a year. Both the starting pay as well as the ultimate figure to be gained are relatively lower in welfare agencies, government departments, and educational institutions.

Community regard. Public relations work gains in prestige as the field itself draws closer to the dignity of a profession. Early personalities in the field like George Creel and Ivy Lee made a favorable impression on the public mind, and that public attitude is being strengthened through the work of the leading contemporary practitioners. The whole concept of public relations is too recent as far as the general public is concerned for any set state of mind to have developed towards it, but success and affluence here as in other lines gain the successful and affluent public relations man the esteem of his community.

The Media of Journalism

Communication Through the Spoken Word, Newspapers,
Magazines, Books, Motion Pictures, Radio and Television

Journalism utilizes the chief media of present-day mass communication. These include the spoken word through its various channels, notably radio; the printed word in the daily and weekly press, in pamphlets, magazines and books; and the visual media—the motion picture and television.

The public gives to these media of journalism one-fifth of its waking hours, and it apportions this time among them according to its tastes.

More Americans read newspapers daily than read magazines or books, attend movies, listen to the radio, or watch television. However, as the following table indicates, they spend more time with other media.

TOTAL U.S. PERCENTAGE OF DAILY TIME SPENT WITH MEDIA [1]

	Male	Female	Total
Total of all Media	100.0	100.0	100.0
(Sum of 1 through 5)			
Broadcasting:			
1. Television (Total)	33.8	36.3	35.2
Movies on TV	4.2	4.3	4.3
2. Radio (Total)	28.3	29.5	28.9
Automobile Radio	8.6	4.1	6.2
Publishing:			
3. Newspapers	10.5	9.0	9.7
Sunday Magazines *	5.2	5.6	5.4
4. Magazines	4.1	3.7	3.9
5. Theatre Screen Adv't.*	23.3	21.5	22.3

[1] This information has been extracted from "National Media Activity," August, 1960 (a monthly report). Copyright 1960 by Sindlinger & Company, Inc. Reprinted by permission.

* Represents total weekly time.

25

In the beginning was the word. Even before the dawn of history men spoke to inform, to convince and to persuade their fellows. Men today are still hard at it and with the same ends in view. Through the centuries the spoken word has lost none of its power, and in our own century science and invention have widened the range of its influence by increasing its audience a millionfold.

History is not only written in words, it is made with words. The man whose garbled gutturals nearly brought our world to ruin understood their potency. Writing in *Mein Kampf*, Adolf Hitler said:

The power which set sliding the greatest historical avalanches of political and religious nature was from the beginning of time, the magic force of the spoken word alone.

Men communicate information and ideas through the spoken word to individuals, to small groups, to large audiences in schools, in churches, in town meetings, and in crowded auditoriums. The effectiveness of men's words with any audience depends quite as much on the way speakers say what they have to say as on the contents of their talks themselves. At its best, the superior influence of speaking over writing lies in the ability of the speaker to impress his audience with his personal characteristics and his manner of delivery.

Communication Through the Spoken Word

In the early days in New England, even before 1690 when Benjamin Harris in his *Publick Occurrences both Foreign and Domestick* made the first fleeting adventure in printed journalism, mass communication had one chief medium—the pulpit. The Puritan divines at the end of their lengthy discourses had a habit of tacking on public announcements and similar items of general concern.

The pulpit remains a means of communication today though its power has waned. One reason for this is that church attendance itself has fallen off since colonial days. Nevertheless, statistics also record that some twenty million sermons and religious addresses are delivered during the course of the year. The subject matter of much of this discourse falls directly under the head of journalism, based on note and comment in newspapers, magazines, and books.

In schools and colleges the spoken word still remains the chief medium of communication. Teachers speak; students listen. In the old days the process was one of intellectual feeding. The teacher told his students what to think. The trend today is to send students to sources, to show them not so much *what* as *how* to think, and to utilize all available media of communication in addition to the spoken word. Much of the reading matter assigned in schools and colleges consists of contemporary journalism. Current events, as reported in the press, form the topic of much classroom discussion.

It is through the lecture platform that the spoken word has grown in prestige and inflence. As a people, Americans have developed a high saturation point for talk. As an observer in *Harper's New Monthly Magazine* of April, 1861, remarked: "Whenever there is an argument about anything everybody in America listens."

The lecture platform developed side by side with the improvement in transportation facilities in the early 1820's. By 1828 there were roughly 100 branches of the American Lyceum, and by 1834 there were 3,000. During the 1860's the lecture bureau appeared and made lecturing a profitable business.

Henry Ward Beecher, who gave 1,261 public lectures during the last twelve years of his life, received as much as $1,000 a lecture. Charles Dickens gained $228,000 on his American tour in 1867–68.

The Chatauqua circuit followed the old Lyceum and lasted well into the present century. At its peak the Chatauqua influence reached an estimated annual audience of 40 million.

Today public lecturing continues to grow in popularity and power. The W. Colston Leigh Bureau books annually more than 5,000 lectures; this is the largest of several hundred bureaus.

Upton Close, writing in the *Saturday Review of Literature*, notes the impact of the public lecture on contemporary society.

The lecture business . . . is one of the deepest-rooted institutions in American life, and is now becoming one of the widest-spread. Today it is giving birth to new crusades, creeds, cults, and organizations, just as earlier it gave the popular impetus to abolition, prohibition, woman suffrage and circulating libraries.

The late Professor W. Norwood Brigance points out the change in attitude and technique which has come over the public lecturer in our time. Because he now faces a public of higher educational and intellectual attainment than even a generation ago, and a public influenced by the spirit of scientific inquiry, "the speaker is less of an oracle than formerly and more of a plain man talking." Writing in *The Annals of the American Academy of Political and Social Science*, Dr. Brigance says:

Before educated audiences today speakers more frequently use the conference technique of "co-operative dialogue" than the orator's traditional "dogmatic monologue." The speaker takes hold of the problem at issue, states it honestly and then stimulates his hearers to think their way through it.

Today the public platform has been widened. It now includes business associations, labor organizations, conventions and congresses, women's clubs, service clubs and civic organizations.

Each day in New York City alone some 300 reunion banquets and lunch and dinner meetings bring thousands to listen to the spoken word. The development of the electrical public address system not only makes listening easier, but increases considerably the size of the speaker's immediate audience. A crowd of 110,000, for instance, in Soldier's Field, Chicago, can hear a speaker with ease and comfort.

COMMUNICATION AND RADIO

People are no longer limited to direct listening. Radio and television now carry the human voice around the world. Through them, the speaker who formerly reached the few thousands within hearing range now influences a national and even an international multitude. Abraham Lincoln spoke to 15,000 at Gettysburg; Franklin D. Roosevelt spoke in person to 150,000 at Gettysburg on July 3, 1938, and more than once he spoke by radio to 50 million.

This miracle developed in the present century. Marconi began it all when he demonstrated the possibility of wireless telegraphy in 1901, and when he later transmitted the first news report by wireless to the New York *Times* in 1907. But radio as we know it now dates from the 1920's.

For a time after radio was born its sheer novelty was enough to win and keep the attention of listeners. People sat tied to their receivers by earphone cords, spellbound for no other reason than that there was something to hear. Soon the number of listeners swelled to millions, the number of broadcasting stations grew to thousands and the variety and pretensions of programs spread beyond the bounds of the normal imagination. The effect of all this has been to saddle radio with one of the greatest responsibilities ever assumed by any invention of mankind. Taken at first for a curious toy, broadcasting has become a vital force in the political, social, economic, religious, educational, and cultural patterns of human life.

Today, the National Association of Broadcasters contends that the number of radios in use has reached 150 million, with 100 million in homes, 38 million in cars and 120 million in bars and other gathering places.

As yet there is no completely satisfactory answer to the question of the control of radio. In the United States, private enterprise operates and controls the stations and networks, with national and local advertising footing the gigantic bill and providing a handsome profit. Congress has set up a Federal Communications Commission to remind radio companies that they have responsibilities to the public as well as to their program sponsors.

Remember, too, that while the audience is measured in hundreds, thousands, and even millions, the appeal is to the *individual* in his own home. Psychologically, this is speech at its best.

Finally, it is a *unique social instrument* in that the radio speaker is blind and deaf to his audience, and the listener is blind and dumb to the radio speaker, yet the two-way power of the human voice is such that it suggests imaginative pictures which more than compensate for the lack of sight. The image occurs in the listener's mind unrestricted by specific detail; it is therefore a perfect picture, for the listener can tailor it to his own taste. Radio exhibits these interest-compelling properties in the odd medley of programs one gets by traversing the dial. There are more than 22,000 different program offerings in the United States every day; eight million a year. They are supposed to provide satisfaction for any listener's mood of the moment.

What does the listener want to hear, and what do the stations supply to fill his needs? The first question presents a difficulty to anyone surveying radio, because there is not one "public" but many. True, some listeners may like both symphony concerts and baseball games, but for the most part these programs appeal to different audiences. The consensus of radio opinion apparently is that the public chiefly wants entertainment; and that is what the networks and stations chiefly supplied before the leading comedy shows and comedians left radio for television.

News reports get a high radio rating. As we have just shown, 15 per cent of evening time goes for news broadcasts and for commentators' interpretation, but over the whole broadcasting day, 10 per cent of the radio's time would come nearer the mark. This is high, and the increasing amount of time being given to radio journalism constitutes the greatest change in programming that radio has experienced in recent years. Before the outbreak of World War II in 1939, only 8.55 per cent of radio time went for news broadcasts.

According to the Associated Press, radio news has a higher percentage of general listeners in all age groups of any type of radio program.

Today when listeners are asked to name the type of program they enjoy most, 65 to 75 per cent say they prefer the news. Measurement studies show that women prefer *hearing* it to *reading* it. Those in the lower income groups prefer radio to newspapers. Farmers and young people say the same thing. But people who have a deep interest in events continue to read the newspaper because there they get the whole story and not a fifty-word highlight version. It is in this instantaneous "bulletin" quality that radio news excels. The listener hears of an event sometimes within seconds after its happening. He finds his interest piqued and stimulated by the bare announcement and buys the next newspaper as it rolls off the presses to satisfy the curiosity which the radio has aroused. Publishers who first feared radio as a rival find that it frequently increases newspaper circulation and now regard radio as an ally. Today newspapers own or control upward of 750 radio stations.

In Great Britain, radio has public rather than private ownership and exists without benefit of advertising. The British Broadcasting Corporation operates under a royal charter which comes up for renewal by Parliament every five years. Canada has devised a system which is something of a compromise between the American and English extremes. The Canadian Broadcasting Corporation comes up annually for review by a parliamentary committee. It operates the networks and some stations and its programs go out across the Dominion without advertising. However, local stations which transmit the Canadian Broadcasting Corporation's features also broadcast sponsored programs and profit through advertising revenue. The result of this method is that radio is carried to parts of the country where commercial operation would not be feasible; on the other hand, private stations provide variety and competition. This middle-of-the-road plan has so far won the approval of each successive parliamentary committee on radio.

The immense popularity of radio has placed it well in the forefront of all the media of mass communication. Why this popularity? How could anything so new have captured so much attention and public confidence in so short a time?

Kenneth G. Bartlett, Vice President & Dir. of Radio-TV Ctr., University College at Syracuse University, an authority on radio who has written extensively on this subject, supplies an answer by pointing out radio's unusual properties: its *universality*, its *contemporaneous* nature, its direct and *individual* appeal and its characteristics as a *unique social instrument*.

An examination of the daily schedule will show a *universality* that encompasses almost every taste. The radio tries to be all things; and it probably has had its greatest success in appealing to lower income and educationally less fortunate groups.

Listen to a program, and with the sound dying in the fraction of a second, the listener will sense that radio is *contemporaneous*. It deals with "now." Once broadcast there can be no correction—once released the signal is gone forever! This is a characteristic that makes radio exciting and always new and fresh.

Communication Through the Written Word

Man alone of all the animal kingdom has devised the knack of translating sound into written symbols. First man communicated to his fellows through gestures; then he learned to speak, to use words; then he discovered how to turn his words into written symbols which others could see and understand. He scratched them first on cave walls or carved them deep in stone columns and monuments, and still later he wrote them on light and portable materials such as leaves—papyrus—which could be carried around or sent from place to place. Untold centuries went into the perfecting of this unique achievement, but its possession has done more for the human race than any of man's other skills.

Journalism began when man learned to write; the newspaper began when man learned to write at regular intervals. It is this element of periodicity which stands out as a basic characteristic of the newspaper and sets it apart from mere sporadic writing even if such effusions deal with timely topics.

An early series of writings which boasted periodicity and covered current happenings was the *Acta Diurna* or Daily Acts which Julius Caesar, around 50 B.C., ordered to be publicly posted each day in the Forum at Rome. If we regard this as the first newspaper we can draw some parallels between it and its present-day successor. First, this bulletin gave information; it published news—the accounts of the goings-on in the Senate. Second, it recognized the value of publicity, for Julius Caesar hoped that when the Senators saw their actions and words recorded they might act and speak in a more worthy manner. The *Acta Diurna* demonstrated the use of the newspaper to secure results through propaganda. The Emperor Augustus, who followed Julius Caesar, used the bulletin in his crusade against race suicide and published "features" praising Romans with large families. This forerunner of the newspaper, however, was not a business proposition, though it had a wide circulation. Each day scribes would copy it when it was posted in the Forum, and then send these copies along those Roman roads which stretched from the Eternal City north to the Baltic Sea or through Gaul and across to Britain, wherever the Roman armies marched or their eagles rested.

We can take the newsletter as the prototype of today's newspaper. In fact, the first continuing newspaper in the American colonies, which John Campbell began publishing in 1704, took the name, the Boston *News-Letter*.

NEWSPAPERS

Today the newspaper ranks as the chief medium of communication through the printed word. In the United States, there are some 14,000 papers of which some 1,750 are dailies, with an aggregate circulation of approximately 55 million. More than 70 of these daily papers appear in tabloid size. Then, throughout the country, there are some 150 foreign language daily newspapers. In addition, the smaller communities are served by weekly newspapers, some 8,500 of them. These weeklies move at a slower and more sedate pace than the dailies but play an important part in community life. Their chief concern is local news and they print items about residents and about local events.

In Canada, the combined circulation of the 95 daily newspapers reaches a total of 2.8 million, actually higher than the number of families in the Dominion. Also, there are 1.5 million persons in Canada who subscribe to 750 weeklies.

Together the papers of the North American continent bring their readers the news of the town, the nation, and the world with a speed, an accuracy, and a comprehensiveness unequalled elsewhere.

The newspaper's chief importance lies in its primary function of furnishing news to readers. Years ago, Thomas Jefferson saw clearly the value to a democracy of unfettered information when he made the extraordinary statement, "Were it left to me to decide whether we should have a government without newspapers or newspapers without a government, I would not hesitate a moment to prefer the latter." And in our time, Herbert Brucker, editor of the Hartford *Courant*, has re-emphasized this aspect of the press in the nation's life:

. . . In the United States there are not only the three component parts of the national government—legislative, judicial, executive—about which we learned in school. There is a separate and unofficial but nevertheless essential fourth part. This is the press, the machinery of information which is charged with the duty of making the citizen's mental world bear at least a familiar resemblance to reality. Without this, the accepted trilogy of Congress, President, and Courts could not function.

All newspapers supply news to a greater or lesser degree, but papers differ in the type of news to which they give prominence and in their treatment of it. Daily journalism falls roughly into two main classes: the papers which make it their chief aim to inform and interpret, and the papers which place emphasis on entertainment. By entertainment we mean not merely comic strips but "features" of one kind and another, serial stories, gossip columns, puzzles, competitions, and the like. Some papers have achieved success by uniting these two aims. In addition, there is a smaller class which specializes in crusading.

Newspapers in the first category become journals of record like the New York *Times*. In the second group we find papers with vast circulations like the tabloids. The crusaders model themselves on the policy of Joseph Pulitzer's late lamented New York *World* in that they seek out wrongs to set right and worthy causes to champion. A present-day example of the crusading type of newspaper is the St. Louis *Post-Dispatch*, published by Joseph Pulitzer, Jr.

New York City is the newspaper center of the American continent. Its presses turn out thirty-five English language daily papers in all—regular, tabloid, trade, and financial.

The New York *Daily News*, the first successful tabloid in the country, leads the field with a daily circulation of 2.7 million and a Sunday circulation of 4 million. This paper boasts the largest circulation in America.

When professional journalists are asked from time to time to pick out the outstanding newspapers across the country, they usually come up with a list that includes the following:

New York *Times*.
St. Louis *Post-Dispatch*.
Christian Science Monitor.
Louisville *Courier-Journal*.
Kansas City *Star*.
Chicago Daily *News*.
New York *Herald Tribune*.
Washington *Post*.
Milwaukee *Journal*.
Baltimore *Sun*.
Cleveland *Plain Dealer*.
New York *World-Telegram and Sun*.

Then, among many other important papers, there are the New Orleans *Times-Picayune*, the Portland *Oregonian*, the San Francisco *Chronicle*, the Des Moines, Iowa, *Register* and the *Deseret News* of Salt Lake City, as well as distinct and distinguished journals in smaller cities and towns.

In Canada, among the leading papers are the Toronto *Globe and Mail*, the Toronto *Daily Star*, the Ottawa *Citizen*, the Montreal *Gazette*, the Montreal *Star*, the St. John *Telegraph-Journal*, the Halifax *Chronicle-Herald* and, in the West, the Winnipeg *Free Press* and the Winnipeg *Tribune*, the Edmonton *Journal*, the Calgary *Herald*, the Vancouver *Province*, and the Victoria *Colonist*.

THE BRITISH PRESS

It is the constitutional guarantee of freedom of the press and the manner in which American newspapers use that freedom that come to the fore in any comparison of American and foreign newspapers.

Of all major powers the United States permits most freedom in actual practice, and as a result the American people have the opportunity of being the most enlightened in the world.

With the exception of the United Kingdom, where newspaper censorship in normal times is largely self-imposed, virtually every other major nation outside of the United States exercises some form of control over the newspapers, direct or indirect. In some countries the governments also control the press associations and in this way control the passage of news from state to state.

In the United Kingdom, the newspapers published in London dominate the field. Because of the compactness of the British Isles and the rapidity of distribution, a morning newspaper published in London can reach subscribers anywhere in the country on the same day and, in most cases, in time for breakfast. This means that the London papers work as national papers and that the most popular of them achieve vast circulations.

Among the papers of the conservative type we have *The Times*, *The Daily Telegraph*, and *Morning Post*, and in the mass circulation field we find *The Daily Mail*, *The Daily Express*, the *Daily Mirror*, the *Daily Graphic*, and the *Daily Herald*. These last five all have vast circulations, the *Daily Mirror* topping the list with a daily circulation of 4,566,000. However, a weekly newspaper, *News of the World*, leads all contenders with its circulation of 8,382,356.

Despite the dominance of London, some so-called "provincial" papers exert a profound influence not only in the districts in which they circulate, but nationally and even internationally. Four such papers come inevitably to mind. They are the *Manchester Guardian*, *The Yorkshire Post* (published in Leeds), *The Scotsman* (published in Edinburgh), and *The Birmingham Post*.

JOURNALISM IN RUSSIA

In Russia, all forms of journalism are strictly controlled. This falls in line with Soviet policy from the beginning. Lenin once described a newspaper as "not only a collective propagandist and a collective agitator, but also a collective organizer," and Stalin defined the press as "the one weapon with whose help the party speaks to the working class in its own language daily and hourly."

Although there is lack of freedom of the press in the U.S.S.R., Russia has no lack of newspapers and magazines. In fact, there are some five thousand newspapers and some one thousand magazines published in the Soviet Union. The newspapers range from *Pravda* and *Izvestia*, with circulations running into the millions and with a country-wide distribution, to the small local newspapers in towns and rural districts. These appear not only in the Russian language but in the languages of most of the chief minority nationalities which make up the Russian sphere. The magazines, too, have not only general but specialized appeal. There are publications for farmers, for service men, for writers, for railroad men, for teenagers, and for youngsters under ten. All, of course, speak with one voice—the voice of the Kremlin.

THE MAGAZINE: HISTORY AND TYPES

In this field of mass communication through the printed word, the magazine in the United States ranks second only to the newspaper. From the day when Benjamin Franklin first published his *General Magazine* in 1741 to the present, this type of periodical has operated as one of the most persuasive instruments of communication. Through each succeeding generation the magazine has exerted a strong influence on the American social and economic structure by establishing tastes, stimulating trade, and molding public opinion. Today in the United States, over three billion copies of 7,000 different periodicals are read each year and influence in very substantial measure what Americans wear, eat, think, and believe.

Like the newspaper, the early colonial magazine modeled itself after the English forerunners in the field, but also like the newspaper, the magazine soon developed native characteristics. It offered a sure appeal to the American temperament which loves variety and conciseness and hankers after self-improvement. Benjamin Franklin, who understood the public taste without the aid of surveys or polls, early put an emphasis on educational content. Later publications such as *The Port Folio* and its contemporaries developed this phase and turned themselves into national educators. Through each generation the magazine has kept aware of the public's needs and tastes and has played successive roles as literary arbiter, as crusader, as "muckraker," as entertainer.

Here are some high points of magazine achievement:

Harriet Beecher Stowe with her serial "Uncle Tom's Cabin" made the magazine a potent propagandist for the abolition of slavery.

Godey's Lady's Book put the emphasis on feminine fashions and taste and made popular the woman's magazine which now as a class leads the whole magazine field.

Thomas Nast, through his devastating cartoons in *Harper's Weekly,* led the journalistic campaign which overthrew the notorious Tweed Ring.

Ida M. Tarbell, with her "History of the Standard Oil Company" in *McClure's Magazine,* not only precipitated the era of muckraking but influenced both the practices of big business and legislation affecting these practices.

Edward Bok, when editor of the *Ladies' Home Journal,* made over the American home from its architecture to the pictures on its walls.

Although during the nineteenth century the American magazine developed much along the lines of the British publications overseas, original leadership developed in the beginning of the twentieth century with several important results. First, it developed a new type of advertising about 1900 which made use of pictorial and psychological appeals and banished forever the mere "listings" and announcements of former days. The new advertising had such a marked effect on American buying preferences that both its volume and the revenue reaped therefrom increased prodigiously and resulted in developing the advertising agency as it exists today. Then, after World War I, American publishers initiated several new types of magazines. These included the news magazines such as *Time* and *Newsweek,* the digest magazines such as *The Reader's Digest* and *Magazine Digest,* and the picture magazines such as *Life* and *Look.*

Among these newcomers, the news magazines have made the

greatest impact. Their conciseness and their lack of convention in regard to vocabulary and stereotyped methods of presentation have had a marked influence on general journalistic style. This impact has been noted in the conventional newspaper lead paragraph. Many one-edition newspapers in particular have borrowed the news magazines' technique of a swift and arresting approach to the material in hand and have dropped the frequently dull summary beginning, long customary across the land.

We can classify magazines as *slicks* or *pulps* when we refer to the quality of print paper stock used in their manufacture; as *weeklies*, *monthlies*, or *quarterlies* when we stress their frequency of publication; or as *general* or *trade* when we take note of their content, which covers hundreds of fields of human activities and interests.

1. GENERAL:
   a. The Popular Magazines: This group includes weeklies such as *The Saturday Evening Post* and monthlies such as *Cosmopolitan* and *Redbook*. These magazines furnish the reader with fiction in both serial and short story form and articles on current topics and personalities.
   b. The Women's Magazines: This group is also "popular" in the appeal of fiction, articles, and illustrations, but slants its material to interest the feminine taste. Such magazines invariably include departments on cooking, patterns, home decoration, and so forth. Leaders in this group are the *Ladies' Home Journal*, *Good Housekeeping*, *McCall's*, *Mademoiselle*, *Charm*, and *Glamour*.
   c. The "Quality" Magazines: While they also provide fiction and articles, the "quality group" which includes *The Atlantic Monthly* and *Harper's* appeals to readers with more mature and cultivated tastes. Such journals maintain a high literary standard.
   d. Magazines of Criticism and Opinion: This group includes *The Nation*, the *New Republic*, the *Saturday Review*, *The Commonweal*, and such quarterlies as the *Yale Review*. These magazines seldom print fiction. They limit their content to

reviews and opinions. As was the case with a former magazine, *The Nation*, edited by Edwin L. Godkin in the 1880's, these magazines exert an influence far greater than their limited circulation suggests.

e. The News Magazines: Here, condensed in size, but limitless as the news itself in range, such publications as *Time* and *Newsweek* and their imitators present each week a record of that week's happenings. Here too we can list *U. S. News & World Report*. In circulation as well as in content, each approximates a national newspaper.

f. The Digest Magazines: The policy initiated by *The Reader's Digest* has been to reprint articles abridged from other magazines. This publication, conceived as a serious periodical for a comparative few, has rolled up an international circulation of over 15 million. Both the digest formula and the pocketsize format have had a multitude of imitators.

g. The Picture Magazines: *Life*, which took over its title from an earlier magazine of satire and humor, has initiated a new departure in picture journalism. Along with *Life* we can place *Look* as well as their less serious contemporaries.

h. Fashion Magazines: Here we have class publications such as *Vogue* and *Harper's Bazaar* in the women's sphere and *Esquire* for male consumption.

i. Special-Interest Magazines: Members of this group devote themselves to some special subject such as the theatre, the motion picture, child care, and the like. They include *Theatre Arts, Etude, Arts and Decoration, House and Garden,* and *Sports Illustrated.*

In addition, wide circulations are enjoyed by magazines each of which seems in a class by itself. *The New Yorker* indulges in satire and humor; *Fortune* transfigures big business; *The American Mercury* combines fiction with criticism and comment; *Coronet* is digest in form but original in its text and illustration, as is *Pageant.*

2. TRADE, TECHNICAL, AND CLASS:

The technical and trade magazines are what their names imply. Each profession, business and trade now has its own publications, in some cases a dozen or more. These periodicals run into the hundreds, including those on advertising, banking, canning, drugs, embalming, education, food, geography and exploration, hardware, insurance, journalism, labor, machinery, nature, oil, pets, radio, shoes, temperance, et cetera.

The 7,000 or so American magazines listed in *N. W. Ayer & Son's Directory* do not include the vast number of house organs and other publications which the directory excludes, because they do not accept advertising.

THE BOOK, THE PAMPHLET, THE NEWSLETTER

Books. Since Stephen Day printed the first book in this country, *The Bay Psalm Book,* on the Cambridge Press which he set up in Harvard College in 1640, book publishing has grown side by side with the ever-widening reading public and has today become a vast business. Millions of copies on thousands of topics pour from the presses annually and keep statisticians working overtime merely tabulating their multitude.

There is no end to the making of books. All that has ever been thought, felt, seen, discovered, and imagined—"the funded capital of civilization"—now finds its way between covers of books. Never before has the result of scholarship been so readily available to everyone. Merely by reading in our homes we can gain insight into knowledge which in former days would have cost us endless time in lecture rooms and libraries.

Today the book-reading public constitutes a mighty army. Surveys place the number of readers in the United States at 100 million, assuming that the literate population above the age of ten reads something.

All people read to satisfy a variety of purposes and fill a variety of needs. Publishers see to it that any number of titles appear to meet each reading aim.

Why do people read books? If we give a moment's thought to the question we can list at least six specific reasons:

1. Many people read in order to gossip. They like to be "in the know" or perhaps they want to be thought to be in the know.

They like books that are in the news, "best sellers," or books by highly publicized authors.

2. Many people read to obtain precise information. They seek knowledge to enrich themselves as individuals or to advance themselves in their businesses or professions.

3. Many people turn to books for inspiration, guidance, and what they term "comfort." They find inspiration for their own lives by reading of the achievements of others.

4. Some read for esthetic enjoyment. They enjoy a book for its style as much as for its content.

5. Some read for relaxation. This class includes many "brain workers" who wish to rest their minds with some piece of humor or some mystery or puzzle.

6. The vast majority of readers read to escape. They want to leave behind the humdrum of everyday life and enter some enchanted make-believe universe.

To all readers books have a way of communicating ideas and stimulating thoughts. "The power and glory of literature will always be that it enlarges and enriches life."

One of publishing's important contributions to our time is the availability of worthwhile low-cost books of both past and present.

In the introduction to his *Modern English and American Literature,* W. Somerset Maugham points out the significance of this trend. He sees the American people possessed of a boundless curiosity and an eager desire to learn. He notes, too, the availability of reprints of fine books at low cost. Since in reading, he says, perhaps more than in anything else, appetite grows with what it feeds on, "it may be hoped that they [the readers] may discover how great may be the delight of reading books and as their reading grows more extensive and their taste widens, learn how much enjoyment may be found in great literature." The resulting acquisition of breadth of vision, independence of judgment, and the growth of tolerance and magnanimity may, he suggests, be looked upon in time "as one of the most important events of our day."

A significant trend of the times is the growth in the popularity of nonfiction over fiction. Based on the aggregate number of titles published in 1950, nearly five times as much "general" literature reached the bookstores as fiction—8,101 books of nonfiction as compared with 1,746 novels. Fifty years earlier, in 1900, the proportion was almost reversed.

Literary commentators explain this swing to nonfiction by stating that more and more evidence points to the fact that competitive entertainment media have taken over much of the public which used to spend its time reading the light popular novel. People nowadays get their entertainment "on the run."

Pamphlets and Newsletters. Although it lacks the book's dignity of fine binding, the pamphlet, too, has an honorable background and can stand side by side with its weightier relative as an important medium of communication.

Historically, the pamphlet precedes the newspaper as a purveyor of opinion. In the days when news reached the readers through the newsletter, opinion reached the public through the pamphlet. John Milton showed how forceful the pamphlet could prove as a formulator of ideas, a force which later Thomas Paine demonstrated in his pre-Revolutionary publication *The Crisis* papers.

Today, under various names, the pamphlet rolls off the presses in a steady stream. As tract, booklet, brochure, it tells its readers what to believe, where to travel, what school or college to attend, what candidate to vote for, what cars to ride in, and what merchandise to buy. If you obey the invitation: "Send for our literature on the subject," you will find that this so-called "literature" will consist of pamphlets often elaborately printed and illustrated.

A form of journalism unknown outside the United States is the Washington newsletter; the 35 published in the capital today are the survivors of approximately 700 started there since 1918. All the newsletters interpret trends and forecast conditions and events; but the majority specialize in one field, such as oil, food, or aviation, and are issued daily or weekly. Written by some 200 experts, these letters have a combined circulation of around 200,000, range in subscription price from $15 to $175 a year, and do an annual gross business of about $4 million. Getting its impetus in Washington, the newsletter as a medium of communication has grown prodigiously since World War II. There are now newsletters of all kinds. Virtually every general circulation magazine now has a newsletter section, and a multitude of organizations put out newsletters.

Communication Through the Cinema

Approximately 45 million people attend 13,000 regular motion picture theatres and 4,400 "drive-ins" throughout the country each week. These figures show something of the impact which television has made on the "movies." Before television the weekly movie attendance stood at approximately 65 million and the number of regular theatres neared 20,000. Since then only the "drive-ins" have increased in number, an increase of 1,000 in ten years. Uncounted thousands more watch the cinema unfold its entertainment or its "message" in schools and colleges, in army bases, in hospitals, in churches, in community halls and in shops. This fascination which the motion picture has come to exert in the short half century or so of its existence has led Dr. Alvin Johnson to declare that the motion picture "represents potentially the greatest advance in human inter-communications since the invention of printing."

Like other media of communication, the cinema serves the journalistic trinity of purpose: to inform, to influence, and to entertain. Frequently it combines all three functions.

With Hollywood as the headquarters of a still vast industry, and with eight or nine major companies and many lesser ones manufacturing and distributing their wares, it is nevertheless true that a great change has come over the once dominant movie capital. Elements of this change include the growth of the independent producer, the tendency to "shoot" many major films in Europe, and the fact that Hollywood itself has become the center for the filming of many television shows. The leaders in the field include Columbia, MGM (Metro-Goldwyn-Mayer), Paramount, RKO (Radio, Keith, Orpheum), Warner Brothers, 20th Century-Fox, Universal and United Artists, and Universal.

The vast proportion of motion pictures which Hollywood turns out fall within the entertainment field, and since the advent of the sound film in the 1920's both the technique and the taste of these productions have shown improvement. Comedy, melodrama, romance, and crime make up the standard ingredients of a motion picture, and although avowedly turned out for no other purposes than to amuse or thrill, this run-of-the-mill product has exerted its influence for good or ill. A criticism of Hollywood which frequently crops up is that these films by and large convey to audiences in other countries a distorted, exaggerated, and therefore incorrect picture of American life.

Many entertainment films undoubtedly have educational value. For instance, Hollywood has given celluloid production to both the classic and contemporary drama. Audiences which have no way of seeing a living theatrical performance can, through the film, enjoy the work of playwrights old and new. Similarly, it has bestowed a new life on many a classic that grew dusty on the library shelves. At the movie director's bidding, the characters of Charles Dickens, of Victor Hugo, and of Tolstoy cease their existence between the covers of books and live and move and have an actual being on the theatre screen.

Similarly real lives—the whole rewarding realm of biography— become animated and vocal as Henry VIII, Rembrandt, Louis Pasteur, Abraham Lincoln, Alexander Graham Bell, Thomas A. Edison, or Woodrow Wilson appear before us in their habits as they lived.

In book form the dramas old and new, the fiction of past and present, and ancient and modern biography all run to volumes of considerable bulk. Few could be read at a single sitting. The motion picture manages to convey their contents in "features" of conventional length.

NEWSREELS, DOCUMENTARIES, AND TRAVELOGUES

It is, however, in what we can loosely call the nontheatrical film that the motion picture becomes journalism. The first "flickers" at the dawn of the twentieth century pictured actual events and personalities and foreshadowed the newsreel of today.

The newsreel, as its name implies, is one reel (approximately fifteen minutes of playing time) devoted to the picturing of news and the people who make it. The conventional newsreel deals chiefly with the top headlines and headliners. The specialized newsreel devotes itself exclusively to sports or to fashions. In this way the newsreel covers much the same territory as the newspaper with the exception of the newspaper's editorial page. This opinion-forming function the cinema approximates through its documentaries and other "shorts."

One type of documentary, the pictorial essay, has an importance all of its own. The vanguard in this line, "The March of Time" sponsored by *Time* magazine, initiated the type and broke new ground for cinema journalism. It is a topical two-reel film which both presents and interprets, pictorially and on the sound track, subjects of current interest for American and export distribution. Similarly, the Canadian-made "World in Action" series falls within this category and receives wide distribution in North America and overseas. In the United Kingdom, the J. Arthur Rank organization has devised a somewhat similar two-reeler, "This Modern Age," and a one reeler, "Looking at Life," for the British Commonwealth and the colonial market.

The documentary film bases its appeal on the assumption that fact can be both as interesting and pictorial as fiction. Its development in recent years has made both cinema and educational history. Today the documentary film is widely used in schools, colleges, and churches, and it has become an accepted vehicle for the national and international communication of ideas.

Akin to the documentary, because it utilizes the same technique, is the special-purpose film. This is avowedly a "message film." Making use of it for their own particular propaganda are churches and religious groups, hospitals and charitable causes, manufacturers, business big and little, railroads, and organized labor.

Long popular as a short feature in motion picture theatres is the travelogue. Audiences enjoyed it in the days of the silent screen. Now, with the added dimensions of sound and color, the travelogue with its vivid scenes of the life and customs and beauty of other lands acts as a pleasant yet potent aid to the better understanding of the world in which we live.

Communication Through Television

Television, the most recent of the media of communication, has already shown signs of becoming one of the most important. It is the most dramatic of all the wireless inventions. It adds motion to the pictorial content of facsimile and vision to the immediacy and intimacy of sound broadcasting. Having extended his voice and hearing to the ends of the earth, man is now able to extend his eyesight also.

While yet in its infancy, television transmission attained almost the instantaneous quality of radio. A picture can be picked out of the air, processed within sixty seconds, and screened immediately.

Television's rise in importance has been phenomenal. Its commercial use began in 1945. By 1951 there were 107 stations operating in 63 cities within range of roughly 62 per cent of the country's population. Of the sixty-three cities, however, only twenty-four had between two and seven stations, and a choice of programs has been a prerequisite for the medium to exercise its full impact on competitive media. Each succeeding year sees television grow in size, with an increasingly marked effect on the social life and political thinking of the nation. The plans of the Federal Communications Commission envisage ultimately perhaps 2,000 stations serving ultimately several hundred communities.

The A. C. Nielsen Company estimates that some 48 million television sets are now in use and places some 44.5 million of them in homes. Eleven per cent of these homes own more than one set.

As for its present and potential importance, here is what Jack Gould, radio and television critic of the New York *Times*, says in a front page story:

The now familiar dipole aerial perched on the rooftop symbolizes a fundamental change in national behavior: the home has become a new center of interest for the most gregarious people on earth.

Reports by correspondents of the New York *Times* in more than

100 cities, town and villages over the country show that the impact of pictures sent into the living room is being felt in almost every phase of endeavor.

The ability of television to conquer time and distance together, permitting millions of persons to see and hear the same person simultaneously, is having its effect on the way the public passes its leisure time, how it feels and acts about politics and government, how much it reads, how it rears its children, and how it charts its cultural future. The country never has experienced anything quite like it.

3
The Craft's Style and Argot

Trends in Style—Basic Style Requirements—Some Spelling
Pitfalls—A Typical Style Sheet—Journalistic Terms and
Expressions

In the writing field the word "style" boasts a variety of
meanings. When the professional writer talks of his
style he refers to his manner of writing—the unique
twists and rhythms which he as a unique individual
gives to the words and phrases he uses. When the critic
writes of style, he also has manner in mind—the varying
ways in which schools of authors have expressed themselves in writing. In the publishing field, however, the
word sheds such esoteric overtones and becomes at once
precise and practical. Style to the editor and publisher
simply means the coordination of physical symbols used
to transfer the author's "copy" into print. It deals with
such mundane matters as spelling and punctuation,
with capitalization, with abbreviations, and with the
typographical practices of a particular publication.

In this sense most newspapers and magazines have
definite styles. The editors of such periodicals show
preferences one way or another in these mechanical
matters of presentation in print. Many of them publish
their own style books. Others compile less impressive
style sheets. All such publications stress a basic theme—
uniformity.

Legibility—easy-to-read type—is the first fundamental in good typography. Readability—easy-to-understand
"copy"—is the first fundamental in good journalistic

49

writing. Lack of uniformity in physical presentation puzzles and often baffles the reader and tends to defeat the aim of all concerned —writers, editors, printers—to turn out readable, understandable journalism. Lack of uniformity not only perplexes the reader but leaves a trail of confusion all along the line. Lack of uniformity slows up the original writer; it hampers the editor; it hinders and delays the printer. Frequently the net result is that haphazard copy has to be reset, which means both time and money lost. No wonder that publishers and editors insist on strict adherence to the style rules which they formulate or adopt.

Trends in Styles

Along with the aims of legibility and readability goes the desire to conserve space. A capital letter, for instance, takes up more room in the line than a lower case letter. Therefore the tendency is growing to curtail the use of capitals unless definitely called for. Some publishers, however, notably book publishers, cherish a fondness for capitals. The argot of the craft has its own terms for these preferences.

The emphasis on capitalization is called the "up" style, as, for example, Lincoln Street.

The preference for lower case letters and de-emphasis of capitals is called the "down" style, as, for example, Lincoln street.

The majority of newspapers now favors the "down" style.

Another trend, also guided by the space-saving motive, tends to use more and more abbreviations. The danger here is that although abbreviating words saves space, some abbreviations, if odd-looking and unfamiliar, confuse the reader. To avoid such confusion, the New York *Times*, which for some years omitted periods in abbreviations of government bureaus, companies, and organizations, has returned to the use of periods in these instances. Robert E. Garst says in his foreword to the revised edition of the style book of the New York *Times*, "The experience of several years in which periods in such abbreviations have been omitted leads to the conclusion that the former rule (to omit periods) produced confusion and oddities both in headlines and text which were unintelligible to readers."

Basic Style Requirements

All style books and sheets have several basic requirements. They are professional in their inception, and merely by following them the writer gives immediately a professional look to his copy.

The first requirement calls for proper identification. In newspaper offices, the reporter puts this "slug" on the upper left-hand corner of each page. The slug line may read "Bank St. Fire" or "Mayor's speech," but it immediately serves to inform rewrite or copy desk of the story's subject. Under this slug, the reporter writes or types his own name.

The second basic style rule requires the writer to begin his copy well down—somewhat less than half-way down—the first page. By doing this he takes the appearances of his copy out of the amateur class and also leaves ample room for the editor to change the title, if the copy boasts a title, or to indicate or even write an appropriate head, if the copy calls for a headline.

The third universal style rule insists that all writers double-space their copy whether handwritten or typed. The reasons behind this rule are clear. Double-spacing not only adds greatly to the legibility of the copy but leaves sufficient room in most cases for the editor to edit. For the same reasons, the writer should make a point of leaving fairly wide margins on each side of his page.

The last requirement of this general quartet has to do with word division and applies to writer as well as to copy desk and composing room. It rules that when words break at the end of a line, they be made to break at the syllable. The dictionary is the authority on syllables. This rule has several attendant "don'ts." Don't separate a one-letter syllable, such as *y* or *a*, from the remainder of the word. Don't divide a word of one syllable. The rule also has a brace of "*do's*"—(a) divide between a prefix and the following letter and (b) divide between the suffix and the preceding letter.

In revising his copy before submitting it, the writer usually finds that the standard copyreader's symbols and practices come in handy. As, for example, if he wants to change a capital letter to lower case, he draws a line through it slanting downward from right to left. If, on the other hand, he wishes to turn a lower case letter into a capital, his procedure is to draw three horizontal lines under it (two for small caps). If he wishes to put a title, phrase, word or letter into italics, he draws one horizontal line under the phrase or word or letter. For boldface, he draws a wavy horizontal line under the material he so designates, and so it goes.

A most useful symbol is the word "stet." This Latin command "let it stand" is placed opposite a word or phrase or sentence which the writer wishes printed as originally written. Stet has come to mean: Disregard all corrections and editing and print it as was set down in the first instance.

Writers will find it good practice, in any copy they submit for publication, to see to it that, if possible, their paragraphs end on the page. The way to achieve this, of course, it not to start a new paragraph at the bottom of a page if there is room there only for a line or two. The reason behind this suggestion is mechanical, not literary. When the copy arrives in the composing room to be set in type, the copy-cutter divides it into "takes" which he distributes among the linotype operators. If the take ends with a half-finished sentence or paragraph, he may have to cut and paste a section from the following page to achieve a paragraph unit. This takes time.

Some Spelling Hazards

All style requirements insist on uniformity in the matter of spelling. Office practice usually settles on one or other of the recognized standard dictionaries as the criterion and follows its usage. When in doubt the copy desk then turns to, say, *Webster's New International Dictionary* and accepts its rulings as final.

Here is a list of ordinary words which the copyreaders of newspapers find most frequently misspelled:

rarefy	sacrilegious	inoculate
kimono	picknicking	harass

tranquillity	naphtha	innuendo
supersede	liquefy	plaguy
paraffin	repellent	accommodate
	vilify	

Without expressing more than an implied opinion in the debate between "simplified" and correct spelling, we can state that in most cases the simplified form succeeds in shortening the word count and presumably for that reason is favored by many tabloids. Most of the outstanding papers of the country, however, still prefer *thought* to *thot* and base their spelling style on some standard dictionary.

A Sample Style Sheet

This is a style sheet for all classes in the Department of Journalism at New York University. This style sheet, which is based on standard newspaper practice, is aimed at achieving uniformity in the preparation of class papers in respect to format, punctuation, capitalization, abbreviations, and use of copyreading symbols.

FORMAT

All assignments must be typewritten.

Place on the upper left-hand corner of each page, the page number, the "slug" to identify the copy and under that your name. This is the professional procedure.

For class assignments, place in the upper left-hand corner the following notation:

Page #—slug.

Last name, first name, seat #.

Class, day and hour, date due (date submitted).

On first page, begin almost halfway down the page; on subsequent pages leave about an inch of space at the top. Use 8½ by 11 typing paper (white unlined). *Never* use both sides of paper. Double-space all copy. Leave wide margins on both sides of paper and at bottom of sheet. At the bottom of each page, with the exception of the last page, type the word "more." On the last page indicate "the end" with the proper symbol.

In general, follow the rules of good standard English.

PUNCTUATION

The Comma

Members in a series:
   She played with force, fire, freedom and feeling.
Preceding modifiers of length:
   As I stood watching, a boy ran out of the house.
   At the beginning of the football season, classroom work suffers.
                                        But:
   Today I feel very well. (No comma after today.)
*Independent clauses connected by any of the five simple
coordinating conjunctions (and, but, for, or, nor):*
   We need the money, and we mean to get it.
                                        But:
   Because we are building a house, we need the money; and we
mean to get it.
Direct Address:
   Sir, I greet you.
Appositives:
   His first statement, that he was ill, was found to be untrue.
Addresses and dates:
   John Jones, 561 Blackstone Avenue, Chicago, Ill., was born July
1, 1910.
Nominative Absolute:
   New automobiles being hard to get, secondhand cars are selling at
a premium.
Non-restrictive clauses:
   "Tales of the South Pacific," which won the Pulitzer Prize, is
colorfully written.
                                        But:
   The novel which won the Pulitzer Prize is colorfully written.
Parenthetical and transposed sentence modifiers:
   He was, it was said, a man of means.
   Beyond, the horizon stretched unbroken.

Quotation Marks

Quote names of books, dramas, essays, lectures, magazines, newspapers, nicknames (except personal nicknames in sports), pictures,
poems and songs.

Position of quotes when used with other marks of punctuation:

"I'm going out for a walk," she said. "Do you want to come along?"

"Did you say 'alone'?" he asked.

"Of course!" she replied. "Maybe we'll drop in to see 'Hollywood Follies.'"

CAPITALIZATION

Capitalize the names of political parties, all governmental bodies, presiding officers and permanent committees, corporations and firms, military, naval and similar bodies, races and their languages, religions and geographical divisions. Do not capitalize "p.m." and "a.m." when referring to time of day.

ABBREVIATIONS

Titles when preceding personal names:

Dr. Robert Brown

The Rev. William Johnson

Mr. Harold Green

States, territories and provincial names following names of countries, cities and towns of the United States:

Philadelphia, Pa.

Following personal names, abbreviate names of scholastic degrees, decorations and branches of military and naval service:

John Doe, M.A., Ph.D.

Commonly recognized organizations and programs with long names (except when mentioned for the first time), such as:

YMCA, WCTU, FRP, UN, NLRB

FIGURES

In general, spell out numbers below 100.

Use figures for street addresses, time of day, percentages, sports scores.

Never begin a sentence with a numeral.

SPELLING

The spelling, division and hyphenation shall be those of *Webster's New International Dictionary*.

COPYREADING SYMBOLS

Abbreviate, or make figures:	(Captain) John West
	(Eighty-one) Students
Spell out:	(Prof.) Winters
	(4) new classes
Capitalize:	president Morris
Make lower case:	the Football Coach
Close up:	curri culum
Separate:	high school
Comma:	Curley ‸ who entered school
Delete:	The new student council
	president, who is well
	qualified, took office
End of Story:	(30) or (#)
Ignore correction (let it stand):	He left a good job when (stet)
	he went to college.
Insert letter or word:	the ‸new botany labor‸atory
Paragraph:	¶ Lutz looks good.
No paragraph:	This is the reason:
	Lutz pitched a no-hit game
Period:	(X) or ⊙
Quotes:	ʽʽPinkieʼʼHarris
Transpose letters:	histroical
Transpose words:	girls' varsity team

The Argot of Journalism

Most arts, crafts and trades create their own particular patois. This develops as each calling itself develops, and new terms appear from time to time to swell the unique vocabulary. People in "show biz" talk to each other in a vernacular which probably has some roots in the amphitheatres of ancient Greece as well as of Broadway. Navy men, whether topside or stateside, use a language which mere landlubbers fail to understand. Similarly journalists through their history have built up their own individual jargon of words and expressions.

Here is a comprehensive list of newspaper terms:

A.B.C.   Audit Bureau of Circulations.

AD   Advertisement.

ADD.   Additional news material to be appended to a story.

ADVANCE   A story concerning a future event.

AGATE   Type measuring 5½ points in depth. Newspaper columns and advertisements are measured in agate lines.

ALLEY   Print shop aisles.

ANGLE   Aspect of a news story.

AP   Associated Press.

ART   Newspaper illustrations.

ASSIGNMENT   A reporter's designated task.

BANK   Lower section of a headline; a table on which set type is placed.

BANNER or BANNER LINE   A page-wide head in large type.

BEAT   A reporter's regular territory for news coverage; a story published solely by one newspaper.

BEN DAY   Term referring to mechanical process for shading line engravings.

B.F.   Bold or black face type.

BINDER LINE   One line of large type, on an inside page, over an especially lengthy story or a number of stories on one general topic.

BODY TYPE   Type in which the major part of the newspaper is set.

BOILER PLATE   Syndicate materials in metal plate form.

BOX   Type bordered by rules.

BREAK   The point at which a story goes from one page or one column to another. A story "breaks" when it is available for publication.

BULLDOG   Early edition of a morning paper.

BULLETIN   Significant last minute news.

BUREAU   News-gathering body organized in a center of importance.

BY-LINE   Signature above a story.

CANNED COPY   Material received from publicity offices or press agents.

CAPS   Contraction for capitals.

CAPTION   Explanation of a photograph, illustration, or a diagram.

CASE   Cabinet of type where printer works.

C.G.O.   Can Go Over—meaning that the story is such that it can be printed at any time.

CHASE   Metal frame used for holding, in page form, type and cuts ready for printing.

CIRCUS MAKE-UP   The use of many headlines of various sizes and many kinds of type to create a bizarre effect.

COMPOSING ROOM   Department where type is set.

COMPOSITOR   Person who sets type.

COPYCUTTER   Employe of the composing room who cuts up copy for rapid setting and who distributes copy among typesetters.

COPYHOLDER   Proofroom employe who reads aloud to the proof-reader from manuscript.

COPYREADER   Newsroom employe who reads, edits, and head-lines manuscript.

COVER   To get the facts or be responsible for a story.

CREDIT LINE   Line acknowledging source of a story or cut.

CROSSLINE   Portion of a headline differentiated from the top and banks.

CRUSADE A newspaper campaign for reform or improvement.

CUB An unseasoned reporter.

CUT A newspaper engraving; to shorten a story.

CUTOFF A rule across a column or columns to separate one part of the page from the rest of it.

DATE LINE Place of origin and date put at the beginning of non-local news; the top line of a page giving the publication date.

DEADLINE The time when a story must be completed or an edition go to press.

DECK Part of a headline.

DISPLAY TYPE Large, prominent, or ornamental type used to make headlines or advertisements conspicuous.

DUMMY Diagram showing the layout of a page.

EARS Small boxes appearing in the upper corners of any page.

EM A measure of type width.

EXCLUSIVE A story published by only one newspaper.

FILE To dispatch a story by cable or telegraph.

FILLER Material that can be used at any time to fill space.

FLAG The newspaper title appearing on the first page.

FLASH A message giving the first brief news of an event.

FOLD Place where the half-fold is made in a newspaper.

FURNITURE Wood or metal pieces, less high than type, used for packing type in order that a form may be locked.

F.Y.I. For your information.

GALLEY An oblong metal tray for holding type.

HANDOUT Statement prepared for publication.

HANGER Headline which appears below banner head and belongs to the same story.

INSERT New copy to be incorporated in a story that has gone to the composing room.

JUMP The carrying of a story from one page to another.

JUSTIFYING or JUSTIFICATION Spacing out a line to fill a column or type to fill a form.

KILL To exclude from copy; to destroy a story in type.

LEG MAN   One who gathers news but does not write it.

LOBSTER SHIFT or TRICK   The late watch; on an evening paper the early watch.

MAGAZINE   Section of a linotype machine containing matrices.

MAKE-UP   The placement of stories, pictures and advertisements on a page.

MASTHEAD   The editorial page heading that supplies information about the paper.

MAT   Matrix: the papier-mâché mold of a page of type used for making a stereotype plate; the linotype brass mold for casting type.

MUST   Instruction on copy meaning that it must be printed without fail.

PIED   Type that is in disorder or unusable.

PLATE   A page of type which is cast in metal and is ready for locking on the press.

PLAY UP   To display a story prominently.

PROOFREADER   One who corrects proof against the copy.

PUT TO BED   Locking up the forms in preparation for printing an edition.

QUERY   Correspondent's telegraphic synopsis indicating existence and nature of a story. On the basis of the summary the telegraph editor designates the number of words desired.

QUOIN   Device used for locking type in a form.

RAILROAD   To rush copy in an emergency to the composing room without careful editing.

RELEASE   An instruction to print a story set earlier and held for later disposition.

REWRITE MAN   One who writes stories from facts taken over the telephone; one who revises other reporters' copy or clipped stories.

RIM   The outer edge of the desk, usually in the shape of a horseshoe, where copy is edited and copy editors sit.

RULE   A metal strip which is the height of the type and prints as a line. Column rules make the printed lines separating the columns of a paper.

RUNNING STORY   A news story that continues over a period of time; a story sent to the composing room in sections.

SCOOP   An exclusive story printed by only one paper.

SHORTS   Relatively unimportant brief stories.

SKELETONIZE   Framing a cabled story so as to omit unimportant words.

SLANT   Emphasis placed on a particular aspect of a policy story.

SLOT   Position where the copy desk editor sits.

SLUG   Notation placed on copy to identify the story; a guide line in type.

SOB STUFF   Stories that are sentimental and designed to appeal to the sympathy of the reader.

SPLIT PAGE   First page of second section.

SPOT NEWS   Unexpected, live, important news.

SPREAD   A chief story and its auxiliary stories; a story requiring a head at the top of a column; also used at times to indicate the head itself.

STET   Let it stand.

STICK   A measuring unit for type equaling about two inches; a type holder.

STONE   A stone- or metal-topped bench or table upon which a page is assembled.

STRAIGHT NEWS   An unembellished account of news facts.

STREAMER   Same as banner.

STRING   Newspaper clippings pasted together in a strip or scrap book.

SUBHEAD   A line of type differing from body type and used to break up a long story.

TAKE   A section of a story sent to the composing room by the copy-editor, or given to an operator by the copycutter.

THIRTY   The end.

TIME COPY   Copy held for later use after it has been set.

TYPO   Typographical mistake.

WHEN ROOM   Story may be used at any time.

4
Understanding the Public's Tastes

The Psychological Reasons Behind "Popular Taste"—Why Action Stories, True-Romance Stories, and Success Stories Have Their Vogue—Satisfying the Reader's Frustrated Impulses—Deductions Applicable to Both News and Fiction Writing

Men judge an individual by his friends. A man is known by the company he keeps. Closer observers gauge an individual's taste by the books he reads, the pictures that hang on his walls, the phonograph records he prefers to play. Similarly we, as writers, have an infallible guide to the average reader's likes by surveying the content of the written matter he purchases. What the public wants we have to construe in the economic sense as being what the public buys.

The wise reporter always keeps a steady eye on the market. One of these days he may, if he becomes interesting enough as a writer, give the public what he likes. He may write to please himself and make the public like it. At the start he has to remember that he writes to please his editors who are better judges than he of what the readers want.

Popular Types of Reading Matter

Studying this market then—the avalanche of printed matter that chokes the presses and gets distributed by the carload all over the continent—the reporter finds that several clearly distinct classes of reading predominate in the popular field. He needs no magnifying glass to see the newsstands weighed down with action stories, truelove romances, success stories, and detective tales.

He finds the first class—action stories—has to do with characters engaged in arduous physical exertion. Many of these stories he can classify as adventures. They tell tales of men who go down to the sea in ships; they deal with clashes and pursuits on dark continents. Some chronicle the triumphs of champions in the prize ring; others, the adventures of the cowboy who traces and reclaims the stolen cattle. All have the common denominator of intense physical action, whether accompanied by gunplay or the crueler conflict with the elements on the stormy ocean or the parched Sahara, or the hazards of outer space.

If he can wade through the true romances, he discovers that as a rule they deal with the girl who got her man or with the man who got his girl. The periodicals which publish this material announce to prospective writers that such stories must have a "deftly handled sex motive." But whether deftly handled or not, most of them have to do wholeheartedly with good old-fashioned, unpsychoanalyzed love.

Perusing the success stories in the various types of fan magazines, the reporter finds that time has gone back in its flight. He recalls his boyhood days, when he raced excitedly through such classics as *Paul the Peddler, From Bootblack to Merchant Prince,* and *The Young Millionaire.* Here he reads, almost without variation, of the triumph of ordinary mortals over the adverse circumstances that befall them. He reads of their steady scaling of the ladder till they reach that ultimate golden rung—success. If he is just ordinarily astute, he discovers that one variation to this general theme leads all the rest. He easily identifies it as the "worm who turned" formula. He reads story after story about the "poor nut" at whom the world laughs almost pityingly. And then, hey presto! The scene changes. Something happens, something usually attributed to the poor nut's "personality." Our much-laughed-at hero now laughs last and best. For the feminine counterpart of all this, substitute any variation of the sure-fire Cinderella theme.

When he turns to detective stories, the reporter finds that he himself gets a definite mental exhilaration from them. He enjoys tracing the problem step by step, clue by clue. He likes the way the super-sleuth on the case takes the reader into his confidence. He feels, moreover, a glow of satisfaction and an almost personal feeling of achievement when the criminal is run to earth in the final chapter entitled "Dawn."

The Reading Public's Psychology

These types of writing, then, represent what the average reader wants. The writer asks himself, "Why does he want it?" He finds his question answered readily if he penetrates into the reading public's psychology.

An early tenet of that new and nimble science dealt with the blocked or thwarted impulse. Whenever an impulse, an appetite, or a desire runs up against a stone wall and fails to find outlet, satisfaction, and fulfillment, it seeks to discover the next best thing. If, in turn, the impulse finds the next best thing to be out of the question, it tries to discover the second next best thing, and so on, down the line. This one tendency sums up the whole law and the prophets, or rather, profits, as far as the mass of popular writing is concerned.

Once an impulse finds itself thwarted, four definite psychological reactions occur. Of these four, one stands out as of paramount importance to the writer.

Suppose a man loses a position which he likes very much. He will carry around with him the thwarted wish to regain that job if he gets the chance. This thwarted wish may take four forms: that of simple rebellion, that of "sour grapes," that of cynicism or that of dream life.

If he rebels, he throws up his second job. For him it is his first position or nothing. If he enjoys the "sour grapes" reaction, he attempts to satisfy himself by saying that his first job cannot compare in value with the job he now holds. Perhaps he becomes cynical on the subject and, if so, makes himself unbearable to his family and friends by blaming all the other people in the world for his plight. The chances are that he will drift off into a state of dream life and enjoy himself imagining all the satisfaction he would like to have achieved. In this blissful state he can picture himself with all the emoluments and pleasures of his former job and completely eliminate the many unpleasant features and the actual drudgery which also figured in it in its actual form.

Naturally, writers find their chief concern in the dream-life reaction. The conditions of modern life tend to make dream life popular. Few people achieve the opportunity to do everything they want. Whenever a human desire receives a setback, it immediately seeks satisfaction in dream life.

Referring to our four main reactions, we can see that most people become either cynical or addicted to dream life. Experience has shown that the openly rebellious usually come to grief.

The writer, then, can consider that the general public consists mainly of three types of people:

The intellectuals—a relatively small group who tend toward cynicism.

The practical—a group wrapped up in the affairs of the world; they have no interest in cynicism or art. They achieve success in their chosen line.

The nonintellectuals—the largest group of all. They read the cheaper magazines, enjoy the "soap operas," and get a thrill from run-of-the-mill motion pictures.

How, then, can the writer best satisfy the needs of these special groups, all of which join in making up the newspaper-reading population of the country? He can do it by analyzing their tastes and needs and by remembering them when he embarks on even the simplest news story.

Interesting Three Types of Readers

Let us consider first the intellectual group. This group finds its enjoyment in mental stimulation. It reads with interest the articles dealing with foreign affairs, politics, government, finance. It enjoys entering the new doors opened to it by each successive scientific discovery and all articles that deal with exploration and man's domination in the universe. It appreciates music and art as much from the intellectual as from the emotional standpoint.

In fiction, this group prefers urbane, sophisticated writing. It takes to books which show significant insight into character. To use a convenient tag, it appreciates the psychological novel, the type of novel that passes by mere gunplay and "sweethearting" to elucidate the counterplay and interplay of impulses, motives, desires. For relaxation this group often turns to detective fiction. And why? We find our answer in the true nature of detective fiction. The basic appeal in the well-written detective story lies in the riddle it propounds. Intellectual humanity's delight in riddles goes back beyond the Sphinx. The Old Testament abounds in illustrations of this liking. The Queen of Sheba went to Solomon, as she said, to try him with hard questions. At least that was one of the reasons she had in going. The intellectual reader's zest in the present-day detective novel is chiefly his zest and eagerness to solve the riddle, to unravel the skein of circumstances which the writer has devised.

What of the practical group? As the individuals who make up this "go-getter" class usually have no interest in art, we can eliminate from their needs all writing that makes an appeal to the imaginative faculty. The practical man wants to read articles which he feels will help him in his business or profession. He turns to the technical article in his own field, to all writing that points the way to better production and better marketing and to health information which promises him a better physique. The practical reader feels he has no time to waste on merely entertaining stuff. He wants the real goods. Often, to catch his interest, the writer must appeal to his cupidity. He must suggest that his article gives subject matter that the practical man might well heed, that it holds out chances for improvement and furnishes a formula of real, practical value.

And now we come to the largest and, for the writer, the most important group—the many who desire outlet for their thwarted wishes, who crave a dream-world release.

Here we can set down four main types of frustrations, and indicate the kind of reading matter in which each finds an outlet.

1. **Frustration of the simple motor impulse.** By "motor" we merely mean action and movement. If we prevent a child from being active, it gets into a tantrum. If we thwart an adult, he goes into a dream life of motion. Now, modern conditions keep many young men tied to their desks when what they crave is some physical outlet for their youth and spirits, some work or play which will exercise their muscles. Since these men are themselves unable to lead lives of action, they take their activity vicariously by reading action stories which, in the newspaper, they find on the sporting page, in the adventures of explorers and aviators, in the physical achievements of mankind around the globe.

2. **Frustration of the play impulse.** Everyone enjoys the carefreeness implicit in play. Yet the daily grind involves duty; things must be done, and done at a certain time. The individual goaded by routine dreams of an escape from the daily round, an escape from responsibility. He takes delight in slapstick comedy, particularly in that form of writing or that comic strip in which the writer or cartoonist takes a play attitude toward reality. He likes to see Old Man Drudgery whacked soundly on the head.

3. **Frustration of the masterful impulse.** Most men and women desire to become leaders. Lack of education, lack of social embellishments, lack, primarily, of the ability to lead—all thwart them in this ambition. This disappointment gives place to a series of dreams which gives them the fulfillment of their hopes. They like to read of others who succeed. All newspaper stories and interviews which deal with success in business, in society, on the stage or in Hollywood help in enabling this group to escape reality. They ally themselves with the story's protagonist and succeed vicariously in that protagonist's success.

4. **Frustration of the love impulse.** Thwarted sex attempts to satisfy itself in romantic dreams. These take an infinite variety of forms. Perhaps the commonest finds itself related to the masterful type, and the man dreams of some bright idea which enables him to win the girl, or the girl dreams of securing "charm" or "appeal" to help her get her man. Many murder stories, many human interest stories, even some obituaries have a strong romantic content, and,

in their own way, aid the thwarted love impulse to escape vicariously.

Popular writers achieve their success by carefully catering to these blocked desires. Sometimes they cater strongly to one or to another. More often they blend several satisfactions together. When they evolve a judicious blend of all four appeals, the resulting royalties jingle a cheerful chime in their personal cash registers.

Before psychology laid bare the workings of our mental processes, the older authors had to proceed mainly by guesswork. By sheer, innate gumption they had to foresee what the public wanted without quite knowing why. In a good many instances their blending of material appears to be a stroke of sheer luck.

Take for example one of the outstanding best sellers of former years, *Ben Hur*. As a story in printed form, the book sold by the million. As a play it toured and toured the country with much of the excitement and ballyhoo that usually attend the circus. As a film it achieved vast profits in recent times. Wherein lay its appeal?

The shrewd old advance agent who used to go ahead of the road company of *Ben Hur* as publicity man supplied the answer. "*Ben Hur*," he said, "could never fail. If you mix a horse race, a ballet dance, and religion, you are bound to catch the American public." Herein lay three potent satisfactions. It released the action impulse, the sex impulse and gave that outlet for dream-world desires which all religions hold in common.

So it goes. The reporter can find no better preparation for a real understanding of the public for which he writes than by tabulating the appeals made to readers by past and present successes.

While the novelist and the feature writer have exploited the foregoing principles more extensively than the newspaper writer, the reporter should never forget that their reading publics are one and the same. His province, just as much as the novelist's province, lies in interesting the reader. Fact remains stranger than fiction. Much of the daily grist which comes to him in the course of his assignments contains all the appeal which the fiction writer has to invent. The knowing reporter, conversant with reader psychology, develops these stories in a way so absorbing that mayhap he can hold children from their play and old men from the chimney corner.

5
The Average Reader
and His Interests

Reader Interest the Basis of Successful Writing—The Average
Reader Considered—How to Attract, Stimulate, and Hold
Reader Interest

All journalistic mass media depend for support on the
average man and woman and have from their beginnings made a determined effort to appeal to the tastes
and interests of average individuals. Editors, because
they have been in the business longer than motion
picture producers and radio and television directors,
had worked out a rule-of-thumb procedure based on
experience and gumption. They knew that local stories
held more interest than foreign stories, that picture
pages were a big drawing card, that obituaries apparently attracted women readers, and that the weather
news outranked even their banner-headline stories in
its universal appeal. In recent years scientific research in
the field of reader preferences appears to bear out these
old rule-of-thumb ideas.

The Bureau of Advertising of the Newspaper Publishers Association and the Advertising Research Foundation, for instance, interviewed 62,487 readers of 138
United States dailies, and found among other things
that only about 14 per cent of general news stories
were read by men and 11 per cent by women; that the
highest score was that of an Indianapolis *News* war
story which was read by 94 per cent of all the inter-

viewed men readers of the *News*. Women readers gave top individual attention to the obituary of a local judge, published in the Lima (Ohio) *News*. This article was read by 91 per cent of that paper's women readers.

Most journalistic media have writing at their base. Accordingly the present-day journalistic writer makes it his paramount aim to interest the average reader. Who is this average reader who looms so large in the scheme of things? To find him we have only to look around us. The average reader resembles us all so closely that to discover what holds his interest in reading matter, we have only to ask ourselves what each of us finds interesting in the stories and articles we read.

If we answer our own question thoughtfully and carefully, we find that interest attaches itself to four main elements in writing. We discover our delight in what is novel or in any way unusual. We notice that our interest quickens when we turn to writing that has a direct appeal, that seems aimed at us or that sometimes seems to include us in its range. We prefer prose which runs along smoothly and has pace. And then we know that our interest never flags if what we read boasts the element of variety.

The Interest in Novelty

The new and the unusual hold an interest for everybody. Haven't we all felt it? From the days when, as youngsters, we stood open-mouthed outside the circus side show longing to see the marvels within, the new and the unusual have gained our interest. This craving for novelty, for news, draws most readers to their daily papers. Knowing this, the reporter strives to satisfy this craving at every turn. When the story he has to tell contains the element of freshness or of the unusual, he rejoices. He knows that he will not have to bother with his style—the story will carry itself. If, on the other hand, his story has no inherent interest-provoking qualities, the good reporter seeks to impart freshness through the method of presentation. He knows that trite or dull writing makes tedious reading. To say the same old thing in the same way comes easy to all writers. The wise ones realize that saying the old thing in a new way will stimulate interest and startle readers into understanding the thought behind the word symbols.

Like everything else we use, words and phrases cannot stand up forever under constant wear and tear. If writers use and overuse them, they must expect to find that their meaning and their pattern become worn and frayed. How can they renovate this pattern? How can writers bring back the picture which the word originally conveyed? They can do this by getting back to the word's primal meaning. They discover, if they bother to look into them, that words start out by reflecting ideas. Time in some cases has dulled this reflecting quality. They can bring back this shining mirror surface by releasing in their writing a hint of the word's original picturesque meaning. The word "exorbitant" shows something outside the normal track or orbit; "emolument" projects the image of a mill with the ground wheat. As words constitute the chief instrument with which writers work, the wise writer uses constant study and research to keep it sharp and pointed.

The Interest in Directness

Much writing fails to hit the mark because it is aimed at no mark in particular. It strives apparently to reach the wide, wide world, but unfortunately the wide, wide world, as such, does not read. The most interesting matter which we peruse each day is in the form of letters which reach us in the mail. Why? We find them interesting mainly because they are directed definitely at us. Their thought comes direct. Note the straightforward manner in which the sentences in letters run along. Each one fairly races from its capital letter to its full stop to bring us its message.

Writers can incorporate this element of directness into their journalistic style. Often they achieve it by the simple process of addressing their readers individually as "you." Take, for example, this opening sentence of a human interest story:

If you have ever been a five-year-old counting the days before Christmas, you will understand how Johnny West felt on Thursday night when . . . .

The same direct writing focus may be obtained and a similar reader interest created merely by asking a question. A question implies that the readers can supply the answer. Naturally they feel flattered that the writer has asked them, in a sense, to act as collaborators. But another interest element attaches itself to the question—the element of curiosity. Here the readers claim brotherhood with the whole human family. The customers outside a drugstore phone booth, if the door to the booth is open, give ample proof of this. Outwardly they may be going through the motions of drinking orangeade or buying soap; inwardly, they follow every nuance of the one-sided conversation and even make up answers to the questions asked.

The Interest in Pace

Nowadays the newspapers try to adapt their style to the hurried rate at which readers live. They aim at putting across their information with directness, conciseness and pace. They employ preferably the short declarative sentence which their readers use normally in conversation. They comb the language for verbs of terse telling and swift announcement. In fact, the newspaper writer can be most successful in his effort to acquire an interesting style if he models it on the spoken word. He should copy its crispness, its directness, its simplicity. He will find that the most striking conversation is that which conveys the sense of rapidity, of swiftness, of pace. Centuries ago, popular sentiment linked rapidity with wit and slowness with dullness. This remains the modern attitude.

Studying modern conversation and its reflection in modern newspaper prose, one can without difficulty analyze the causes behind the effect of rapidity. For one thing, the short word takes precedence over the long word. For another, the popular connectives have emerged as the trio "and," "but," and "then." Who in conversation now uses the once popular "albeit," "notwithstanding," "nevertheless"?

Anything that calls upon the mind to halt and wonder what is meant naturally impedes the writing pace. Readers often spend precious seconds figuring out for themselves just which is the "former" and which is the "latter" in the sentences they read. Many modern writers follow Macaulay's lead, do without the pronoun as much as possible and repeat the noun or some variant of it.

The effect of rapidity in writing bears no relationship to the actual tempo of the writer's typewriter. Often writing which in the reading runs along smoothly and quickly has been arrived at laboriously.

While on this general question of pace in style, we suggest that a sure way to hold reader interest is to inject action into copy. Readers like action and the sense of the up-and-doing in what they read. They react immediately to writing which contains a variety of quick, nervous little verbs that run around and do things. Nothing picks up flagging interest so quickly as an apt and active verb. Naturally writers must use the passive construction when it is definitely called for. But they use it advisedly. If they write for long in the passive form, they put their readers in a passive mood. If they write too long in it, they put them to sleep.

To make slow and tedious writing interesting, writers can try the simplest of all devices. They can go through their copy, comb out all the passive constructions and substitute for them lively, active verbs. Immediately the writing picks up and becomes animated. Immediately the reader-interest also picks up. The verb writers use most is the verb "to be" in its various forms. Writers find it the easiest to use because it requires no thought. The verb "to be," therefore, is a lazy verb. Often writing which contains every element of good writing misses fire. Why? It simply buzzes with is's and was's.

The short active verb fits in admirably with current newspaper practice. All papers aim at easy readability to minimize the reader's effort. Accordingly, they prefer the short word to the long word and the short sentence to the long sentence. If we analyze any newspaper column which we have read with ease, we will probably find few words over two syllables.

The Interest in Variety

The wise showman knows that nothing pleases his public more than variety. In fact he uses that attribute to describe a whole class of entertainment. The showman has found that his audience grows restive if he gives it too much of the same type of thing. In arranging a successful television revue, he sees to it that no act plays for more than a few minutes; in constructing a popular musical comedy, he works on the same cut-and-dash principle—a zig-zag outline plan which rapidly cuts to new material.

The writer may well take hints from the showman, as indeed he must take hints from every person and method which successfully interest the average public. We can apply the interest-provoking qualities of variety immediately to the written word. In the case of the actual vocabulary used, the need for change and variation becomes readily apparent. A primary aid to arousing and holding reader-interest lies in just this matter of verbal variety. No two words carry exactly the same shade of meaning. Each word, no matter how nearly synonymous it is with another, conveys its own unique idea. Accordingly, the more words the writer uses, the more ideas he uses. The piece of writing which shows a varied vocabulary boasts also a varied thought range. It attracts a greater reader interest because it provides a greater mental stimulation owing to this variety in idea.

The use of the same word over and over again is the chief device which writers employ to convey the sense of monotony, dullness, sameness, drabness. Recall Rudyard Kipling's poem, "Boots," with its recurring iterations—"Boots—boots—boots—sloggin' over Africa." Now these qualities of monotony and dullness are precisely those of which writers in all journalistic fields seek to steer clear. They can avoid the danger of this tedium by seeing to it that their vocabulary reveals an infinite variety.

Writers can cater to the reader's desire for constant change by varying the form which the copy takes, by making it continuously appealing to the eye. They are wise if they take into account this whole element of visual appeal.

Suppose we open a novel or magazine or newspaper page at random. The page or column which attracts us has on it probably a great deal of conversation. We see whole sentences in quotation marks. Sometimes the lines consist of a monosyllable, a "Yes" or a "No." "This page," we say to ourselves, "looks easy to read." In that comment we have a real clue to that page's reader interest. *It looks easy to read.* As a matter of fact, it *is* easy to read. It has what we have called visual appeal. One turns to the page or column which boasts variety, which is broken up, rather than to a page which confronts him with a solid array of type. Why? In many cases he comes to his paper or his book tired. He doesn't want to bother. He doesn't want to exert any more effort than is necessary. He prefers to see a page which as he says looks easy to read.

Advertising copy writers keep the element of visual appeal much to the fore. By the use of differing types and colored inks, by the clever spacing and arrangement of their written matter, they attract sufficient readership to their layout to make worth while the vast sums expended in the publication of the advertisement. Journalistic writers in all fields may well study with profit the devices which expert advertisers unearth and exploit. They rest their bag of tricks on sound psychology.

How can the writer transfer this element of variety to the printed page? What are some of the ways in which his copy can achieve visual appeal? A simple way in which to achieve it lies in varying the sentence lengths. Sometimes a writer falls into a rhythm of a jog trot in which he finds that each of his sentences runs to about the same number of words. If his style tends to the long and balanced sentence, he should practice conciseness. If he types out staccatos, he must vary them occasionally with a phrase or two of amplification.

A similar effect of variety comes when we consider paragraph lengths. A writer can see to it that his paragraphs differ in length. In so doing, let him err if necessary on the side of brevity. He should never forget that the reader prefers something that looks short to anything that looks long. What an author may write may be as clear and uninvolved as the next man's writing, but if it looks long-winded it defeats its purpose.

Punctuation provides another method of varying the written word. The present-day sentence tends to race along to its conclusion. As a rule this eliminates the many commas so frequent in old-fashioned writing. But other punctuation points remain. If the sentence construction calls for a semicolon, use one. This breaks the effect of too many short sentences together. We have the device which gives special prominence to the words coming after it—the dash. Usually before a quotation or insert there comes the colon. Quotation marks themselves invariably catch the eye. Also the newspaper rule which makes a separate paragraph of each phrase in quotes, sometimes even the single words, "Yes" and "No," insures a certain amount of visual variety. The use of parentheses has fallen out of favor. The present tendency limits their use to sentences in the text which correspond somewhat to stage directions.

Many papers and magazines vary the type in which they set the story. Often they print the leading paragraph or two in a type larger than the body type used in the rest of the article. Occasionally they will set up inserts—long quotations—in type smaller than the body type. The publication's own rules decide this, and the copyreader rather than the writer carries them out. But it all helps in achieving this surface effect of visual variety and appeal.

Style in Newspaper Writing

For the newspaperman, style consists in getting across the facts as accurately, as quickly, as readably, and as entertainingly as possible. The best newspaper stories and leads exemplify the best newspaper style. How can the young reporter acquire it? If he looks to one school for the answer he finds that style is the man. This means, presumably, that an instinct implanted in a man's personality grows to fruition as he puts pen to paper. He seeks his answer elsewhere only to find that style is playing the "sedulous ape." This means that he can acquire it only by laboriously copying someone else's models. Probably both theories have truth, but not the whole truth. Let us take a fifty-fifty break and assume that style is half creation, half imitation.

With the purely creative part, no outside agency should meddle. That little personal twist, that unknown quantity, that spark or twinkle from inside which makes a writer himself and nobody else— that remains up to him individually to guard and develop. He must nurse that spark along, feed it with fuel from his imagination, shelter it from the wet blanket of discouragement, and fan it from one direction with encouragement and from the other with salutary criticism. Who knows? In time the spark may grow into a steady flame.

With style on the imitative side, he has excellent models to guide him. They stand as signposts and milestones along the road leading to the acquisition of a fine journalistic style. But they can after all only stand and point. The young reporter himself must do the walking. He must write, write, write.

No royal road exists to the achievement of facility with words. The young reporter must practice constantly. No six- or eight-hour day need hamper his progress. He can work, if he will, the round of the clock. He can obtain excellent practice by assigning himself professional stories to cover. Then he can compare his work with the accounts of the same stories as they appear in the leading metropolitan papers—compare them as to manner of treatment and length; see what the skilled reporter has included and what he has left out; see which features the paper plays up and those which it plays down or ignores altogether. By doing this over and over again, the young reporter will learn more than by reading all the books on style ever written or by listening to all the lectures on the same esoteric subject, however eloquently delivered.

In analyzing this professional work, the young reporter will note a number of things which will not fit into cut-and-dried categories. Oddly enough, he may find that the element he cannot poke into a pigeonhole stands out as the best part of the story and is the element which gives it distinction.

6

The Nature of News

**Definitions of News—Factors Which Determine News Value—
Elements of Newsworthiness—Big News and the "Big Story"—
Present-day News Emphasis**

What is news? When asked this question the average person might answer, "News is what the newspaper prints," or "News is what we hear over the radio." Such replies, though partial and incomplete, are nevertheless on the right track. For news is not an event, however stupendous, but the report of that event; not the actual happening but the story or account of that happening which reaches us. If we keep that fact in mind we are well on our way to a correct answer to the initial question.

Many newsmen and others have tried their hand at defining news.

Charles A. Dana, when editor of the New York *Sun,* declared that news was something that made a person exclaim. Later he improved on his first notion and decided that "news is anything which interests a large part of the community and has never been brought to their attention."

Stanley Walker, when a city editor, defined news with the succinct summary: "Women, Wampum, and Wrongdoing"—sex, money, crime.

The United Press Associations,* in the manual

* After merging with the International News Service, a new manual was compiled in collaboration with Associated Press and was released September 5, 1960.

78

issued to its correspondents, told them that "News is anything and everything interesting about life and materials in all their manifestations."

Gerald W. Johnson, after his years with the Baltimore *Evening Sun*, gave his opinion a professional shading. "News," he wrote, "is such an account of such events as a first-rate newspaperman, acting as such, finds satisfaction in writing and publishing."

According to Neil MacNeil, formerly assistant night managing editor of the New York *Times*, in his book *Without Fear or Favor*, news is "a compilation of facts and events of current interest or importance to the readers of the newspaper printing it."

All these definitions have a common denominator in that they indicate the idea of interest, but all except Mr. Dana's ignore the element for which the city editor looks. He hopes the news he publishes is the *first* report. Accordingly, he must introduce the notion of timeliness, and with that incorporated, we can arrive at a workable answer. When again asked, "What is News?" we are now able to reply, "News is a timely report of anything of *interest* to humanity and the best news is that which *interests* the most readers."

We place the words "interest" and "interests" in italics in order to emphasize from the start the primary element in newsworthiness, for interest rather than importance is the touchstone.

What type of news holds the chief interest for the average reader? As each of us comes under the head "average reader" we can phrase the question more precisely, and ask "What holds the greatest interest for us?" That's an easy one to answer. "The proper study of mankind is Man." Certainly, mankind is the individual's chief concern. The news, then, which most interests the average reader consists of anything that affects himself—his health, his wealth, his safety, his well-being. This news which the reader relates to himself may not be the first to catch his attention; nevertheless the rule holds. He may scan the front page, with its alarums and excursions from near and far, and say to himself, "What in all this concerns me?" "Nothing," he concludes, but he is wrong. True, the report from London of the Prime Minister's last speech, the graphic account from Japan of a shattering earthquake, news of a strike on a railroad in a far-off section of the country and half a dozen other headlined stories may not concern him though they may interest him; but, up at the top of the page, his eye catches the weather report and, reading it, he decides whether or not to go through with his plans for tomorrow. The news which most concerned him proved to be the news that most interested him.

Side by side with the individual reader's natural self-interest stands a number of closely allied basic human appeals to which every individual responds. *The American Weekly* lists twelve such which it utilizes and cites its vast readership as proof of their potency. Here they are: achievement, culture, faith, tragedy, health, heroism, mystery, self-improvement, recreation, romance, science, security.

As the chief worth of news rests in its ability to interest, all who write and publish it keep in mind the attention-provoking qualities of such basic stimuli.

Factors Determining News Value

Four main factors determine the value of news.

We have already mentioned the first one, *Timeliness*.

The reader wants his news to be new. That is why he buys his paper or listens to the broadcast. The miracle of present-day communication frequently makes the announcement of the news almost coincide with the instant of its happening.

Another is *Proximity*.

The reader finds more interest in a minor event close at hand than in a more important event miles away. James Gordon Bennett, Jr., when he first published his Paris Edition of *The Herald*, gave his reporters this principle in the epigram, "A dead dog in the Rue de Louvre (the paper's address) is of more interest than a flood in China." Today news of purely local concern is the bedrock on which the publishers of American newspapers outside the largest cities build their circulation, and surveys show that news of international importance, except major events, is of interest to only 10

per cent of readers in large communities and to so small a proportion of readers in the small cities that no percentage figures have
been worked out.

The third factor is *Size.*

The very small and the very large attract attention. We find
interest in minuteness as well as in magnitude—but chiefly in
magnitude. Accordingly, when we hear of an accident or a catastrophe, we ask for the number of lives lost and the extent of the
damage done. We want to know the amount of the philanthropist's
bequest and the dimensions of the new airliner.

The fourth factor is *Importance.*

Is the news reported important or in any way significant? We
might naturally think that this factor should head our list, but news
practice decrees otherwise, for the touchstone, as noted before, is
interest. The trivial story, if imbued with interest, frequently ranks
in newsworthiness above announcements which are important and
significant, but dull. This is no new thing. Away back in 51 B.C.
Cicero complained that his professional news correspondent was
giving him too much of sporting events and not enough about the
political situation. Editors get the same complaint today from their
thoughtful readers. They know they can't satisfy everyone. They
know, also, that "interesting" news, which encompasses much that
is trival, attracts the mass audience, while the merely important is
addressed to a small public. Nevertheless, the better papers and the
better newscasts seek to give news that holds significance and importance in its proper place and treatment.

Elements of News Interest

History never actually repeats, but it does seem to repeat tendencies. Similarly, news stories never duplicate each other, but they
do have a way of falling into definite categories. Analyzing them
as we read them from day to day or listen to them as they come
over the radio, we can easily discern elements of news interest which
recur constantly. Sometimes a story will contain several of these

interest-provoking elements, sometimes but one. In each instance the dominant element present gives us the clue to that story's type and category. Here are twelve chief elements of news interest:

Self-interest. Topics related to the individual reader or listener, to his affairs, his family, his hobbies, and his well-being make the strongest appeal to his interest.

Money. The love of money may be the root of all evil; it certainly lies at the root of much news interest. Stories with economic appeal attract us, rich and poor alike.

Sex. Sex curiosity stimulates interest from childhood on. It draws us to many crime stories, as well as to those with a more wholesome romantic appeal.

Conflict. Struggle always secures our interest. Big news is news of battle, of flying fists. It is hard to hold readers with an account of a love feast. Many types of stories have conflict as their underlying element—the struggle against odds.

Here are several of these types:

1. Man's struggle with Nature.
2. Struggle between individual and organized society.
3. Struggle between political and economic groups:
   a) Wars;
   b) Campaigns;
   c) Strikes.

The unusual. Novelty, strangeness, incongruity form the basis of much that we consider news. Departures from the expected fascinate us. Variations from the norm often amuse us. This element led the editors of the Minneapolis *Morning Tribune* to print this item from a city far away:

REVEALING ACCIDENT

Boston, Mass.—Struck by a motor-cycle, 8-year-old Timothy Todd was taken to a hospital where doctors discovered he had:
1. Possible fractures of the nose and knee; 2. Chickenpox.

Hero worship and fame. Big names not only make news, they are news themselves. We all find interest in what a well-known person does or thinks or says. Under this head fall stories of the "success" and achievement type, as well as many interviews and personality sketches.

Suspense. Stories which make us wonder what will happen excite a continuing interest. Here we find those stories involving the rescue appeal—will or will not the trapped miners survive?—stories of adventure and exploration.

Human interest. News of fellow human beings or of animals which touch our emotions come under "human interest." Such stories have a way of appealing to such primary emotions as love, pity, horror, fear, sympathy, jealousy, sacrifice.

Events affecting large organized groups. We are all "joiners" to a certain extent and accordingly find interest in any item that concerns our political party, our church, our fraternity, our scout troop. These groups may be:

1. International.
2. National.
3. State.
4. Civic.

Contest. The struggle to win allies itself with the conflict element as previously noted but deserves an individual listing, for it forms the basis of much of the appeal of the sports pages. It also enters into accounts of danger and daring where man pits his strength against great obstacles.

Discovery and invention. "Eureka!" exclaimed Archimedes. "News!" says the editor.

Crime. Wrongdoing holds a fascination for saint and sinner alike. Frequently we hear editors criticized for publishing "too much crime news." Too much or too little, they wouldn't publish it at all unless readers found absorbing interest in it. The "best" crime stories, from the news point of view, unite many of the foregoing elements such as sex, conflict, suspense, human interest and sometimes even big name and fame appeal.

The four factors of news value and the dozen or more elements that stimulate reader and listener interest play their parts in determining an item's newsworthiness.

Elements of Newsworthiness

Editors would be hard put to it if asked to give a crisp and comprehensive definition of "newsworthiness." Yet most of them know unerringly what constitutes it. To prove this, we have only to study the page one headlines on American newspapers from coast to coast on any given day. They are remarkably similar, as if in general agreement as to what constitutes newsworthiness—that standard which determines what to choose and what to discard from the vast record of the day's happenings which reaches editors from North, East, West, and South.

Ignoring theory and basing our selection solidly on the day-by-day procedure of representative editors from coast to coast, we can set down at least a dozen rules and principles governing news selection and answering the question: "What is news?"

1. Anything touching a person of prominence or one who has become a public character.
2. The very unusual. Anything that can't happen and yet does happen is news.
3. Anything vitally affecting the government of the country or city.
4. Anything which directly or indirectly affects the pocketbook. (This is the reason why stories of city budgets are played up to such an extent.)
5. Any injustice. Anything which rouses the temper of the reader is a story.
6. Catastrophe. Anything involving great loss of life or property. Accidents as news vary directly in proportion to the distance involved.
7. Anything involving universal consequences, like the tie-up in transportation.
8. Any story which affects the emotions of the reader—which makes him sorry or pleased.
9. Any event which vitally interests a large number of people, such as a world gathering of a large religious denomination.
10. Anything to do with large amounts of money.

11. Discovery in any line—or achievement—the first time anything big has been done.
12. Murder. In a small town or community a murder is always a story. In a larger place it depends on the amount of mystery it possesses. It has definite news value

    a. if it involves a person of importance;

    b. if at all unusual—i.e., if a woman murders a man;

    c. if the people involved are upper class people; here the interest centers on the motive;

    d. if it involves the "unwritten law."

    The great murder stories in the history of journalism—such as the Thaw case and the Hall-Mills murder—have had all the ingredients: mystery, woman involved, prominent people, scandal.

The reader has his reasons for selecting what he reads in the paper or listens to over the radio. He may select from the mass offered him, perhaps, one-fourth in a daily newspaper or perhaps one-half of the items in the newscast.

Why does he select what he does? What factors govern his choice?

Psychologists as well as editors seek the answer.

One important reason for selection is the physical presentation of the news—its position on the page or in the newscast, size of the headline, or timing and voice. A reader is likely to select a story with a large headline or listen carefully when the newscaster announces "Flash" or "Bulletin." These correspond in a way to personal endorsements from editor or newscaster, as if each announced, "This is a story you had better read or listen to." Getting beyond and behind such obvious stimuli, we may find other reasons.

Wilbur Schraam, former Director of the Institute of Communications Research at the University of Illinois, has an hypothesis based on experimental evidence. Here is his theory:

I think it is self-evident that a person selects news in expectation of a reward.

This reward may be either of two kinds. One is related to what Freud calls the Pleasure Principle, the other to what he calls the Reality Principle. For want of better names, we shall call these two classes *immediate reward* and *delayed reward*.

In general the kinds of news which may be expected to furnish immediate reward are news of crime and corruption, accidents and disasters, sports and recreation, social events and human interest.

Delayed reward may be expected from news of public affairs, economic matters, social problems, science, education, and health.

Big News and the Big Story

Having raised and answered the question, "What is news?" let us raise and answer another, namely, "What is big news?" We live in an era of big stories. The era began in the first quarter of the present century when the press generally developed an amazing concentration of effort upon a succession of news events—reporting, photographing, eyewitnessing, high-spotting—to the end that circulation figures passed into the mass millions.

It is, as all commentators agree, the big story with its streamer headline and full-page display with "art" and attendant features that determines what a large section of the American public reads from day to day, thinks about, and talks about.

What are the elements which enter into the making of the big story?

For the surest answer let us fall back again on actual procedure.

Each year representative editors from coast to coast are asked by pollsters and article writers to pick out what they consider to be the ten biggest stories of the preceding twelve months.

A typical year's list runs along these lines.

1. A murder that combines such choice ingredients as prominent names, mystery, sex, and scandal.
2. A country-wide strike or a war, if one is in progress.
3. The death of a "glamorous" movie star, male or female.
4. A notable long-distance flight.
5. The visit of some outstanding royal personage.
6. A great disaster of nature such as a flood or a hurricane.
7. The World Series.
8. A struggle between ideologies along the line of church versus state.

9. A highly publicized boxing event—world championship at stake.
10. A story of endurance, achievement, or adventure.

If we analyze this list we find that the elements of crime, sex, novelty, disaster, human importance, and conflict enter in varying degrees.

Let us look at our list of a year's ten biggest stories and pick out the dominant element in each.

In the murder story crime and sex can both enter, but conflict is there, too, both in the pursuit of the criminal and in the legal proceedings after he is caught; it is the struggle between lawbreaker and the law.

In the strike or war story we find conflict from the outset and raw conflict at that.

The death of the glamorous movie personage may rank chiefly as a sex story.

With the notable long distance flight we find conflict again; man pitting his puny strength and the instruments of his invention against time and space.

The royal visit can rank as novelty.

The disaster story is another conflict story—the fists of nature unleashed and on a rampage against a peaceful world.

In the World Series we have team pitted against team.

In the struggle between ideologies we find a similar pattern—conflict clearly defined.

The world championship boxing bout gives us flying fists in dead earnest, and in our final story, that of endurance, achievement, or adventure, man our hero is again matched against odds on mountain, in the air, or on the sea.

In eight of the ten stories we find conflict as the fundamental pattern. Big news is news of battle.

Present-Day News Emphasis

Big news is growing bigger, not so much in itself as in the journalistic treatment of it. The growing tendency now is to emphasize one important story a day. Actually this tendency stems from long-held journalistic practice; the novelty about it lies in the present-day methods of emphasis. Newspapers for many years have had "lead" positions, and the editor had always to decide which of his available stories merited that position. Today, the big story gets not only the lead position but streamer headlines, the embellishment of "art" and the display techniques possible because of the modern newspaper's typographical facilities.

Out of this tendency has grown another one—the tendency to make high-spot newspapers. Editors rationalizing this tendency argue that too much is happening in the world to make it possible to report any considerable part of the news. Therefore they have to pick out a few of the things which they believe to be the most interesting and important. The newspaper in the old days could be compared to a mirror—like the one the Lady of Shalott had—which would reflect everything that went on. Today the comparison would more truly be with an artist's landscape which featured the significant and suppressed or eliminated the infinite mass of detail.

Back of all the rationalizing and back of all the featuring, emphasizing, suppressing, and eliminating stands the economic factor. As Fremont Older of the San Francisco *Call* once plainly put it:

Competition is growing and there is more pressure on all of us as time passes. We editors select news according to the appeal in it, trying always to play the story that has the widest appeal. Sometimes it is a football game, sometimes a prize fight, sometimes a murder mystery and sometimes a scandal, but we are always trying to estimate as near as we can the story that will sell the greatest number of papers.

"Spot" and "Spread" News

Two designations relating to news crop up so constantly in city room lingo that they may logically find a place here. They are "spot" and "spread" news. The first term has to do with the type of news and the second term with its treatment. When we seek to define "spot" news, several adjectives rush to the fore to help us. Here they are: unexpected, live, recent, important, immediate. Spot news then is an unexpected, fresh, live, important happening, not an event that has been planned for and scheduled. Spot news if it comes in even a few minutes before press time, makes the paper if only in the form of a bulletin. If it is of extreme or extraordinary importance, the whole front page may be hastily remade.

Spread news refers to the type of story to which the paper gives emphasis by position, display, typographical embellishment, illustrations and the like. It tops the column, has the ballyhoo of a striking headline and may even have auxiliary stories adjacent to it as part of the "spread."

7
The News Story: Its Construction

The Importance of the Lead—Main Types of Newspaper Leads—
Present-Day Story F itterns—Writing the Story—The Rewrite
Man and His Work

The newspaper story in America has evolved to meet
the requirements of everyday life as lived by everyday
readers. It relies on the elements of novelty, directness,
pace and variety, and it strives to convey its information
in the form most in keeping with the tempo of our
times. It aims to state its facts quickly and clearly.

We can divide the newspaper story as it strikes our
eye on the newspaper page into three parts:

1. The headline.
2. The first paragraph.
3. The remainder of the story.

The headline first attracts us. It stands out in bold
black type. Its message is terse, abrupt and often
startling. It makes us stop and look. It tells us quickly
what the story covers. Its primary function is to attract
our attention. It corresponds to the beat of the drum
outside the side show. But we will not consider the
nimble art of headline writing here. As we have seen,
headline writing belongs to the copyreader's province
and not to the reporter's.

The First Paragraph or Lead

It would be difficult to overstate the importance
of the opening paragraph or lead. Always this lead

remains the primary concern of the newspaper writer. In any form of writing the writer tries to put his best foot foremost. In journalistic writing, this first stride has unique importance.

Because the present-day reader resembles the man who both runs and reads, present-day newspapers seek to facilitate his getting his information quickly. The convention has developed of telling the main facts of a news story in its first lead paragraph. Read any American or Canadian newspaper today, and you will find that by glancing at the headlines and through each lead you get, substantially, all the important news, although you may miss many interesting details.

This convention requires that in the lead the reporter answer the questions which would occur to any normal person when confronted with the announcement of an event. These questions, called the five W's, are:

Who? What? When? Where? Why? and How?

Suppose the news story concerns a fire. In writing his lead the reporter would answer the question, What? "Fire broke out," he would write. He would answer the questions, Who? and Where? by telling whose premises were burned and giving their location. He would answer When? by telling the time the fire broke out and how long it lasted. Why? In this case the cause, the inevitable carelessly tossed cigarette butt. Our reporter can answer the How? in this story in several ways—by describing the type of fire, "flames fanned by a stiff breeze," or by answering How much? Here he would estimate the probable financial loss and find out to what extent the premises had been covered by insurance.

This simple illustration shows us some of the things which a good lead is required to do. It summarizes the story for the reader. It identifies the persons concerned. In this case it gives the full name of the owner of the premises and the address of his property. It fixes the locale of the story. It gives the reader the latest available information—in this case probably the extent of the damage. Yet so far it has neglected another very important function of the lead. It has failed so far to stress the story's news "feature."

What is a story's news feature? It is that angle or twist which differentiates the story from any other of its particular type. Let us illustrate. Our fire story so far appears merely as a run-of-the-mill item. Blazes of this kind unfortunately happen everywhere, every day. But, suppose the burned premises temporarily housed important works of art which likewise went up in smoke and were lost to the world; or suppose the building was the property of some well-known person, a statesman, a Hollywood star, a baseball hero; or suppose again that next door to the burning premises stood a theatre, crowded at the time by people unaware of their danger. Each of these suppositions would satisfy as the story's news feature. Each would supply the necessary element of uniqueness.

But whether it be run-of-the-mill or outstanding in its impact, the lead should cover the story's essential facts. The city editor enunciated the alpha and omega of the craft when he shouted to his inquiring cub reporter:

"Spill the whole story in the first paragraph, and maintain the interest for the rest of the column."

The best-written lead not only satisfies the reader's initial curiosity, but whets his appetite to read more. Summing up, we may say then that the newspaper writer must see to it that his lead does five things: presents a summary of the story; identifies the persons and the places concerned; stresses the news feature; gives the latest news of the event; and, if possible, stimulates the reader to continue the story. And the present-day tendency is to achieve all this as quickly and as briefly as possible.

Rudolf Flesch, author of *The Art of Plain Talk* and a consultant on readability to the Associated Press, insists that the traditional Who, What, When, Where and Why lead is antique. However a great many antique traditions still persist. Nevertheless, newspapers have been stimulated by the radio and television newscasts and also by the news magazines and are consciously striving for more readability. This stimulation shows its effects in the continent-wide tendency to shorten the lead paragraph.

Today the practice on outstanding dailies throughout the nation indicates that the average lead should not be more than thirty words. The former International News Service's style book instructed its staff to write the lead in three lines or less. Usually the news can be told effectively within these limits. The man in the street can recognize the facts in most leads after reading or listening to them in twenty words. Most headline writers can tell the story in ten words.

This new lead trend simply points out the story's significance and prepares the reader's mind for details to come. Here is such a one:

> Brunette, Cathy Emanon, 23, and "the best looking woman in the police lineup in years" was arraigned yesterday before U.S. Commissioner Jones. She was accused of cashing stolen treasury checks in Chicago three years ago to obtain heroin.

Then more details follow.

A reporter may write his lead in a variety of forms. Editors welcome originality. Several types, however, have proved their readability and have become almost standardized.

Main Types of Leads

1. The digest lead. This lead summarizes clearly and plainly all the principal facts. It remains the simplest in construction and forms a basic part of all lead variations. The typical news item or dispatch starts off with the digest or summary lead. The following is a fair example:

> LONDON, Jan. 23—A silver cup nearly two feet high, standing on a bar at the Olympia Exhibition Hall here, awaits the winner as 375 bartenders from all over the world submit their prize original cocktail formulas in a contest for the world's championship that began today.
> —New York *Times*

2. The direct appeal lead. This form borrows the interest-compelling device of the personal letter. It addresses the reader directly or by implication as "you," and has the effect of making the reader a collaborator in what follows. It often begins with such phrases as "If you have ever thought," or "If you have ever seen or read." Here is a typical direct appeal lead.

If you think you've got it tough when you have to listen to your little sister practice the piano, take pity on Alfred Jay Smith. In the last 30 years he's had to audition 20,500 child performers. And he likes his job.

3. The circumstantial lead. Here we have a beginning which stresses the circumstances under which the story happened. It crops up usefully when the story has a human interest slant.

> CHESTER, Pa., Feb. 20—The cries of a pet cat into the mouthpiece of a telephone at a house in West Third Street today brought out a detachment of police and plain-clothes men bent on frustrating a burglary and possibly saving a life.
>
> A telephone operator at the central exchange called the police department and informed the desk sergeant that cries of distress were coming from the telephone at the Third Street house. A patrol wagon full of policemen was hurried to the scene and they surrounded the house. Repeated knocks at the door brought no answer and they forced an entrance.
>
> They found the cat with one of its feet caught in an ice chest. In its struggles to get free it had knocked the receiver from the telephone, which was lying on the floor, and was crying into the mouthpiece. The family was away.
>
> —AP Dispatch

Here is another *circumstantial*-type lead. Although the body of the story is about a fatal auto crash in which two of five sisters were killed, the emphasis in the lead is placed on the circumstances which lead up to the accident—the heart attack of the driver. Without this emphasis on circumstances under which the story happened, it would have been just another "run-of-the-mill" account of an auto accident.

> A heart attack suffered by Mrs. Mary White, 60, of 5 East 37th Street, Waverly, was believed by the police today to have caused her to lose control of her car in Cedar Village last night with resultant death for herself and one of the

four elderly sisters who were with her. The three remaining sisters suffered severe hurts.

4. The statement or quotation lead. This type of lead starts out with an enunciation which, as often as not, occurs in quotation marks. In speech reporting particularly, a succinct, epigrammatic sentence often puts in capsule form the gist of the speaker's remarks. When the reporter has added to this the inevitable five W's, the resulting paragraph coincides with the digest or summary lead.

> A "large percentage" of the persons over 60 years of age in state mental institutions "do not belong there," Abraham Cohen of the Mayor's Advisory Committee for the Aged declared yesterday. He spoke at a plaque-dedication ceremony at the Walter S. James Community Center for the Aged, 23-12 Second Avenue.

5. The descriptive lead. This form of beginning presents a picture. The reporter may set the stage for the action of his story or he may present in detail one or more of his chief actors. In other words, this lead can describe the scene or it can describe one or more of the people involved.

> FORT LEE, N.J., Oct. 23—When the sun is right, it projects the swooping cables and tapering verticles of the George Washington Bridge to the surface of the Hudson River in the pattern of a mathematical graph.
>
> If the dark band slicing across fainter parallel lines were taken as a symbolic instead of a scientific curve, it could represent the traffic over the bridge and its earnings in its first twenty years, and it would show that 200,811,678 vehicles have crossed the graceful span since its dedicatory ceremonies on Oct. 24, 1931. The gross tolls have been $109,866,465.
>
> —New York *Times*

and again:

> Dressed in similar grey gabardine coats and grey fedoras and wearing false rubber noses attached to lenseless spec-

tacles, three armed young thugs invaded the third-floor offices of the Anderson Jewelry Company, 24 Main Street, Beverly, early yesterday afternoon, held up seven persons and escaped with $5,920 in cash.

6. **The suspended interest lead.** This type of lead serves as a stimulator of interest. It gives the reader enough information to whet his appetite, and no more. After the lead, the story usually runs along in chronological form, so that the reader must read to the very end to get the climax. Reporters use this type of lead chiefly for short bits, on the theory that if used on longer articles, readers would not bother to wade through paragraph after paragraph. Here is a typical suspended interest lead, used in a typical way.

The quick action of John Lowell, a baker, probably saved this city of 16,290 inhabitants from disaster today.

At 4 A.M. he noticed that the gas flames in his bread ovens had flickered out. Ten minutes later gas again hissed through the pipes, unlighted.

Lowell reasoned that many unattended gas appliances in the slumbering city might be pouring unburnt gas into homes and apartments. He called Fire Chief Charles Albert.

Fire trucks, police cars and ambulances sped through the darkened streets, sirens screaming. A sound truck blared, "check your gas! Check your gas!"

Chief Albert said that the cacophony which woke the population saved many lives as his men found about 200 gas-filled homes and he personally awakened "at least fifty" groggy citizens. No one was overcome.

The light and heat company serving the area laid the gas interruption to an air pocket in the lines.

7. **The tabulated lead.** Occasionally one runs into a story in which no one fact is prominent. Each facet of interest has about the same value. In such instances, a practice has grown up of tabulating each item in the lead—one, two, three, four.

A major scandal has erupted in the 3rd Internal Revenue District, the *World-Telegram* learned exclusively today. It involves:

1. Suspension of a five-man "fraud squad" suspected of shaking down 12 firms for $50,000 to cover up income tax discrepancies.

2. Implication of a high city official who is a Tammany stalwart.

3. Exhaustive investigation by intelligence agents of the Treasury Department. Their findings have been turned over to U.S. Attorney F. X. McGohey's criminal division for presentation to a grand jury.

—N. Y. *World-Telegram*

8. **Various "stunt" leads.** All editors put a premium on novelty, and some even on the bizarre. Accordingly a variety of what we can call exclamation point leads crop up from time to time and have been dubbed, "astonisher," "punch," and "teaser" as the case may be. Originality knows no pigeonhole and refuses the standardization of definition beyond the generalization that such leads are eccentric variations from the norm. When successful, a stunt lead has its own reward.

Bertram Walker today had a fishing tale to top them all.

Out of the icy, wind-whipped waters of La Crosse Channel, Centralia, yesterday, he caught a man—an all-weather swimmer who had been floundering in the fast-running ebb tide.

Robert Jackson, 57, a 170-pound hod carrier of 122 Manchester Street, North Port, was losing his fight against the currents when the fisherman heard his cries for help, uncorked a 50-yard bull's-eye cast, "hooked" the swimmer and reeled him to safety.

Mr. Jackson was released after treatment at St. Mary's Hospital, Centralia, for exposure, submersion, cuts and bruises.

Mr. Walker, an electrical engineer for the Calco Engineering Company, went back to his fishing.

We start the normal story at its beginning and trace it step by step to its conclusion. The newspaper convention of the lead, however, makes the news story an exception to this general rule. This lead demands that in most instances the news story begin with its climax. Two reasons lie behind this formula: the desire to catch the reader's attention; the desire to save the reader's time.

The lead forms the springboard for the reporter's leap into the story. From a springboard wholly adequate, he can make a graceful dive; from one even partially defective, he may sadly flop. Often the impetus given by a successful lead carries him with fine tempo and gusto into the remaining paragraphs. Sometimes when fumbled over, the lead throws a disheartening shadow ahead.

This lead business makes even the practiced journalist pause. While covering a story he carries in the back of his mind the consciousness that a suitable beginning for the story must somehow evolve within him. He keeps on the watch for that element or those elements in the assignment which would make a good lead. A feeling of rare content creeps over him when he tucks the sought-for start away in his mind for eventual use. The best way to gain journalistic facility is to practice the writing of leads.

The Remainder of the Story

From the headline and the lead we come to the rest of the story. The reporter constructs the model news story after this pattern. He selects the most important incident or fact for his lead. Then he proceeds by selecting the next most important incident, fact or detail; then the next important; then the next important after that, and so on till he reaches the least important phase of all. Guided by his idea of news importance, the story assumes graphically the shape of an inverted pyramid. To the most important element of the story, the reporter has given the greatest space and prominence. To the next most important, he gives somewhat less prominence and space, and so on down the story. He ends up at the apex of the inverted pyramid with the facts or incidents of least value.

Obviously, he can best shorten his story by cutting off the last paragraph. Herein rests the technique's chief virtue from the make-up editor's point of view. Most papers receive far more news than they have space to publish. Stories must often undergo a last-minute shortening if important late news demands inclusion. The make-up editor knows that he can slice one, two or three paragraphs off any story written in this inverted pyramid form without depriving the reader of the story's chief news elements.

This story from the New York *Herald Tribune* illustrates the "inverted pyramid" construction:

2 IN GYPSY GARB
TRICK PAY-ROLL
CLERK OF $196

WOMEN DISTRACT VICTIM WITH
THEIR BEGGING PATTER,
SPIRIT MONEY OFF DESK

Two women in Gypsy costume, out on a begging tour in the garment section yesterday, snatched $196 from a desk in the office of Glamour Togs, Inc., 520 Eighth Ave., and escaped, police reported.

The money was part of a $950 payroll being sorted by Sarah Grossbard, clerk-receptionist, on the nineteenth floor of the building between 36th and 37th St.

Miss Grossbard reported the women kept pestering her for "a handout" and so distracted her with constant chatter that she did not know anything was missing until fifteen minutes after they had disappeared. To cap it all, she added, she had given the pair a ten-cent donation for some unexplained charity.

The women came into the office at 1:45 P.M., Miss Grossbard told police. One of them peered through the glass panel while the other entered through the shipping department and tiptoed into the reception room, where Miss Grossbard was seated alone. The second woman said that "they told me in the back you should give me money."

Miss Grossbard said she gave the woman a dime but could not get rid of her. "She kept fussing with my hands and with articles on the desk and chattering like a squirrel," she said. "All I can remember of her words were: 'Do you believe?' 'Do you have faith?' "

"Then," Miss Grossbard continued, "Lou Grau, owner of the place, came out of the back room and shouted: 'Get out of here!' Then he noticed that the one woman had a dollar bill in her hand and he yelled: 'Put that down!' She did and then ran out."

Miss Grossbard told police that the women were "thirty-ish" and dressed in vivid Gypsy skirts and blouses.

The typical news story takes this graphic form:

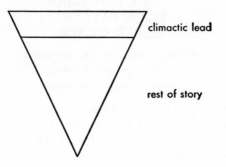

The Chronological Pattern

The usual story pattern is the chronological one. It begins at its logical beginning and ends with its logical conclusion. The usual story or anecdote told in conversation adopts this method. The newspaper uses this pattern chiefly with the human interest story which it regards as a journalistic art form distinct in itself and which therefore seldom runs the risk of being hacked off from the bottom. This chronological pattern is based on simple narrative.

Simple narrative cleaves to the very satisfying and logical procedure of placing incident after incident in the order in which they actually occurred. This time sequence, with each moment unfolding something new in the story's development, has long proved its effectiveness as an interest-holding device. The method holds the reader or the listener through the expectation and promise of what will follow next. Simple street ballads all rely on this narrative method. Time has long proved its effectiveness. E. M. Forster, in his *Aspects of the Novel*, takes this basic and most primitive element of pure narrative as his first aspect. He calls it the "and then—" appeal. It stands out as the one essential. It will always remain as the essence of storytelling; the binding narrative thread.

Scheherazade avoided the fate of her prodecessors because she knew how to wield this weapon of suspense which, as Mr. Forster again points out, is the only literary tool that has any effect upon tyrants and savages.

She only survived because she managed to keep the king wondering what would happen next. Each time she saw the sun rising, she stopped in the middle of a sentence and left him gaping. At this moment Scheherazade saw the morning approaching and discreet, was silent.

We all resemble the listening king in that we want to know what happens next. The oral or written satisfaction of this desire constitutes a story.

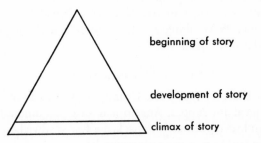

beginning of story

development of story

climax of story

The chronological story takes the graphic form of a pyramid which begins at the top, usually with the story's protagonist, and builds up incident after incident until it reaches the story's conclusion at the base.

Here is how the New York *Times* has used simple narrative technique to tell a human interest story chronologically:

DREAMS COME TRUE
FOR BOY TRAVELER

A 10-DAY SAGA OF FREEDOM
WITH 9 NIGHTS IN A SUBWAY
ENDS IN MORE DREAMS

Sometimes the dreaming of a youngster is abruptly transformed into sweet reality, his world expands beyond the limits of the schoolroom and the home, and, briefly, he travels on a plane that few adults know. It was so with 13-

year-old Angelo Cruz of Brooklyn, whose ten-day saga carried him far afield from workaday pursuits.

His story began on Election Day and ended yesterday in Children's Court. It entailed feasts on frankfurters and candy, explorations of parks and gardens and museums, travels on the subway, and it reached its zenith as he wandered wide-eyed and alone for five and a half hours Thursday night through a large department store.

Angelo is a stocky lad—5 feet 2 inches tall and 120 pounds —with dark hair and dark, inquisitive eyes behind his glasses. He is a first-year student at Metropolitan Vocational High School in Manhattan. According to his mother, Juanita, 37, he is a "better than average student," a "dreamer, who likes to wander and always talks of traveling." His father, Faustino, 49, is a rigger in the New York Naval Shipyard. At the home, 96 Washington Street, there is a brother, Harry, 21, and a sister, Jeanette, 7.

NINE NIGHTS IN A SUBWAY

On Election Day Mrs. Cruz gave Angelo $1.50 to purchase meat for supper. Angelo had an equal amount of his own, and surreptitiously he packed a few sandwiches and his bathing trunks in a worn shopping bag.

For nine nights Angelo slept in the subway. He spent his days in Brooklyn. He visited Coney Island and Prospect Park. He made a survey of the marble passages of the Brooklyn Museum. And he sat for hours in the Brooklyn Botanic Gardens.

But Thursday was chilly. He ventured downtown into Namm's Department Store, Fulton and Hoyt Streets, where it was warm. All afternoon he mingled with the early Christmas shopping crowds. At 9 P.M. the customers were ushered out. All except Angelo.

Now he was alone in the deserted store. He tiptoed cautiously along the silent aisles. "I always wanted to be in a department store alone," he reminisced wistfully, "and there I was, thinking of all the things I could buy sometime."

He passed through the soda shop and past the candy heaped in mountains on the counters. Yet he resisted temptation. He moved on to the toy department on the fourth floor. He gaped at the glittering holiday display, tentatively extended a hand toward the pristine electric trains. But he did not touch them. He only stared and wondered and sighed.

After hours among the toys, Angelo reluctantly left the department. One flight up was the furniture display. And sleep could not be denied.

At 2:30 A.M., night watchman James Carroll, making his tour, could hardly believe his eyes. There, on a couch, was a small, hunched-up figure in a gray plaid jacket, a khaki engineer's cap, a pink shirt and blue dungarees.

From then on the idyll disintegrated, with the help of police from the Butler Street station and another trip to Children's Court. But a sympathetic justice, confronted with an incurable romanticist, could do nothing but parole him in his mother's custody. On Dec. 22 he will come back to court to talk with a probation officer.

As he left the court, Angelo was asked if he would roam again. He looked up quickly at his mother.

"Anyway," he said, "there isn't much more to see in Brooklyn. I want to see other parts of the world. Like the Bronx and Europe."

With increasing frequency newspapers are adopting for some stories a compromise between the conventional "inverted pyramid" structure and the chronological order. This pattern starts off with a climatic lead in the sense that it gives the latest news development on the story and follows this lead with simple narrative in strict time sequence. We can represent the story pattern graphically in this manner:

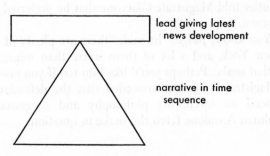

lead giving latest news development

narrative in time sequence

The following news story which originally appeared in the New York *Sun* will serve to illustrate this type:

SNAKE WILL TEST
CHARMS ON COURT

6-FOOT REPTILE TO FACE BAR SO
MAGISTRATE CAN RULE IF IT'S
"VICIOUS" OR "AFFECTIONATE"

Magistrate Francis X. Giaccone was confronted yesterday with the problem of deciding whether a rattlesnake can ever be graduated from the ranks of a "wild and vicious animal" to that of "affectionate pet." Decision was reserved pending court appearance of the reptile on Tuesday.

The trouble began when Robert Butler, 58 years old, of 27 West 139th Street, decided to visit friends at 110 Belmont Avenue in the Brownsville section of Brooklyn. As Butler explained in Brooklyn Week-end Court yesterday:

"Judge, I have had that snake twenty years and brought him with me because I did not want to leave him all alone."

Turned out that Brownsville people, though long accustomed to organizations like murder rings, have no use for rattlesnakes. That brought Patrolman Anthony Anzalone of the Liberty Avenue station into the picture. He investigated, peered into a box and beheld a six-foot reptile. He slammed down the top of the box and took Butler and his pet to the police station.

The snake was left at the station house while Patrolman Anzalone and Butler went to court, the latter charged with violating Section 22 of the Sanitary Code, prohibiting possession of wild and vicious animals.

Butler told Magistrate Giaccone that he preferred snakes to women.

"You know, Judge," he said, "there are plenty of snakes in New York, and a lot of them worse than mine, too. I love that snake. Perhaps you'd like him too if you saw him."

Magistrate Giaccone conceded that the defendant had advanced an interesting philosophy and suggested that Patrolman Anzalone fetch the snake in question.

The newspaper uses the word "story" as an omnibus term to cover all the items it publishes. Many of these articles are not stories at all in the sense that they have no narrative quality. Probably, an analysis of today's newspaper would show that it contained more exposition, interpretation, and opinion than narrative. We may find that the greater part of the news articles have to deal with new tax plans that the paper strives to make clear; new judicial decisions the significance of which the paper attempts to indicate; new scientific theories and inventions that call for explanation. For the majority of these articles, the paper will fall back on the standard inverted pyramid form. In some instances it happens that all sections of the interpretation have equal value and importance. Here we find no tapering off to an apex and no building up in time sequence. These interpretive stories fall into a graphic pattern of rectangular arrangement of equal sections.

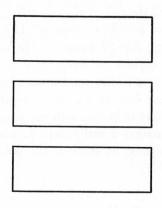

Writing the Story

Back to his typewriter with his notes, the reporter starts to build his story. He already knows, because he has covered it, whether his story will be exposition and interpretation or a chronicle of what happened.

If his job is to explain, he knows from experience that all exposition calls for a definite plan, and that the time he now spends on making an outline will be more than saved when he starts to write. Clarity is the goal at which all explanation aims. No matter how detailed or learned the explanation may be, if it leaves the reader muddled and puzzled, it has failed. The only way to avoid a confused story is to make a plan.

Suppose the writer's assignment calls for the explanation of a process. How will he construct his plan? First, he educates himself. He clarifies the whole process in his own understanding; mentally he takes the whole process apart and then reconstructs it. Only when he knows what it is all about himself, is he ready to start. First he considers the lead which must contain the news of the process along with any attention-getting devices he may have in his repertory. Then step by step, as he puts the process together in his own mind, he outlines it for the reader.

If, on the other hand, his story is a typical news narrative, he knows the ingredients that go to make it interesting. He knows that it consists of the "and then—" or story element, of description, conversation and a certain amount of suspense. The descriptive element comes logically enough into all narrative. The reader wants help in visualizing the scene beyond the precise geographical location. Conversation too enters as a logical constituent of a story which deals with people other than deaf mutes. The reporter sees that this conversation can sometimes help him with his description, but realizes that the best conversation actually steps in and helps the action along. He injects suspense by delaying the point or climax of his story as long as possible.

The Rewrite Man

Perhaps our reporter hasn't the time to bring his notes to the office and bang out his story on the typewriter. The paper's deadline may be too near. Or perhaps he is a "leg man" covering one of the city's police districts—a reporter whose chief ability lies in getting rather than in presenting the facts. In each of these cases he phones his story in to a rewrite man.

These rewrite men are usually experienced reporters who after years of covering various beats have demonstrated facility in news writing. Equipped with earphones, they take down, frequently on the typewriter, what the reporter at the other end of the line has to tell them. They check the spelling of all proper names; they check all addresses given; they get him to enlarge on all details that may add color or significance to the write-up.

Although the rewrite man in building his story lacks first hand acquaintance with the scene and the personalities involved in it, his work frequently turns out to be a story so expert and vivid that the reader would never guess that it had been compiled at long range and at second hand.

For one thing, the rewrite man has had long practice in writing to the newspaper pattern. He knows the tricks that a reporter can inject to arouse interest and to hold it. He can give life and movement to a descriptive bit that sounded static enough when the reporter mentioned it. He can add background to meagre facts, for he has his paper's morgue right at hand to serve him. He can write, and he can write quickly. In fact, his ability to write quickly forms one of his chief assets. As Robert B. Peck, a famed rewrite man himself, puts it in *Late City Edition*, "The rewrite man's value lies in his ability to turn out a lucid story to fit a given space in as short a time as possible."

In addition to his creative job of taking the reporter's facts and whipping them into a story, he, as his name implies, frequently has to rewrite. That is, the copyreader tosses on his desk a clumsy or hurried piece of copy that no amount of editing can redeem. It calls for revamping from start to finish. The result is a readable story.

Second thoughts may not always be the best, but it's a rare piece of copy that cannot profit from rewriting, either by its author or some editor.

The rewrite man is often asked to perform a highly useful but tedious chore; he has to wade through the voluminous reports of governmental departments—federal, state, and municipal—and discover aspects of newsworthiness. He does the same with annual reports of social agencies. Frequently, the result of this tedious digging stands out as a highly readable story of local interest. Why? Simply because the rewrite man has supplied the home-town angle to the Washington compendium. He has shown in the items or the statistics he selects for his story how the findings of the report he has gone through will affect the health, the happiness, or the pocketbooks of the people in the community served by his paper.

When finished, all stories, whether typed by the reporters who cover them or compiled by the rewrite men, are handed in to the copy desk where the process of editing them begins.

8
Main Types of News Stories

Interviewing as the Basis of Most News Stories—Covering a
Speech—The "Human Interest" Story and "Feature Stuff"—The
Obituary Article—Covering Sports—Impact of Radio and
Television on Sports Reporting

If you take an analytical glance through today's newspaper, you will see that at least five types of stories
predominate. They are the interview, the speech report,
the human interest story, the obituary, and the sports
event. Each requires a distinct approach in its preparation; each requires a distinctive technique in its presentation.

Interviews

The process of interviewing lies at the basis of most
news stories. If a holdup occurs in a corner drugstore,
the reporter who covers the story embarks on a series
of interviews—that is, he asks questions and receives
answers. He talks to the clerk who was in the dispensing
room when the bandit entered. He talks with the
nervous spinster who had her handbag snatched from
her as the bandit dashed from the store. He phones the
brother-in-law of the cashier who was shot. He talks
to the youngster who was deep in an ice cream soda
when it all happened. But we would not call the result
of his questionings an interview; we would refer to it
as the holdup story.

The interview proper, which has emerged through

109

the years as a journalistic art form, dates in the American press from the call which Horace Greeley of the New York *Tribune* made on Brigham Young, the Mormon leader. The questions and answers had to do with the slave problem and with secession, and Greeley ran them in his paper in that form. The development of the interview as a newspaper feature stems from the practices of James Gordon Bennett, the elder, in his racy New York *Herald*.

The modern interview as we have come to know it consists of a personal contact between two people: the reporter and the interviewee. It blends the reporter's impressions and his description with the interviewee's own comments in reply to the reporter's questions. Because of the dominant interest which the average reader has in the doings and opinions of his own species, the interview has become so popular with readers that all editors nowadays regard it as a journalistic staple. It crops up as a daily news story and as a Sunday feature; it forms the main stock in trade of the fan magazines; and in its glossiest form it adorns most issues of "the slicks."

We have defined the interview, broadly, as a personal contact between the reporter and the interviewee. By considering each of these agents separately we can go far on our way to discovering the best method of obtaining a successful interview.

THE REPORTER AND HIS PREPARATION

The reporter represents the right of the public to know certain things. Sometimes he thinks he represents the right of the public to know everything, but "everything" occasionally is none of the public's business. But the reporter's place in the scheme of things is well assured, and he need feel no inferiority complex. His physical preparation for the interview is to see to it that he appears neat, clean, and presentable. His mental preparation for the interview, if adequate, will leave him competent and assured.

The person to be interviewed is usually a person of importance. As such he has no time to waste on an ignoramus. He expects the reporter to know something of the subject in hand so that he can ask intelligent questions. The reporter realizes this expectation and spends as much time as possible getting background material for his talk. He has at his disposal the "morgue"—his paper's reference department—where envelopes on all important people and important subjects are filed away for ready survey. These envelopes contain clippings of news stories, earlier interviews, feature articles, and photographs. By going through them, the reporter can bring himself as up to date as the latest published item. He accordingly studies the envelope on the person to be interviewed and also on that person's subject—engineering, motion picture production, sculpture, whatever it may be.

The reporter's perusal of this subject envelope will prove immensely useful. He will find that from this preliminary survey will spring the questions that he must ask. New developments in a particular line or a news dispatch which concerns it stimulate the new queries. What changes will the new method make? How will reorganization affect the average citizen? The wise reporter regards these leading questions as of supreme importance. With them he can keep the interview in hand. With answers to them, even if he gets nothing else, he can write a good story.

Another important preliminary is to arrange for the interview's time and place. Of course, the hour of going to press waits for no man, but if there is not this strict time urgency, the reporter usually arranges for the interview in advance. He does this by note or by phone. If he is acting as an agent of his paper, the thing is easy. If he wishes to write the interview for free-lance sale, he explains this to the interviewee and indicates the type of periodical at which he aims.

THE PERSON TO BE INTERVIEWED

Prominent men and women make excellent subjects for interviews. They have, through their activity in their own special lines, caught public attention. Through their writing, speaking, painting, political sagacity, acting, or executive capacity they have in varying measure appealed to the public imagination. Mere mention of their names arrests the reader. He is in a mood to find interest in what they say before he reads the interview.

Beyond the fact that these men and women lead busy lives and have scant time free from engagements, the reporter finds them easy to interview. They appreciate publicity. They usually meet the reporter more than half way. They themselves know pretty clearly what the public wants to read, and this motivates to a large extent what they say for publication.

A subdivision of this prominent group makes the task more difficult. Many men and women of affairs who bear great names and hold influential positions actually dislike publicity. They are naturally reserved, and even if they consent to be interviewed, their adventures in rhetoric are apt to be monosyllabic. The reporter usually finds in cases like this that he has to promise to submit his interview to them before publication. This is a nuisance, as it takes time, and the consciousness of censorship somewhat cramps the reporter's free spirit. But a promise if given must be kept.

Another type of interview subjects is the suddenly prominent. A quick turn of events sometimes puts men and women into full glare of the limelight. The novelty of it all frequently goes to their heads and the chances are that, when interviewed, they may say some very silly things. The wise reporter usually gives such people a break. He knows that they will aid him and his paper later.

Then there are private individuals unaccustomed to public attention of any kind who, because they have done interesting things or lived unusual lives, make first-rate subjects for interviews. Sometimes through no fault of their own they become interesting to the public because of some member of their family—a son or a daughter may have brought honor or disgrace to the family name.

All these classes may on occasion become gun-shy. For some reason or other they will become taciturn, silent, or perhaps merely diffident. The reporter has to find the reason. Perhaps his note-taking worries them. Note-taking often affects the speaker whose words are being taken down. It gives him an acute consciousness that he is talking for publication. As a result, what he says may become formal rather than natural, stilted rather than conversational. In cases like this, the reporter should fold up his paper, but away his pencil and sharpen his memory. Often successful interviews spring from no scribbled notes but from deep-cut impressions in the mind.

TYPES OF INTERVIEWS

While preparing for the interview, the reporter usually has in mind the general class into which the material he secures will fit. Interviews subdivide into five main types:

The news interview.

The opinion interview.

The personality or feature interview.

The group interview.

The press conference.

The news interview seeks facts. Its field is as broad as human endeavor. Its subject may be politics, education, finance, crime, or invention. A doctor performs a new type of operation. The reporter gets from him the information on how it was done and its results. A firm devises a new method of production. The reporter seeks to find out all about it, how it works, its advantages over the old way, and whether the new system will increase or decrease the number of the firm's employees. In these situations he must know what questions will result in news. He must be quick to get factual matter— names, occupations, addresses, titles, terms—as accurately as is humanly possible.

The opinion interview is sometimes easy, but as a rule it requires more tact on the part of the reporter than does the straight factual one. Some people have a ready opinion on anything that crops up, usually too ready. The opinion interview that is worth while is usually the result of both digging and diplomacy. The reporter strives to learn all he can of the personality of the individual whose views he seeks. He arrives with his leading questions memorized to avoid fumbling and delay. He understands the value of a well-timed and sincere compliment. In cases where the opinion expressed is highly technical or controversial, the reporter frequently asks that the key statements be written down by the interviewee to avoid all danger of misquotation.

The feature interview is usually more interesting to write and more interesting to read than the other types, but because it is less routine it makes greater demands on the reporter's resources. Here, as in a personal sketch, the emphasis tends to stress not so much what the person says, as how and where and why he says it. The reporter attempts to develop the personality of his subject through noting characteristics, tricks of speech, dress and appearance, personal traits, idiosyncrasies, and the like. The net effect, if successful, makes the reader feel that he has almost met the person depicted. In this reaction lies the virtue of the personality interview, and in this fact also lies the reason for its great popularity with readers; they like to meet, if only via the reporter, the great and the near-great.

The group interview, as its name suggests, sets down in one story the facts and opinions obtained by the reporter through a series of interviews with a number of people. Washington announces some price or credit control measure. Immediately the paper assigns a reporter to secure the comments of financial authorities or leading businessmen in the branch of industry concerned. Here the reporter summarizes his findings in a general lead and then quotes in turn the important observations which each expert has given him.

The press conference resembles the group interview technique in reverse. Here, in order to save time, or with the purpose of giving all the journalistic media or all the papers in town an even break, an important individual arranges to give out an important piece of news to the assembled group of newsmen. The interview element enters here in that after the announcement reporters are free to ask questions for further enlightenment. The most famous of these press conferences is, of course, the one which the President of the United States holds when he chooses to meet with the top Washington newsmen.

Frequently the reporter finds the factual interview and often the group interview can best be set down in the conventional inverted pyramid manner of the stereotyped news story. He writes his lead which summarizes the chief news obtained and, of course, gets in all the W's. The succeeding paragraphs deal with lesser news in dwindling importance. He avoids, if possible, printing his own questions and writes his copy in such a way that the answer implies the question he has asked. He makes his story visually attractive by varying the paragraph lengths and by using direct quotation.

In addition to the answers to questions which he has in his notes or his memory, the reporter in writing a good feature interview finds he has to call on his observation and use his knack for description. Even so, he sometimes feels that his story is static, and he wishes he could inject more life into his copy. Actually the device which achieves this is simple. The reporter has merely to record the interviewee's natural actions. By doing this he breaks up the stiltedness of the question-and-answer formula. As, for example:

He turned toward the window and looked out upon the park. For a few minutes he was silent.

"The great trouble with the world is to make it realize that the chief interests of all people are common ones," he said.

"Here in this country we have a shining example of this very fact. People do not realize that Main Street and Wall Street cross each other. . . ."

He got up and walked up and down the room, puffing on a cigarette. Then he went on:

"It is the political leaders attempting to gain popularity in their own parts of the country who run down the other sections, and thus cause the feeling that exists between East and West."

He went to the table, on which was a book.

"Have you ever read Faguet's *Cult of Incompetence?*" he asked.

Here the reporter has given the reader a veritable talking picture of his subject. Our man is animated as well as vocal. We know that we are listening to an interview with a living, breathing individual and not, as we sometimes suspect, with a pompous stuffed shirt.

Reporting a Speech

America has always had a high saturation point for the spoken word. People enjoy speeches, conventions, lectures, and sermons. And they like to read about the talks which they are unable to attend. Accordingly, covering speeches constantly crops up as an assignment on papers large or small. It's a rare reporter indeed who hasn't tried his hand at it.

The newsman can cover a speech in one of two ways. He can actually go to the hall and listen and take notes while the speaker is talking, or he can write his report from the mimeographed copy or "flimsy" of the speaker's talk which has reached the office in advance or which is handed out to the press table before the lecture starts. In these days when so many public men apparently prefer to read from a prepared script to their audiences rather than to talk to them, the "flimsy" is usually available.

Reporters find that by actually attending the event, they are more apt to turn out a good story. For one thing, they are guided in their selection of what to report by the audience itself. Audiences have a way of reacting. They laugh; they applaud; they can even show dissent. Those portions of the talk which stimulate the audience will stimulate the reader, too. The reporter knows this and checks such paragraphs on his carbon copy or in his notes. Also, audience stimulation frequently inspires a speaker to indulge in extemporaneous outbursts which are often more newsworthy than the careful cagey-ness of the planned speech. If the reporter catches this frankness or this indiscretion, he may find himself with a page-one story.

If he takes notes, the novice finds that he is apt to take too many. He dreads the thought of translating or transcribing the hurried scrawl when he gets back to the office. The veteran reporter knows that most speeches, unless they are frankly extemporaneous utterances, are based on a plan. He waits till he hears the topic sentence which initiates one of the subject's divisions. This is jotted down along with an illustration or the few statistics with which the speaker expands it. Then the reporter waits for the next planned point, and so on. He takes especial care to note down the speaker's summation. The reporter has learned from experience that often this summary will make an excellent lead for his story.

WRITING THE SPEECH REPORT

The reporter writes his report of the speech to conform to the pattern of the standard news story. He starts off with what he considers the most important or most interesting aspect, then deals with the next most important point and so on to the end. Accordingly he ignores the speaker's own logical order and must see to it that his own revamping does not result in a disjointed or garbled story.

He can choose from a variety of leads—the "speaker lead," "the digest lead," "the striking statement lead," or the "keynote lead." Currently one of the most popular approaches is the participial beginning, "Contending that . . .," "Denying that . . .," "Upholding that . . ." and so on.

The best speech reports contain full paragraphs and full sentences in direct quotes. After all, the reader of a speech report wants to know what the speaker actually said. Indirect quotes have their usefulness in condensing less important points and also in varying the look of the story. The end of each paragraph is the least important part of it, and when the reporter feels he has to use such mechanics as "he said" or "Dr. Blank added," he had better place them where they show least. Actually, when only one speaker is reported and his name is mentioned in the story's lead, all the quotes which follow presumably emanate from the one source.

Naturally, the reporter records anything that is noteworthy about the speaker's actions, appearance, or method and anything unusual in the audience's reception of the remarks. But normally he will find it unnecessary to describe the ordinary male speaker's appearance and clothes—and dangerous to attempt to do so in the case of a woman speaker.

The Human Interest Story

The standardized newspaper story fulfills its function when it imparts its content of factual information. The human interest story has an entirely different purpose. It need contain no news at all or merely news of very minor import. Its aim is to touch the reader's emotions.

Editors have readily found a place for the good human interest story since the beginning of this century. The reasons for its popularity with editors are both economic and literary.

They saw the fiction magazines develop a vast readership with material which, in most cases, the newspaper passed over. They decided no longer to ignore it.

They felt that stories that had emotional content would attract women readers to the paper and its advertisements.

They realized that the occasional writing of stories from a sympathetic point of view would keep their reporters from developing a callous attitude toward human misery.

They began to appreciate the entertainment value of human interest items which divide evenly between the amusing and the pathetic.

They saw that the inclusion of human interest material gave an element of variety to the literary style and content of the paper.

Because of its special nature, the human interest story runs slight risk of being cut and accordingly need not be written to the stereotype news story formula. Unhampered by conventional rules, the writer can construct his story in any way he pleases. In this way it stands out as a reaction to the usual news account.

Although originality knows no pigeonhole and refuses to be standardized, the human interest story has developed at least certain tendencies which indicate a general, if elastic, pattern. Certainly it must have been the human interest story and not the standardized news story that the Red Queen had in mind when she laid down for Alice the formula for storytelling: "Begin at the beginning, go through to the end, and then stop."

The human interest story, as a rule, does just that and adopts the pattern of simple chronological narrative. Its graphic form takes the shape of a pyramid which starts at the apex and develops downward to the broad climax of its base.

The beginning of a human interest story, while not a lead in the usual sense, usually does certain things. It aims to stress the story's timeliness. Although the story may have no news value, it should be timely. Usually it presents the story's chief characters and gives a sufficient hint of the complications to urge the reader to read further. Sometimes, in the approved O. Henry manner, it leads up to a surprise ending.

Here is the way a reporter began the story of a minor mishap in which no one was hurt and which had no news significance at all, for the people concerned were blissfully unimportant:

> "If anybody should see in the papers," said Al Jenkins, trap-drummer out of work, "that our Katy should be playing in the park—"
>
> "And where should a child play but in the park?" interposed Mrs. Jenkins, as she leaned over to button Katy's red flannel wrapper.
>
> "If anybody should see in the papers," went on Mr. Jenkins, "that our Katy should fall down a manhole and be rescued after a full half hour . . ."

And yet a million or more readers saw just that in the paper because this little newsless incident was written with such artistry and such universality of appeal that it ran for a full column and made a metropolitan front page.

The body of the human interest story usually follows the rules of simple narrative, that is, incident after incident, approximately in the order in which they actually happened.

The appeals of the human interest story are the appeals that prove effective in everyday life. Reader sympathy goes out to helplessness, loneliness, poverty, suffering, sudden bereavement. Reader anxiety is aroused by hearing of the anxiety of others. The fight for life and the struggle for existence are the strongest of all appeals to reader interest.

The artistic quality of the writing in the human interest story must never peter out. It draws the reader on to the climax and perhaps to a flip at the end which may give the key to the whole narrative.

Here we have a typical human interest story from the New York *World-Telegram and Sun* which aims to amuse the reader:

HIS SNOOZE ON GIRDER
OF BRIDGE—'DELIGHTFUL'

> *Oh sleep! It is a gentle thing,*
> *Beloved from pole to pole.*
> Samuel Taylor Coleridge

So far as we know Shipwreck Kelly is the only gent who actually did any sleeping on a pole, but a sailor was found on Brooklyn Bridge this morning knitting up the ravell'd sleeve of care.

George Hayes, 17, was a pretty sight when a bridge patrolman spied him—snoring merrily on a girder no more than 18 inches wide and about 25 feet above the airy bridge.

Fearing to arouse the slumbering gob for fear he might do a Brody, the patrolman summoned Emergency Squads 2 and 4.

They were on the scene in a jiffy with lifenets, but after surveying their project they took a different approach. With delicate care—"Aw, let the guy sleep," one remarked —they lassoed his feet, tied his arms and then slipped a rope around his waist.

Gently they moved him down to where they could get a grip on him and then lowered him to the bridge. Then, finally, Sailor Hayes awoke.

He didn't know where he was, but the nap—"cool and delightful." He piled into a police radio car, wide awake, and was taken to the New York Navy Yard, Brooklyn.

How'd he get up there? All he knew was that he'd started for Greenwich Village and grown tired on the way.

Editors today group the animal story along with human interest stories. Even a casual glance at current newspapers will reveal to the reader how prominently animals figure in the headlines. This interest, of course, is no new thing; it goes back beyond the dawn of history. Long before Aesop, primitive man delighted in picturing animals and in listening to animal fables and legends.

But why should animal stories fall under the human interest head? Simply because many of them are written directly to the human interest formula. That is, the reporter writes them to appeal to his readers' emotions—sympathy, anxiety, sense of humor. Primarily, these stories become legitimate human interest stories because the writer endows his animal actors with human characteristics. This is an old device, but its modern popularity with readers dates from Rudyard Kipling's masterly use of it in his *Jungle Books*.

The human interest story ranks as the main type in a category which the editor refers to in a general way as "feature stuff." In that phrase he includes all the items in his news pages which vary in form from the standard, straight factual treatment written in the inverted pyramid form with the exigencies of editing and make-up in mind.

These feature stories are dominated by elements of emotion. They are often trivial in themselves but when well presented prove bright and interesting. Their success with readers rests on original writing, unusual leads and frequently a surprise climax.

Here, for instance, is how Damon Runyon led off a story on the execution of a criminal: "It is bad enough to watch people live without having to watch them die." And H. Allen Smith chose an arrestingly simple sentence to start a *World-Telegram* feature story on the weather: "This is a nice day."

The astute reporter can find feature stories almost anywhere. Here, for instance, are types of material which commonly contain feature possibilities: children, animals, the exceedingly old, sudden wealth, fall of the mighty, anniversaries, holidays, interesting hobbies, freaks, minor courts, historical landmarks, anecdotes and profiles of the well-known.

Writing the Obituary

News of death, particularly if it be the death of an important individual, ranks as live news. Many persons turn to the obituary columns with an avid interest. In some cases this interest is well rewarded, for over the past quarter century a more marked improvement has been made in obituary writing than in any other one single phase of journalism.

This improvement came not before it was needed. Stanley Walker, while city editor of the New York *Herald Tribune,* probably initiated the trend by assigning some of his top-flight writers to cover deaths.

Up to then the unfortunate practice prevailed, and indeed still persists in many city rooms, of assigning the least experienced reporter on the staff to write the routine obituary material for the day. This young reporter, slavishly afraid to get out of step with tradition in this type of writing, laboriously modeled his output on the time-honored formula.

This formula developed in a more pious and less penetrating age. It coined a variety of mortuary phrases in which it suitably embalmed the memory of the "dear departed." Obituary notices enriched from these sources became so bad that they rivaled home-made obituary verse in adding a new terror to death.

Probably this newspaper heritage springs from the very human and ancient superstition summed up in the Latin proverb: *De mortuis nil nisi bonum* (concerning the dead, nothing but good). As an unfortunate sequel, this pious command flourishes too often as *nil nisi bunkum.*

The good reporter writes an ordinary obituary with ease. If he sticks to the facts and gets them down correctly and simply, he performs a useful and appreciated service. Simple facts, simply stated, have a dignity which surmounts the flowers of mortuary rhetoric. The man in the street gets into the papers normally on but three occasions: when he is born, when he marries and when he dies. Friends of John Doe clip and treasure the journalism which records these three events.

Many papers have a printed form which enables the reported to collect the facts. All of them include the following essentials:

Name.

Address.

Date and place of birth.

Date and place of death.

Cause of death.

Occupation.

Religious and social affiliations.

Names of surviving relatives.

The reporter augments these necessary details with anything he can glean from business or fraternal associates. He secures much of this information over the telephone. He may feel a natural distaste at having to bother the bereaved family at such a time, but he can lay aside any real diffidence in the matter. The man's family is only too eager to do all it can to honor John Doe in death and regards the published obituary as a thing of great importance.

When some world figure or nationally known person dies, the obituary assignment comes to real prominence. Often the metropolitan press devotes many columns and sometimes many pages to chronicling the life and career that has ended. In most cases this material has been written months and even years in advance of the news of death. This is because death may come at any moment to the prominent as well as the rest of us, and the papers wish to be prepared for the contingency. Usually this material, which is filed away in the newspaper's morgue, is brought up to date at regular intervals. Such articles resemble biography more closely than does the personal sketch or profile, for they deal principally with the subject's actual achievements rather than with his personality.

A reporter assigned to an advance obituary of this type has no difficulty in securing the material. His paper's morgue will provide him with bulging envelopes of clippings. His job is to run through these and select from them the most salient and most interesting facts. He will find many interviews and feature articles concerning his subject. He will find reports of the person's actual speeches. The editor has told him the approximate length to which the article must run. He therefore chooses those anecdotes, those sayings, those facts which he feels will most clearly reveal the character of his man. Often he finds he has the old Horatio Alger story over again. What of it? Reader interest always goes out to achievement. Occasionally he finds a variation of this formula. A man may fail in middle life only to succeed later. Or again, the whole character may change and develop. But whatever trend the article takes, the reporter has the satisfaction of knowing that he has produced a distinct, uniform thing from a welter of clippings. His has been the artist's touch in selecting, shading, pointing.

Merely as a guide, and not as a definite pattern, we append an obituary biographical article in paragraph outline:

  I. Who, what, when, where, and how.
 II. Outstanding achievements and honors.
III. Immediate family connections.
 IV. Brief summary of rise to prominence.
  V. The man himself, ancestry, characteristics, point of view, etc. as revealed through personal anecdotes, interviews, letters, including details of his rise to prominence.
 VI. Complete list of honors, club affiliations, etc.

Covering Sports

Beyond the fact that sports represents a news field all its own, the coverage of sports events and personalities does not differ radically in its basic techniques from the covering of news in other departments of the paper. Accordingly, sports pages and sports sections give us straight news reporting in their accounts of specific ball games, boxing encounters, tennis matches, and racing events. Apart from an occasional exuberance in the writing vocabulary, such stories follow traditional news procedure with the lead summarizing each story's chief facts and the later development presented in paragraphs of tapering importance (inverted pyramid style) or chronologically (play by play and round by round technique). Then, we get interviews with leading sports figures. They may be news interviews with famous coaches who agree or disagree over some ruling of the National Collegiate Athletic Association or feature interviews or personal sketches of some colorful sports celebrity, such as a glamorous woman tennis star or a Derby-winning jockey. All follow standard patterns. We get editorials and signed commentator columns in which journalistic sports authorities pontificate in much the same manner as do their opposite numbers on the paper's regular page of editorial opinion.

The main difference between sports writing and that in the regular news page rests in the leeway given to sports writers with regard to space and writing style. Here fancy is allowed a freer rein; here vocabulary can reach beyond the confines of standard dictionaries. However, the influence of outstanding sports writers such as Grantland Rice has tended to discourage the use of a specialized *patois* for sports reporting and has tended to encourage the return to a lively but correct English style.

The fact that so many outstanding writers got their start as sports reporters emphasizes the advantage of the sports field as a training ground for writing talent. Heywood Broun, Westbrook Pegler, Paul Gallico—to name three completely unalike writing personalities— started as sports writers. The advantage which they and many others got from sports coverage was the practice which such reporting gave them in actual writing.

Writers teach themselves to write by writing. Sports reporters as a rule do more actual writing than the average reporter. The high school basketball game story runs to two columns; the parent-teacher association meeting gets two paragraphs. Sports writers also get more practice in writing "running copy"—that is, they write the account of the event while that event is in actual progress and feed each page of their copy as it comes off their typewriters to a copyboy or telegrapher. Accordingly, they gain confidence in their own powers of observation, narrative and description. "Running copy" permits no time out for pondering over the "mot juste." The writer must decide on the instant the aptness of the word he uses—the noun, the adjective, the adverb. Small wonder that such training in speed, precision, and writing confidence confers lasting benefits on journalists exposed to it and aids them to further success in other fields of authorship.

IMPACT OF RADIO AND TV ON SPORTS WRITING

Both radio and television have made a definite impact on sports pages and on the business of writing for sports readers. Today millions of fans follow important athletic contests near their radios or in front of their television sets. In the latter instance they often see, thanks to clever camera work, a closer aspect of some particularly important phase of the contest than the reporter in the press box. Before the advent of these sound and sight media the sports writer featured the news and the drama of what happened. Today the viewer gets the news as soon as the sports writer does, and he has already thrilled to the drama. Accordingly, our sports reporter in the case of fights and games covered by radio and television has had to change both his methods of reporting and his style. He writes now from the "second day" angle and endeavors to answer questions which arise from the sport event. The reader, as a viewer, also knows what happened. The writer accordingly strives to get the inside story from the participants concerned. He interviews the fighters, he follows the players to their dugout or dressing rooms, he seeks out the golfer at the clubhouse. He gauges his questions; he strives to get the "low down."

9
How News Reaches
the Mass Media

Analysis of the Parts Played in Supplying News by Reporters, Correspondents, Press Associations, the Feature Syndicates, and the "Volunteer Staff."—How News Reaches Radio and TV Stations

Each day something like a million words pour into the offices of any great newspaper and into the news-rooms of radio and television networks. Where do they come from? As the newspaper was first in the business of news transmission, let us give it first consideration. In the case of the newspaper then, these million or so words come from the paper's own staff—its reporters and correspondents at home and abroad—from the news agencies and feature syndicates, from press agents and publicity men, and from friends of the paper. The material which comes through these channels may be divided broadly into three classifications:

1. News, features, and illustrations obtained by the newspaper staff within the paper's own territory.
2. World-wide news and features including state and national news supplied by press associations.
3. Features, comics, and illustrations secured from syndicates.

Here again, but this time in outline form, are the main sources which supply this material:

1. The reporter.

2. The correspondent:
   a. suburban, state, national;
   b. Washington;
   c. foreign;
   d. war.
3. The news agency and the press associations:
   a. local;
   b. general;
   c. international.
4. The feature syndicates.
5. The "volunteer staff":
   a. "tipsters";
   b. friends of the staff and paper;
   c. press agents.

Let us take up these sources in turn and see the part which each plays.

The Reporter

The reporter is the essential factor in all news gathering. Whether he works on a local beat or covers a revolution half the world away, his task is the same. He goes to the scene of the event and gets the information which makes the story. Sometimes this amounts to nothing more than a routine question-and-answer job; sometimes it brings into play all the intelligence, persistence, and ingenuity he can muster. In real life he resembles neither the romantic hero of the films nor the tough guy of the radio. At his best he is a hard-working, competent individual possessing in his make-up more than the average amount of curiosity, a certain tenacity of purpose and not a little of the eternal boy. He has above all an insatiable interest in people and events. It is this curiosity and this interest which attract him to newspaper work in the first place. Be he young or old, he enjoys the opportunities which his job gives him to watch the human procession as it goes by, to see the drama of politics from behind the scenes, to put his finger on the pulse of a great city, to get a press pass, as it were, to the ringside of life.

In the past many shiftless, picturesque, and occasionally able bohemians tried their hand at reporting. Today the reporter's job is so exacting and there is so much competition for it that only the individual with sound educational background and keen intelligence makes the grade. According to the late Melville E. Stone, former managing editor of the Associated Press, "an intelligent reporter is far more valuable than an intelligent editor."

All reporters work directly under the city editor who is in charge of the paper's local news. He calls some of his staff "beat men" and others "leg men." These terms in the journalistic lingo indicate different reporting spheres. The "beat man" has spots which he covers regularly such as the city hall, the courts, police headquarters, hotels, et cetera. Through day-by-day association he comes thoroughly to understand the routine workings of his "beat" and he develops an acquaintance with the officials involved. Through these contacts he becomes a specialist in his beat and often obtains information and sometimes exclusive tips from friends he has made.

The "leg man" is the reporter on general assignments who is sent out by the city desk to cover special stories. He may tackle an interview one day, a speech report the next, an investigation proceeding, or a church conclave. He needs a good pair of legs but much more besides, for frequently his work calls for resourcefulness and initiative of a high order. In many cases he writes his own story; in some cases he merely secures the facts and phones them in to his office where a rewrite man whips them into shape. Some leg men limit themselves exclusively to fact finding and leave the writing of the story to other hands.

If we sum up the recipe of what makes a good reporter we can list such ingredients as a good basic education, an interest in life and an insatiable curiosity, a mind that enables one to think clearly in order to write clearly, honesty and reliability and a persistence of effort that carries one through to the story's end. It goes without saying, though we make a point of saying it, that the reporter has to have sound health.

It goes without saying, too, though again we say it, that the good reporter should have a pleasing personality.

The reporter is the only representative of the paper who comes in contact with any considerable part of the public. By these human contacts he creates good will or ill will for his paper. The reporter comes to know large numbers of people in all walks of life. He gains their confidence and not only secures all the available news on his run, but if he does his work faithfully and accurately, he creates that good will without which no paper can really prosper.

He needs all these attributes, for his job today is one of primary importance—the supplying of reliable information on which people can base sound judgments.

The Correspondent

Every paper has its correspondents. Take up a small country weekly and note the columns of personal notes and folksy news items which have been sent into it from neighboring communities. Take up a paper like the Los Angeles *Times* or the Kansas City *Star* and you see a vast amount of material sent in by correspondents all over the nation and all over the world. Either paper points up the general procedure: the paper uses its own reporters to cover the news of its own locality; it uses correspondents outside its town's limits to send in the news of other places.

The suburban correspondent. As we easily surmise, the suburban correspondent supplies the news of the outlying residential districts and the counties adjoining the place where the paper is published. He was formerly under the city editor. Now, neighborhood or community editors handle his news which is either telephoned, telegraphed or mailed in to the city desk. The correspondent knows which means of transmission to use either from instinct if he is an experienced reporter or because definite instructions have been issued to him. Sports results, for example, he phones in; the report of an important speech he may wire; the announcement of some coming event he probably drops in the mail.

He is usually a working reporter attached to a suburban newspaper from which he draws his regular salary. The city paper which engages him as a correspondent pays him at "space rates." That

HOW NEWS REACHES THE PUBLIC

In newspaper plants across the land, reporters write, editors and copy-readers edit, linotype and intertype men turn "copy" into print, make-up men arrange it, stereotype operators fit the page for the rotary presses which turn out the finished product.

This series of photographs taken at the plant of the New York *Herald-Tribune*, pictured above, follows the reporter's story from the time it leaves his typewriter to the moment the reader buys the paper and "reads all about it."

Photo Courtesy of N. Y. Herald Tribune

At the inside center of this big U-shaped Copy Desk sits the copy editor—"the slot man." He passes unread copy to the copyreaders around the "rim" who process it for length and style, check facts and write the type of headline specified. One more quick look by the "slot man" at the final story and headline, and then the copy starts on its way to the Composing Room.

As news copy comes from the Copy Desk to the Composing Room, a "copy cutter" sorts it and apportions stories to individual operators. To save time, urgent stories are cut into short pieces of a paragraph or two and divided among a number of operators. As each sets his "take" the type is assembled on a single galley.

As the Linotype operator here lightly touches the keys of his machine, "matrices" of letters drop from an overhead magazine into a line at his left. When the line is completed, he pushes a lever which moves the line against a mold into which molten lead is forced. The result is a "slug" or solid line of type which quickly cools as it slips into a "galley" beside him.

Photo Courtesy of N. Y. Herald Tribune

When the type has been proofread and typographical errors corrected, make-up men, as here pictured—working under the supervision of a make-up editor—fit type and cuts into page forms lying on the "banks." After a page form or "chase" is filled its contents are securely locked in place and "planed" with a block of wood and mallet to make sure all type is of equal height.

When the flat page of type reaches the Sterotype Department, the smallest details of type and engraving in the original form are impressed exactly in this mat of papier-maché. This is called the matrix or mat. The steel cylinder of the mat-rolling machine exerts a total pressure of 45,000 to 60,000 pounds. This is the first step in preparing the flat form of type to fit the cylinders of the high speed presses.

The mat, dried and curved in a scorching machine, is then placed into an autoplate casting box, the door closes, the box revolves into position and liquid lead alloy is forced into it. The resulting finished plate has been automatically trimmed of waste metal. Before it leaves the Stereotype Department, it is plainly marked with its page number. Here a pressman locks marked plates into position on one of the press cylinders.

In the pressroom—gongs strike, horns blow and the huge machines take over. Result: 100,000 complete, folded newspapers per hour.

And here is the climax of the swift, complicated process of turning out a daily newspaper. The reader buys a copy and reads the story which has gone from reporter to Copy Desk to Composing Room to proofreader; from make-up man to Stereotyping Department—then to the pressroom and then—to the waiting public in city, suburbs and countryside.

means that he is credited with just that amount of his material which the paper actually prints. This is measured up each week and for it the paper pays so much per line. A suburban correspondent may serve two or more papers in the same city, typing out two or more versions of each story he sends.

State and national correspondents. The state correspondent operates in a somewhat similar manner from the state capital or from some other important city within the state's borders. Recent years have marked a steady growth in national news. National correspondents send in their reports from areas beyond the paper's home state. The large papers claim as many as four hundred or more such correspondents across the land, but only the great papers can afford such a corps of them. The lesser papers rely for the most part on that news of the nation which comes to them through the press associations.

Like their suburban *confrères*, the state and national correspondents in general are men who hold responsible positions on their local papers. They may also supply reports from their areas to several papers throughout the land and also perhaps to one of the wire services. The material they send is news from their vicinity which boasts more than local significance. Their copy is edited on most papers by a state editor who handles all news from county, small-town, and country correspondents.

Washington correspondents. Washington ranks as one of the great news centers of the world. Many papers send correspondents there, or share with other papers one of the 1,361 correspondents in the capital.

Approximately three hundred individual papers maintain full-time news bureaus in Washington which employ sometimes as many as twenty reporters. Because the news of politics and of government in all its ramifications is today so complex, the men who cover Washington must be specialists in their line. They must have background and experience not only in American but in world affairs. For instance, the late Bert Andrews, who headed the Washington bureau of the New York *Herald Tribune,* came to it only after seventeen years of experience in the United States and abroad, in Sacramento, San Francisco, San Diego, Chicago, Detroit, Paris, and New York. In addition to background, Washington correspondents must have the ability to win and hold the confidence of men high in the affairs of state.

As a rule the bureau chief determines the assignments of his associates much as a city editor would with his reporters. But Washington men are more than mere fact finders. Their job is also to interpret the news and portray the background of history in the making. Political columnists like James B. Reston of the New York *Times* take this as their special province, but all Washington correspondents are given leeway as interpreters and, indeed, in the expression of opinion.

The top Washington men cover the White House, the presidential press conferences, the State Department, and the more important foreign embassies. The assistants keep tab on the governmental departments and offices.

The presidential press conference is an institution unique in the world. Nowhere and at no time in history have the executives of a great nation made themselves so accessible to newsmen as have the presidents of the United States for the last half century. The present method has been slowly evolving since the days of Theodore Roosevelt. His successor, William Howard Taft, is credited with initiating the presidential press conference as an institution, though it was Woodrow Wilson who established it on a regular weekly basis. During Warren Harding's brief tenure he required that correspondents submit their questions to him in written form a day or two in advance of the conference. Calvin Coolidge, who followed, earned the nickname "Silent Cal." He declined to be quoted directly as the President. Accordingly his economical utterances were attributed to "an official spokesman" or to "someone close to the President," very close, as they came from the President himself. Herbert Hoover, who had the advantage of long experience with newspaper men, codified the presidential conference technique. He ordained three classifications for the information which he gave out: (a) statements and information in which the President could be quoted directly; (b) information which could be published but not attributed to the presidential source; (c) "off the record" comment which was not to be published but given to the correspondents as background material or in anticipation of future news of importance.

Under Franklin D. Roosevelt the presidential press conference came into its full flowering. His personality, his wit, and his belief in the value of publicity all combined to make the conferences stimulating to executives and correspondents alike. During his newsworthy regime, conferences were held twice a week. After his death the White House went back to the once a week schedule.

The number of correspondents who attend the presidential press conferences ranges from 200 to 300 and includes a handful of radio commentators as well as representatives of the British, French, and Russian newspapers and wire agencies. Usually the conferences last up to thirty minutes and then end when one of the wire service men says: "Thank you, Mr. President." After that, the wire service people rush to the phones to call their offices, and the majority of reporters drift off quietly.

Washington correspondents are well paid, highly paid when compared with their fellows on the home paper. In addition they are in a position to write for nationally circulated magazines and to accept invitations for "guest spots" on the radio and on television.

The foreign correspondent. The job of foreign correspondent is the one to which most cub reporters aspire. To them it seems a wonderful thing to live abroad and chase big stories from capital to capital; to be a part of the great international social and diplomatic world and perhaps most of all to be away from home office discipline. And, from points of view other than that of the cub, the foreign correspondent's job is one to be envied. For one thing, he does not have to bother with routine news; the press associations take care of that. This means he can choose his own stories. Then the time element helps him. The mere fact that the sun rises in the East means a lot to him. It means that all the European papers work for him. The London papers, for instance, are on the street at two in the morning which is an hour before midnight in New York. As news transmission is instantaneous these days, any facet of his story which he may have missed and some London paper has printed can be sent along before his own paper goes to press, and the situation is saved.

Like the Washington correspondent, the man who serves his paper abroad makes himself a specialist in the affairs of the nation to which he is sent. Besides the background and knowledge and writing skill which he must possess in order to get the job in the first place, he must possess another knack in order to hold it—he must have the ability to guess correctly what, in the welter of foreign news which surrounds him, will be of interest to the readers at home.

Also, as is the case with the Washington reporter, the foreign correspondent's job is largely interpretative. He must explain foreign situations and personalities so that the reader at home can gain a clear understanding of the significance of the events and of the people who figure in them. From earliest days the foreign correspondent has been not only permitted but encouraged to express his opinions. He is a reporter and an editorial writer combined. Frequently the reader encounters as much opinion in the paper's foreign coverage as on its editorial page. This is fair enough. The correspondent on the scene is often better able to form an opinion than the editor at home.

New factors have entered into this whole field of foreign reporting. Increased facilities for transportation, notably the airplane, have given the man abroad a vastly increased mobility. Means of news transmission are nowadays more frequently available. Chief among these factors, however, is the increased interest of the American reader in the happenings of the world outside his boundaries, an interest awakened by old wars and kept awake by the threat of new ones.

Foreign correspondents of American papers are either Americans who know a foreign language and who have studied and understand conditions abroad, or foreigners who understand American newspaper methods. The recent trend is to send more American newspapermen as correspondents, as most non-American correspondents, however excellent their contacts and abilities, seldom understand American newspaper techniques or needs. A knowledge of the language of the country to which the correspondent goes is now considered essential in every area except the Orient.

Because of his importance in the international scene, the American correspondent abroad has come to hold a quasi-diplomatic status. Most papers see to it that he has the means to maintain this position. As far as journalistic salaries go, that of the foreign correspondent is in the higher brackets.

However large the correspondent's pay may be, he feels he earns it when he comes up against his two main problems. One is the cost of news transmission. The rates for cable, wireless, transoceanic telephone all have jumped high and keep jumping higher. To save his employer money, he condenses his stuff as much as safety allows. The use of code has gone by the board. Experience showed it too capable of error. In its place came "cablelese," a system of skeletonizing prefixes and suffixes that can be easily and quickly translated at the home office. However, airmail has proved a boon. For the price of airmail stamps follow-up material and stuff for the Sunday supplements now come swiftly and cheaply. The chief bugbear in some countries is the official censor.

Other factors, too, enter to make the actual picture of foreign reporting less glamorous than it is believed to be by most moviegoers and by deskbound newsmen at home. Paul Scott Mowrer, long-time foreign correspondent, a Pulitzer prize winner, and a former editor of the Chicago *Daily News*, tells the other side with its loneliness, frustration, and exasperation.

"At home," Mr. Mowrer writes in *The Atlantic Monthly*, "the reporter had a deep sense of being where he belonged. Abroad . . . he is quite by himself, in a strange place of which he can never be really a part. . . . To get to know even Englishmen takes about a year."

Worse than the loneliness, he says, is the treatment of cable news at home. The correspondent looks for his piece. It should have been on page one. He finds it on page sixteen. It appears rather short. That is because they have simply left out the key paragraph. The paper's editorials make him wonder if they even read his stuff.

Papers like the *Christian Science Monitor*, the Chicago *Tribune*, the New York *Herald Tribune*, and the New York *Times* maintain their own bureaus in the main capitals—London, Paris, Rome, Moscow—similar to those maintained in Washington. In lesser places, the "bureau" is a one-man affair. Some correspondents operating in London, say, or Tokyo, send their stories to half a dozen or more papers in various parts of the United States and Canada.

The war correspondent. Since 1900 a great change has come over the war correspondent. He has changed his type; he has changed the manner of his work. This transformation has come about because war itself has altered. Picturesque skirmishes between nations have given place to clashes which involve the whole world.

In the latter part of the nineteenth century and at the beginning of the twentieth, newspapers fitted out their journalistic stars, such as the late Richard Harding Davis, with paraphernalia and retinues that a generalissimo might envy. Thus accoutred, they took the field. Once there they wrote with a free hand. When William Howard Russell covered the Crimean War for *The Times* of London, the government back home read and trembled. In the South African war at the turn of the century, the young Winston Churchill covered the conflict on horseback. Such men took to war reporting as to high adventure.

With the outbreak of World War I, the war corespondent came up against the official censor. Security reasons both limited his access to news and dictated the manner in which he wrote and dispatched it. He could no longer get to the front unless carefully briefed and chaperoned. In modern warfare even Richard Harding Davis, who lingered on to cover World War I, could no longer discover picturesqueness, though in his report of the entry of the German troops into Brussels he achieved a masterpiece of journalistic description.

With World War II, the censorship tightened. The newspapers of the United States covered this conflict with their ablest men. In this service to the reading public forty-four American journalists, armed only with pad and pencil, lost their lives. Two of these—Raymond Clapper and Ernie Pyle—demonstrated through the popularity of their dispatches the type of thing which the public chiefly liked. Readers across the country seemed content to leave the strategy of warfare to the high command experts abroad or in armchairs at home. In its place they read with eagerness descriptive articles, similar to those initiated by Philip Gibbs in World War I, and human interest stories about the men in service which seemed to bring closer to them their own fighting ones far away. Ernie Pyle's stories did this to a marked degree, due largely to Pyle's ability to share his own experiences and impressions with ordinary people.

The News Agencies

The news agencies break down into two categories: local and general. The local agency has a limited field. It can only operate with profit in a large center of population and its function is curtailed to covering that center exclusively. Called by some such name as "City News," it places its reporters at the chief news sources of the town such as the police stations, magistrate's court, main hospitals, city hall, fire headquarters, city morgue, etc. These men phone in their news to the main office. In the old days this news was at once typed up in multiple and copies sent to subscribing newspapers and business offices. Today it is sent by teletype to radio stations, business offices, and newspapers.

In the nation's capital, for instance, the Washington City News Service, which is operated by United Press International, supplies government reports, local news, and highlights of world events to a hundred-odd government offices, executives, and special correspondents as well as to the Washington newspapers.

The newspapers cover the chief news sources on their own account, for each paper wants its news reported in the style it prefers. But by subscribing to the local agency, the papers are able to keep tab on their own news coverage, and they also benefit by receiving a mass of minor news which their own staffs do not get. Great cities like New York and Chicago have as many as 1,000 routine sources of news.

The Feature Syndicates

Let us think of the phrase "newspaper feature" as an elastic term. We can stretch it to include such journalistic material as articles, poetry, short fiction, serial stories, "columns," patterns, recipes, photographs, illustrations, and comic strips. The individual newspaper as a rule does not originate this type of thing itself but buys it from syndicates.

Naturally enough, the material which newspapers first wanted was news and, naturally enough, it was news which enterprising men first supplied—the same news to all buyers. Later, as the entertainment side of daily journalism developed, the news distribution was left to the press associations, and companies or syndicates came into being to provide the jingles, stories, and comics which the public began to crave.

An important name in the history of feature syndicates is that of Ansel Nash Kellogg, who, when editor of a small Wisconsin paper in 1861, showed such initiative and enterprise that he is known today as the father of the newspaper syndicate. To him came the idea of supplying small country papers with "insides"—that is whole papers with the inside pages already printed, but with the front and back pages left blank for the journal's own material, heading, and date. With Chicago as his center of operation, he later offered the first serial stories, the first illustrated articles and after 1875 when the first stereotype plate was introduced, he syndicated these plates in various lengths—column, half-column, and so on—so that they could be fitted into newspaper presses across the land. Irving Bacheller in 1884 began supplying the first syndicate features to metropolitan papers. By 1920, the syndicate was a well-organized business institution and an integral part of American journalism both in the country and city field and indeed in the international field.

Today there are approximately 175 syndicates in the United States. Among the best known are: Newspaper Enterprise Association, King Features, Central Press, McNaught Christy Walsh, and the Bell Syndicate.

From this list we can pick one of the largest, King Features Syndicate, Inc., as an example. This syndicate was organized in 1896 by William Randolph Hearst to sell the features he was using in his own papers to other papers and to devise new ones for the Hearst press. King Features introduced the first comic strip, "The Katzen-jammer Kids," and was well on its way.

Today, from its main offices in the Daily Mirror Building, New York City, it operates through two departments: one specializing in comics and the other, the Editorial, in "columns" and other written features. The Comics Department has to its credit the creation of "Blondie," the popular contemporary strip scanned daily by fifty-two million people, for Blondie and her family travel to newspapers all over the world and find themselves translated into a score of lan-guages. In fact, King Features claims eight hundred newspapers in ninety countries as clients.

The Editorial Department in its time has syndicated such writers as the late William Jennings Bryan and George Bernard Shaw. Today it handles such widely read "columns" as those of Westbrook Pegler, Louella Parsons, and Walter Winchell. It also controls the newspaper serial rights to many best-selling novels.

The Newspaper Enterprise Association does not specialize in any one feature. It sells a complete feature service including a woman's page, a sports page, a comic page, a page of editorial miscellany including cartoons, one or more pages of general news features and numberless pictures which are used on a picture page to illustrate the news of the day or are filed away for future use. NEA puts out service sheets from Cleveland, its home town. In New York, the Bell Syndicate supplies this type of all-round service, and claims to handle "every feature a newspaper needs."

Another general syndicate is the North American Newspaper Alliance which goes in for special articles and interviews and serves members only. It is organized somewhat along the lines of the Asso-ciated Press.

In addition to all this, a number of metropolitan newspapers, among them the Chicago *Tribune* and the New York *Times*, sell their features to papers published in other cities. In such a crowded field, the mortality both of features and syndicates is high.

Through syndicates such as these, the small papers have the same chance as the larger ones to secure these circulation-building features, for rates and fees are usually charged to a paper on the basis of its circulation figures. Syndicates also usually assure newspaper publishers that the features they buy will not appear in rival papers in the same area.

The result of all this is seen in the country's press content. It has been said of the American newspaper that it has become too much standardized with its press association reports and syndicate features; that a paper in Maine resembles a paper in Texas. That is hard on the traveling public who may like variety. For the bulk of newspaper readers, however, the press associations and the syndicates make available news and features which cost hundreds of thousands of dollars to produce and which few single newspapers could afford to develop for themselves. The press associations and the syndicates have made metropolitan papers out of the small-town dailies.

The Press Associations

Although the press association or news agency as an institution began in Europe, it has had its chief development in the United States. The big two in the field, the Associated Press and United Press International, are American in inception, in initiative, and in enterprise, while in scope they are worldwide. We must broaden the term general news, as a classification, to include international. In doing so we parallel the story of the agencies just listed, for each was primarily established to gather and distribute national news. Later each entered the international arena.

Reuters, the British news agency, ranks as the oldest press association in continuous operation. It was founded in the 1840's in Kassel, Germany, by Paul Julius Reuter, a Prussian bank clerk. At first he used carrier pigeons to communicate market reports for a profit. In 1851 he moved to London, became a British subject, and organized the news agency which still bears his name. Operating from London, which was then the world's capital, Reuters developed to the point where it monopolized news gathering and news distribution over wide areas. Before long Reuter brought the continental agencies into a vast cartel and parceled out spheres of influence. Reuter took the United States, Japan, China, and most of the Far East; the Havas Agency of France got South America; other spheres went to Rosta of Russia, Steffani of Italy, Wolff of Germany, and some dozen others. Eventually Reuter sold his agency to British newspapers.

Today, although it can no longer exert a strangle hold on news sources, Reuters continues as one of the largest and most powerful news agencies in the field with some 2,000 reporters in all parts of the world. In 1941, Reuters was reorganized and turned into a nonprofit cooperative by the press of the United Kingdom, somewhat along the lines of the Associated Press in the United States. Reuters now controls a subsidiary company, Comtelburo, Ltd., which deals largely with financial news and, in conjunction with the Press Association, the second largest British news-gathering concern, it operates P A-Reuters Photo, Ltd.

Three of Reuters' outstanding news beats were:

1. The dramatic dispatch of James McLean, New York correspondent, which in 1865 gave the world the news of President Lincoln's assassination. McLean missed the mail boat at New York. He hired a tug, chased the ship and threw his message aboard.

2. The news of the relief of Mafeking, a world scoop for Reuters' Boer War correspondent at Pretoria, W. H. MacKay. He persuaded the driver of a train to Laurenco Marques to hide his dispatch to the Eastern Telegraph Company in a sandwich.

3. Exclusive Reuters reports in 1945 which disclosed Heinrich Himmler's secret attempts to negotiate surrender of Nazi Germany behind Hitler's back. Historians say Hitler heard of the negotiations through a broadcast Reuters report and realized that suicide might have to be his way of escape.

In Canada, the Canadian Press is also a cooperative enterprise. It was organized in 1917 and today practically all the dailies in the Dominion and many weeklies take its service. It likewise operates as an international agency with offices in the United States and abroad.

Next to Reuters, the most important foreign news sources for American newspapers are France Presse, the French agency, and Tass, the Russian; but unlike Reuters, which operates freely, France

Presse and particularly Tass are under the strict control of their respective governments.

After the big two—AP and UPI—a duo so important that we will give a chapter to them, the next leading American agency is the North American Newspaper Alliance (NANA).

The chief papers of the country will subscribe for the services of as many as nineteen separate news agencies. Many of these are in specialized fields such as the Religious News Service; Aneta, the Netherlands News Agency; the Overseas News Agency and so on.

We accept as a commonplace today, as one of our ordinary conveniences, this competitive collection and dissemination of news from all parts of the world by various news agencies. Actually, it was not until 1934 that the system of news monopoly was broken. Up till then American agencies had to contend with an alliance of European press associations—chiefly Reuters of Great Britain, Havas of France, and Wolff of Germany, later DNB—which restricted the flow of news in and out of most countries of the world. In order to operate at all the American associations had to pay heavy premiums. That restriction for the most part is now a thing of the past in all areas of the globe not under Communist domination.

The "Volunteer Staff"

No editor overlooks the importance of his "volunteer staff." He knows from experience how many valuable exclusive stories have originated from "tips" that have come to him over the phone or from hints passed along to his reporters from friends of the paper. Naturally he knows too, also from experience, that the world's population includes many crackpots. When unsolicited information comes in from unknown individuals, the source of each item is checked and rechecked and its authenticity well established before the paper publishes it. The news of the death of an important person is news. When such a death is expected, after, say, a period of illness, the paper is on the watch for it. News of sudden deaths makes up a large percentage of this volunteered phoned-in information.

Individual reporters make friends for themselves and their paper through the excellence of their work or the pleasing qualities of their personalities. These friends from time to time put first-rate exclusive stories in their way.

A vast quantity of unsolicited "copy" reaches the newspaper each day. Much of this consists of press releases sent in by organizations and individuals engaged in public relations. The terms "public relations," "publicity," and "press agent" are not synonymous, but they all have much in common. They all aim at getting information of a project or client into the newspaper and in a way to show that project or client in the best light.

The modern tendency of papers is to welcome reputable press releases. Most editors apply to each release the professional yardstick of newsworthiness. Is it or is it not news? If it's news it goes in; if it's just free advertisement it goes in the wastepaper basket.

The most successful writers of publicity are usually men and women who have had newspaper training and experience, and they know that it never pays to trick newspapers, that a "phony release" would have as harmful a repercussion as a boomerang.

Organizations of every type—universities, business corporations, hospitals, charities, hotels, churches—all employ publicity to put and keep them in the public eye. The news each supplies may be interviews, important pronouncements, striking statistics relating to their work, reports of surveys made, the presentation of awards, and the like. Most events involving important individuals are not spontaneous affairs; they are arranged beforehand. Publicity-minded organizations make news in the sense that they plan and carry through newsworthy occasions.

How News Reaches Radio and Television Stations

Today radio and television newsrooms receive their news much in the same manner as newspapers. Radio and television too have their reporters, their correspondents, their feature syndicates, their press association services, and their "tipsters." This parallel came naturally enough, for the early radio newsmen had their journalistic training on newspapers and were familiar with the methods long established in newspaper city rooms.

From its first important broadcast—the reporting of the 1920 presidential election returns over KDKA, Pittsburgh—radio found itself dealing with important news. But its path from then to the present as a news broadcasting agency proved anything but smooth. Many newspaper publishers, fearful of the impact of so potent a rival in the fields both of circulation and advertising, did their best to prevent radio from obtaining the services of the press associations which the publishers virtually controlled. Radio met this challenge. Led by Paul White, an experienced newsman with the Columbia Broadcasting System, the major networks developed their own news bureaus.

In due course, newspaper proprietors discovered that the bulletin quality of much radio news actually reacted favorably on newspaper sales and did away with the necessity of publishing "extras." In 1933 the Press Radio Bureau came into being with two reports daily to its clients, and was followed two years later by TransRadio Press. Later both United Press and International News Service entered the picture with wire services to radio, and finally the Associated Press. Through this period radio reporting matured. Broadcasters relied no longer on the mere excitement of the news but began putting their stories into perspective and interpreting their significance to their listeners. Among the correspondents abroad, radio pointed with pride to Edward R. Murrow as a newscaster whose whole journalistic training had been in the sound medium.

Today the Associated Press sends reports to 1878 stations, and United Press International to 2,378 stations. In addition, the networks keep their own reporters and commentators at key points at home and abroad. Live local stations have their reporters as well as their newsroom staff to cover local events either with "actuality" reporting or through taped interviews and impressions. Nor should we ignore the "volunteer staff" and "tipsters" who frequently phone in news of traffic snarls in their neghborhoods.

Television news coming later into the field and adding the

arresting dimension of sight had more financial and less journalistic obstacles to contend with. Its reporters, many of them taken over from radio, had at first to struggle with the heavy and unfamiliar equipment of cameras as well as of tape recorders. The advent of the sound camera lessened their load somewhat and led to today's more efficient practice of regarding the television reporter and correspondent as a three-man operation. The reporter, the cameraman, and the soundman each has a unique and different but equally important job to perform. Many television news bureaus both here and overseas now use this efficient three-man unit.

Like the newspaper and the radio, television has syndicates. They provide news programs with film clips, animated cartoons, diagrams, and visual aids. But unlike the newspaper and to some extent radio, television newscasts result from the work of a coordinated team and not from that of a single reporter or commentator.

10
The Major News Agencies

**The Advent of Commercial News Agencies—The Associated
Press: Its History and Distinguishing Features—Picture
Transmission by Wirephoto and Radio—United Press
International: Its Historic Background—Impact of News Agency
Service**

Although the idea of a press association—an organization to gather and distribute news—originated in Europe, its development to its present-day efficiency has been largely an American phenomenon. The speed, expertness, and accuracy exhibited today by the leading news services have come about through American insistence on free competition and through the American ideal of trustworthy and unbiased news. The leading press services in this country—in the order of their age and of their size—are the Associated Press and United Press International, both of which have their headquarters in New York. The leading foreign news service is Reuters, which has its headquarters in London.

The early beginnings of news gathering here had a picturesque simplicity with such media of transmission as rowboats, pigeons, and pony expresses. Samuel Topliff and Harry Blake rank as pioneers in the news-gathering business. Topliff established the first "news room" in Boston early in the nineteenth century and peddled out market reports and shipping intelligence. Blake prowled around Boston harbor in a rowboat, intercepted incoming European packets, and then sold, or did his best to sell, any items of news he managed to pick up. In New York the leading papers had banded themselves together to gather certain types of news. By 1828 they faced the stiff competition of David Hale and Gerard Hallock who bought the *Journal of Commerce* and promptly transplanted to New York the methods initiated by Topliff and Blake. With them, however, the rowboat gave place to a regular seagoing yacht called the "Journal of Commerce" which went out twenty or thirty miles beyond Sandy Hook to meet incoming vessels. They also set up a semaphore telegraph down at Sandy Hook to which their yacht signalled the news, and which in turn transmitted the news to Staten Island from where it was carried to Manhattan. Not content with outdistancing their rivals with European news, this pair established a pony express from Philadelphia with eight relays of horses. By this means they were frequently able to publish news of Washington and of the South a day or so in advance of their competitors.

The pigeons come into the picture with D. H. Craig, who succeeded Topliff and Blake. Craig, too, went out to meet incoming ships, but took carrier pigeons along with him. Having secured the news and attached it to his winged messengers, he released the birds forty or fifty miles from port. The year 1844 saw the advent of Morse and his telegraph. Craig desired to use this novel agency, but found his desire balked by those holding the Morse patents and a group of New York newspaper owners. He and his birds outwitted this opposing faction so successfully that it capitulated and took him into the fold.

The Associated Press

About the time the telegraph was beginning to take over from the rowboats, the pigeons and the ponies, in 1848 to be exact, six New York newspapers joined to collect news on a cooperative basis. This was the inception of the present Associated Press. The idea of having identical dispatches published simultaneously marked a forward step in journalistic principle, for news that was acceptable to papers holding various opinions had to be unbiased and accurate. The papers behind this new enterprise might have political and religious diversities and print their own editorial views on these, but they all agreed that the world's happenings should come to the reader without any show of bias. There was, too, the element of cost. No paper could afford to maintain correspondents all over the map and also pay the enormous toll bills. A mutual effort was necessary and from it developed the AP. Newspapers of all creeds and politics and of varied races ultimately pooled their needs and decided to prorate the cost of world-wide news gathering. At first only a few great eastern dailies participated, and then gradually the effort included more and more newspapers published to the westward and southward.

Papers in the hinterland found that the New York hierarchy sent them little beyond routine bulletins of events. They wanted the colorful stories of the type that eastern paper readers enjoyed. Finally they brought sufficient pressure on the New York press potentates to secure a more adequate service. Today papers over the entire country are linked together in this organization. Mark Twain, speaking of the final consummation of this effort, said that "there are only two forces that can carry light to all the corners of the globe—only two—the sun in the heavens and the Associated Press down here."

The Associated Press has been reorganized several times. The AP as we know it now dates from 1900 when it was incorporated under the laws of the State of New York as a hunting and fishing club. This incorporation as a club was not as farfetched an idea as it sounds, for the AP from the first was a membership association for the purpose of collecting news in a joint effort on a nonprofit basis. Papers were elected to membership in the AP as individuals would be to a club; similarly some papers were refused membership. The news secured by each member paper was made available to the Associated Press for the benefit of all other member papers. With this reorganization, the AP took accuracy as its keynote and sent out a service distinguished for its objectivity and completeness, as far as its American coverage was concerned. As far as foreign news dispatches were concerned, the AP labored under inherited disadvantages from its pre-1900 beginnings. In 1893, it had negotiated an exclusive tie-up with the Reuters cartel which gave it a clear field with its foreign news coverage. Through this arrangement the AP traded its domestic news for the cartel's news. This exchange arrangement saved the AP the expense of maintaining its own foreign correspondents but hardly sustained its ideal of accurate, unbiased news. The incoming news was apt to be laden with propaganda; and its own American news which reached the world through London did not always reach the world as it was sent. Instead the United States was depicted in an unfavorable light because of the emphasis which the transmitting agencies put on its riots, murders, tornadoes, floods, and railway accidents. Melville E. Stone and later Kent Cooper and other Associated Press executives labored tirelessly to remedy this situation, and it was remedied not only through their efforts but through the beneficent effect of competition, first from the United Press and later from the International News Service. Up to the advent of the United Press in 1907 and the International News Service in 1909 (now joined as United Press International), the AP had everything more or less its own way and counted the country's leading papers in its membership. It displayed ingenuity and enterprise but naturally lacked the incentive to continuous effort which competition supplies. Many of its stories in these days, although accurate and informative, lacked liveliness and color. It denied its writers by-lines, and it looked askance at features.

The competition of the newer and livelier services made its impact on the AP, and today the country's senior news service holds the premier position through the excellence of its all-round service as well as through the prestige it has gained in the course of its history.

As the largest of the press associations, the AP of necessity works under a peculiar and unique pressure. Minimizing time and tolls makes for simplicity; the all-important member newspapers and radio stations make for accuracy. Somewhere a paper is always going to press or a newscast going on the air, every hour, every minute, it has been calculated. There are no breathing spells between "editions." Edition time is always now.

The AP reports that newspapers throughout the country are

constantly writing for its "style book." It insists in reply that it has no "style book." The nearest to a rule is good English and tacit understanding on the part of AP writers that their copy is for the "average newspaper," not the metropolitan papers, and yet it must please the metropolitan newspaper as well. That this makes no drift toward dryness, the AP contends, is shown in the humor and human interest, copied from coast to coast, that they have to their credit.

If the Associated Press has nevertheless produced a "style," it says the style is based upon preparation for contingencies in which it may have to tell the biggest story in the world in fifty words. Furthermore, these fifty words must be told so they will serve without change as a cornerstone for 5,000 words to come, if need be.

The Associated Press is a nonprofit membership organization. It does not sell its news to all comers. Its aim, as Quincy Howe once put it, is to give its restricted membership better service than they can get anywhere else. The cost of this service to an individual paper is based on the literate population in the area that each member paper serves. When two or more Associated Press papers flourish in the same area, they divide the cost equally. Because of the club-like organization of the AP, a paper desiring its service has to be elected to membership. For years a paper holding an AP franchise could blackball the application for membership of a competing paper in the same district. This monopolistic situation no longer exists. In 1945 the Supreme Court of the United States upheld a lower court ruling that the Associated Press' membership by-laws violated the Sherman Anti-Trust Act and ruled that the Association, in passing on application for membership, must disregard possible competitive effects on existing members.

An outstanding contribution which the Associated Press has made to modern journalism is its Wirephoto Service, developed in collaboration with the Bell Laboratories and successfully initiated on January 1, 1935. Through this "miracle" service, news and pictures ride the wires side by side for simultaneous publication in newspapers from coast to coast. Its inception has revolutionized the news picture business, and its development to an everyday function has been recognized as a step equal in significance to the introduction of the Morse telegraph in 1844, the telephone in 1875, the linotype machine in 1885, and the development of high-speed presses.

Today Wirephotos are sent around the world daily by radio. The quality of radiophotos is excellent, but atmospherics or temperamental ionosphere sometimes make reception difficult. However AP engineers foresee the day when radiophoto will not be subject to interference from nature. This will come about through the use of cable or by bouncing radiophoto signals off satellites spinning around the earth.

The Associated Press began regular transmission by radiophoto in 1951 to South America. This has expanded to daily transmissions to Europe and the Far East. The system is still growing. Today it is possible to send a photo from Europe to Japan in about 12 minutes.

The AP transmits color photos both by radio and Wirephoto. The color separations are made at the sending point and the print for each color is sent as a separate transmission. This radio transmission of color separation prints was inaugurated in April of 1959. The pictures were of the wedding of the Japanese Prince Akihito. They were radioed from Tokyo and received directly by AP's domestic Wirephoto network.

Another outstanding development is the AP Photofax. Photofax, introduced in 1952, receives pictures on a continuous roll of paper. It requires no attention, and pictures need no processing. They are ready for the engraver. The majority of the more than 500 AP Wirephoto subscribers now receive their pictures on AP Photofax machines.

United Press International

Up to 1958, the Associated Press had two wire service competitors—one characterized by speed and color and the other by its partiality toward the sensational. But in that year and with the dateline "New York, May 24, UPI" the teletypes across the country clattered out this news:

"The United Press Association and International News Service joined forces around the world in the creation of a single news agency named United Press International."

The merger had sound economics behind it. Although the United Press had grossed some $28.8 million the year before, it had a slim profit margin. With the merger, the United Press at one stroke eliminated a rival and added that rival's 120 client papers to its own total.

As for the International News Service, the amalgamation was even more beneficial for it took it out of the red. For some years, INS had averaged an annual loss of $3,000,000 and found its professional reputation dwindling with its earnings. As *Time* magazine (June 2, 1958) put it:

"To compete with the AP's thoroughness and the UP's color, INS fell back on splash-and-dash journalism. On a coronation story, editors could rely on the AP for the dimensions of the cathedral, the UP for the mood of the ceremony, and the INS (sometimes) for an interview with the barmaid across the way."

By the merger, the United Press president became president of the new agency, and the International News Service general manager became vice-president.

As it happened, the AP beat UPI on its own birthday story. The AP picked up the news from the Dow Jones wire and sent it out nineteen hours and seven minutes ahead of the announcement from the new rival agency.

Each of the two wire services which now join to make United Press International could boast a colorful and useful past history. The initials U.P. had come to connote speedy, lively, and readable reporting. The United Press, which they signified, came on the news scene in 1907. E. W. "Lusty" Scripps established it by buying the Publishers' Press and uniting it with two services he already owned, the Scripps-McRae Press Association and the Scripps News Association. These services had been separately supplying telegraph news to newspapers on the Atlantic Coast, in the Middle West, and on the Pacific Coast respectively. He founded the United Press to meet a very definite need and to establish a principle in which he firmly believed. In 1907, as we have seen, world news was dominated abroad by agencies which were for the most part subsidized by governments and at home by a single large cooperative, the Associated

Press. All were joined in a vast news service cartel which assigned priorities, often amounting to monopolies, to certain agencies to operate in certain countries. Members of this cartel exchanged news with each other. Since the foreign agencies reported only what their government wanted reported, the news which came from Europe and the Orient was far from complete or impartial, and since the Associated Press here limited the number of papers it served, very many American newspapers found it difficult to get world news.

Scripps rebelled against this monopolistic situation. He felt that news was a commodity that should be gathered and sold in an open market, and with his United Press, he proceeded to challenge the established services. Adopting the policy of complete independence and open supply, the United Press sent its own American-trained reporters to foreign capitals to report the news independent of foreign agencies. From the start it made its news available on a nonexclusive basis, a practice which proved a powerful stimulant to the newspaper industry.

After competing with the AP on the home front and in Europe, the United Press widened the field of competition in 1916 to include South America. Since then, it built up an increasingly impressive reputation for its service there and for the amount and quality of the Latin-American news which it offered here.

As a competitor of the solidly entrenched Associated Press, the United Press from the year of its inception strove for originality. It was the first to use the by-line in telegraph news. It introduced the big-name interview as a means of getting important people's ideas and points of view into the news. It developed the feature story as an important part of press association copy. It encouraged its writers to tell their stories in terms of people and people's interests. Its outstanding attributes were speed and liveliness.

The second member of the United Press International, the old International News Service, had an aim parallel to that of the United Press—to gather news and sell it to clients as a business proposition. This service, established in 1909 by the late William Randolph Hearst, was perhaps primarily intended as a news source for the newspapers in the Hearst chain. It soon, however, began to furnish news and features to a wide variety of papers throughout the land, many of which held to policies which hardly coincided with some of the Hearst editorial ideas. For this reason, the desire to please as wide a clientele as possible, INS kept itself free from any overt slanting, though in its news selection and treatment it did not forget its founder's predilection for the sensational. In its heyday it gained prestige in its field because of its energy and resourcefulness and because of the excellence and variety of its service.

Effects of Competition

The competition which results from having these major agencies active as news gatherers has proved beneficial not only to the news agencies themselves but to the reading public and to the whole journalistic field.

For one thing, the competition insures *accuracy*. No news service would think of deliberately sending out an inaccurate story when it knows its details will be checked against the story submitted by a rival service.

For another, the competition insures *completeness*. No two reporters or correspondents cover an event in an identical manner. Therefore, each story coming from these great services will add its own unique information. The reports taken together achieve a reasonable completeness. This is why the larger papers subscribe to a variety of news services and frequently print side by side dispatches from rival news agencies. Actually only some 450 of the nation's 1,750 daily newspapers subscribe to both wire services. Latest figures show that some 45 per cent are members of AP, while 30 per cent subscribe to UPI, and 25 per cent get their news from both AP and UPI.

Stylistically, the competition has inspired brighter, brisker writing in all wire services. In the old days the Associated Press sent out dispatches which were accurate and dignified but dull. As a reaction to this conservative handling of news, the United Press from its inception deliberately made its copy bright and scintillating. The International News Service followed suit with its smart, snappy, and exciting prose. This effort to inject readability into news copy caught on, particularly at a time when papers had comparatively few straight entertainment features. Today, with all services, the light touch is the rule when it can be used appropriately.

In recent years the wire services have greatly increased the attention they give to sports news. Sports writers with not-too-long memories recall the time when even World Series reports were crowded in on the straight-news wire. Today both the Associated Press and United Press International send box scores of all major league games and a daily roundup of major league activities. They give similar attention to football, basketball, and the whole area of activity covered by the sports editor or broadcaster.

11
The Newspaper: Its Purpose and Organization

The Functions of the Newspaper—Publishing as an Industry—
Types of Newspaper Organization—The Newspaper's
Essential Divisions—Newspaper Executives and Their Duties—
Distribution and the Newsboy

The newspaper as we have seen started out merely as a bulletin board. Its purpose at the outset was to inform. Through newsletters and broadsides it brought short items of importance—political announcements, shipping intelligence, and the like—to its readers. This business of conveying news gives the newspaper its name and still remains its basic job. Through the years, however, the press developed other functions and today's newspaper, as we have previously mentioned, has four outstanding reasons for being.

The modern newspaper is published:

1. To inform.
2. To interpret.
3. To serve:
   a. the community—by keeping a critical eye on civic government and public services; through its charitable funds and through its crusades for betterment;
   b. the reader—through providing information on health, education, and problems of the home and family;

c. the advertiser—through bringing seller and buyer together in its advertising columns both classified and display.

4. To entertain. Today's newspaper brings a wealth of entertainment to amuse and divert the reader: funny stories, comic strips, competitions, puzzles, "hobby" departments, and the like, all aiming to provide recreation and enjoyment.

Edmund Burke, who first called the newspaper "the Fourth Estate of the Realm," also hit on an equally cogent phase of the newspaper's importance when he described it as "the history of the world for a day." It is this conception of its role as a recorder of history which makes the scholar sometimes say: "If only the daily newspaper had been developed in Shakespeare's time what a world of wealth it would contain."

It would indeed. For the newspaper is a source book of real value, not only as a magazine of material for future historians, but as a living promptuary of human nature here and now. It takes us everywhere. It tells us everything. Small wonder that Clarence S. Brigham in the introduction to his *History and Bibliography of American Newspapers, 1690–1920* has been led to conclude:

If all the printed sources of history for a certain century or decade had to be destroyed save one, that which would be chosen with the greatest value to posterity would be a file of an *important newspaper*.

We place in italics the last two words of that quotation, for it is the *important newspaper* which gives daily journalism its prestige and its power. A newspaper's importance bears slight relationship to its circulation. It has to do with its purpose and its integrity.

It is this *important newspaper* which commentators have in mind when they call the daily press "the average man's university." If used intelligently, the newspaper can indeed be a source of knowledge.

Publishing as a Business

Is Publishing a newspaper a business, a profession, a game, or an art? The history of the craft would seem to provide arguments to back up the claim of each member of this quartet in turn. But this same history as it develops tends to put an ever-increasing emphasis on newspaper publishing as a business. This trend is easy to follow.

In the early days it took very little capital to get out a paper. Back in 1835, for instance, James Gordon Bennett could start publishing his saucy New York *Herald* with $500, two chairs and a dry-goods box. By 1841, Horace Greeley found that in addition to his own printing press, he needed to borrow some $1,000 to initiate the *Tribune*. By the time Greeley's early associate Henry J. Raymond was ready to begin the New York *Times* in 1851, Raymond found he had to call in the bankers, for the sum required was $100,000.

Today any man is still free to start a paper, but if he wants to start one in a fair-sized city, he must have millions in capital behind him. He needs this vast amount because times have changed since Bennett's day. Such factors as a huge increase in population, the development of railways, the invention of the telegraph as well as other means of swift communication and industry's increasing faith in newspaper advertising have entered the picture. Editors and writers may talk fondly of newspaper work as a profession, but the publisher knows that getting out a paper is business, big business.

Journalistic history, too, shows how newspaper publishing has followed the tendencies of American industry. Many large manufacturing concerns can trace their start to the single artisan, just as a paper can go back to the printer-publisher in his shop; then came the small company, frequently a partnership; and then developed the large corporate organization of today.

Similarly the newspaper in its evolution has paralleled the main phases of growth of the country's industries. With Joseph Pulitzer, from 1883 on, came the development of mass circulation, a development accentuated by the arrival on the scene of William Randolph Hearst in 1897; with the Scripps brothers came the idea of the newspaper chain, long before that plan became common in retail merchandizing; the growth of press associations and feature syndicates brought the standardization of newspaper content, and even before Frank A. Munsey became the arch-killer of newspapers, the era of mergers and consolidation had begun. It is hardly surprising then that the organization of newspapers should be along the lines of business organization in general.

How does a business concern operate? The usual manufacturing concern employs a staff to design its product, a production division to manufacture the commodity, a sales organization to place it on the market, and an office setup to coordinate this routine and keep records and accounts. The newspaper too has its planners, its manufactured product of news, features and advertising turned into the printed paper, its sales force to distribute the product and sell its advertising space, and an office organization for supervision and accounting. So far, the parallel holds.

But a newspaper is a living organism and not just a cake of soap. Accordingly, newspaper organization differs from common industrial practice in several respects, a difference due in large measure to the nature and history of the newspaper itself. For one thing, this living organism balks at standardization, with the result that there is no one uniform way of organizing a newspaper property. Then too in the newspaper personal factors have a way of displacing organization principles. However the very nature of the newspaper enterprise decrees that there has to be one very general organization, even if it is capable of many variations and minor differences. The newspaper organization has to have two "sides"—editorial and business. In a small concern these two divisions can be run very simply; in a large concern they immediately become complex.

Today most daily newspapers are owned by corporations, because corporate enterprises have many advantages over individual or partnership enterprises.

Types of Newspaper Organization

There are four main types of newspaper organization.
1. The president and publisher type.
2. The general manager type.
3. The owner-operator type.
4. The employee ownership and control type.

The president and publisher type of organization is the most frequent. It is headed by a president and publisher under whom there are two or three major executives. In a two-phase organization, the editor and business manager are the major executives, while in the three-phase organization the major executives are the editor, the managing editor, and the business manager.

With the general manager type of organization, this official, the general manager, is directly under and responsible to the board of directors and the president of the corporation. Under him and responsible to him are all other executives of the paper. Sometimes one individual is both editor and general manager.

The owner-operator type of organization is today chiefly limited to the smaller papers on which the owner-operator is president, publisher, and editor all rolled into one.

The employee ownership and control type in which the workers on the paper share in the profits and in the responsibility of management has, when successful, developed marked teamwork and cooperation among all of a paper's departments. Such a plan has been in operation with the Milwaukee *Journal* since 1937, and on that great paper the employees control 55 per cent of the capital stock of The Journal Company. This majority interest places control of ownership in the hands of the employee group. Employees participate in the management of the company, and their dividends are just the same as any other of the company's stockholders. This plan gives the president of The Journal Company full discretion in the allocation of units of stock to employees, and requires that when an employee-stockholder wishes to sell his units, he must offer them through the trustees to other eligible employees.

Except for the overhead organization, chain newspapers are organized in much the same way as nonchain newspapers.

Basic Departments and Divisions

In addition to the essential "sides" previously mentioned, the editorial and business sides, most papers add a third, the mechanical side. These three departments together really constitute the complete newspaper plant, though some papers leave the mechanical end—the actual printing of the paper—to outside concerns.

In a general way, we can say that the editorial department looks after the paper's content—news, editorials, art work, and features; that the business department takes care of the circulation, the advertising, the promotion, and the office routine; and that the mechanical department prints and dispatches the complete product.

Although there is no standard way of organizing a newspaper plant, all newspapers, be they large or small, which do not have their printing done elsewhere have six general divisions. In a small plant they may exist side by side on the same floor; in a large one they may need a skyscraper. These six general divisions are:

1. **Executive.** This division handles the general administration of the publishing company. It may be a board of directors, a president and publisher, or an owner-operator.

THE NEWSPAPER ORGANIZATION
PUBLISHER OR OWNING COMPANY

Editorial Division

Executive Editors	Editorial Writers	Department Editors
City Room	Telegraph & Cable	News Photographers
Art	Morgue	Library

Business Division

Auditing	Advertising	Circulation
Promotion	Sales Promotion	Radio & Television

Mechanical Division

Composing Room	Stereotyping	Engraving
Press Room	Mailing & Delivery	Service Department

2. Editorial. This division looks after the writing end of the paper. It attends to the production not only of editorials but of all news and features including the pictorial ones.

3. Business. The business office gets the money which the other divisions spend. It develops the circulation, secures the advertising, and undertakes the promotional activities of the paper. The promotional function is a new thing with newspapers and is just beginning to have a well-defined place in the scheme of organization. Its purpose of course is to build good will for the paper.

4. Mechanical. This division handles the composition of the paper, which means setting the written copy in type and placing it into page forms; stereotyping, which transforms the page forms into metal half-cylinders for the rotary presses; press room operations, which nowadays not only print but fold and count the newspapers. The mechanical departments are the most standardized parts of the newspaper from the standpoint of organization.

5. Auditing. This division takes care of financial detail—the bookkeeping, the billing, the credits and adjustments.

6. Service. This department has four main functions. It provides janitor, garage, stockroom, and shipping service.

Visitors to great metropolitan newspapers like the Los Angeles *Times* or the Chicago *Tribune* who see a large plant from top to bottom quickly note that newspaper production works on the law of gravity. On the top floor they find the executive office of the publisher; on the floor below the editor-in-chief and his editorial writers; on the floor below that, the city room where the news comes in not only from city and nation but from all over the globe; below the city room is the composing room where the news copy is set in type; on the next floor, the business office; and on the last floor of all the press room from which the paper emerges as the finished product. Thus starting at the top, the production of the news progresses each time it is dropped a floor. By the time it reaches the bottom, it has been transformed into a paper.

Let us list the duties of the chief officials whom we may encounter on such a trip through the newspaper's plant.

The chief operating executive of the newspaper is usually the publisher or general manager who may or may not be the president of the corporation. Most papers, too, have a secretary and a treasurer, but the office of vice-president is sometimes left vacant. This elimination of the vice-president in many newspaper organizations is one of the ways in which the newspaper differs from industrial concerns. These chief operating officials are ordinarily responsible to the board of directors. It is the publisher who sets the paper's policy. Whether the paper puts its emphasis on the editorial and news side of the paper or on the business side depends frequently upon the training and experience of the chief executive. The Springfield, Massachusetts, *Republican* has stood out for many years as an organ of information and discussion. On this paper, the management works for the editors. In some instances, the business management dominates the organization, as is the case with some of the Hearst papers. Here the chief executives have had their training in advertising, circulation or other phases of the business department and the papers, like industrial concerns, are run as profit-making organizations with the news, editorials, and features considered as means to that end.

EDITORIAL EXECUTIVES AND THEIR ROLES

The editor-in-chief, known sometimes just as "the editor," controls the editorial page. On small papers he writes all the editorials himself; on larger ones he heads up an editorial staff and directs its work. In each case, his is the sole responsibility for the way in which the paper's opinions are expressed. His personal responsibility is to the paper's directing executives.

The managing editor has as his province complete control over the news and features that go into the paper. Under him are the city editor and the various departmental editors; over him, as a rule, is the paper's chief executive. Indicative of the lack of uniformity and rigidity in newspaper organization, are those papers on which the managing editor is responsible to the editor-in-chief. The managing editor designs the over-all plans for news coverage. He decides the layout of the front page.

The city editor heads up the paper's local news. His sphere extends beyond the town's actual boundaries and includes the suburban areas. It is the city editor who makes out the daily assignment sheet which allocates to each reporter the story which he is to cover. His duty is to gauge the importance of each local story, determine its length and the amount of play to be given it. On some papers the city editor controls all departments except sports; on others he directs all news except telegraph. In general he supervises all the paper's local coverage. He is under and responsible to the managing editor.

On morning papers, the night city editor takes over when the city editor's working day is done. The night city editor gets the day's assignment sheet and usually verbal comments from the city editor on the stories being covered and written, and from this he makes out his own schedule. He in turn assigns reporters to cover any story that may break between the time he takes over and the time the paper goes to press. The larger papers have assistants to both these executives—assistant day city editors and assistant night city editors.

The work of the news editor differs from paper to paper. His office illustrates the lack of standardization of titles and functions which exists in newspaperdom. On some papers the news editor may control copyreaders and features, on another he may control the entire news department. A typical news editor has charge of copy desk, make-up, and composing room.

The telegraph editor handles the copy that comes in from Washington and from all parts of the United States outside of the local area. He and his assistants on the telegraph desk, which is sometimes called the national or domestic desk, copyread this news, write the headlines for it, and in general prepare it for publication.

The cable editor, sometimes called the foreign editor, edits the stories that come from all countries outside of the United States. When a world war breaks out, a special cable desk is set up to handle the war news.

The sports editor and other specialized news editors, such as financial, real estate, society, and school, act as city editors within their own departments. On large papers each has a staff to which he assigns stories to be covered. These stories when written are in each case edited and prepared for publication by the departmental desk. Apart from the sports editor, who usually operates independently, most department editors work under the city editor. All are responsible to the managing editor.

The good make-up editor, according to Al E. Davies in *Late City Edition*, is "part printer, part reporter, part editor, and part alarm clock." It is his job to fit the news and features which have been set up in type into the page forms of the paper. As noted elsewhere, a "dummy" of page one is okayed by the managing editor. A "dummy" is a diagram of the layout of a page which shows position of stories. All pages which carry advertising are dummied by the advertising department. In addition, most departmental editors prepare department dummies. It is the make-up editor's job to translate all these various directives into readable realities. To the tick of the clock he fits stories, pictures, advertisements into their allotted columns and pages. Often this entails last-minute decisions. Stories are cut in the composing room or left out altogether; headline type is changed to suit the "look" and readability of the page.

The art editor, often called the picture editor, works in close conjunction with the city editor, for many stories these days are covered by the cameraman as well as by the reporter. On metropolitan papers the art editor may have as many as twenty men under him to assign to stories. The public's growing delight in pictures is enhancing the art editor's position on most papers. In some instances, as in the case of tabloids, the space allotted to pictures is greater than that assigned to text. On smaller papers which do not maintain their own photographic staff, the art or picture man has the job of selecting photographs from the number submitted by a picture agency such as Associated Press Pictures.

ON THE BUSINESS SIDE

The functions of the business manager vary widely. On some papers he may be in charge of all activities outside of editorial and news matters; on others he may be simply in charge of office routines such as collections, credit, and similar servicing. Where his duties are those of general supervision over the business activities of the company, such officials as the advertising manager, the circulation manager, the promotion manager, the mechanical superintendent, the auditor, and the building superintendent are responsible to him, and he in turn reports directly to the chief executive. This means that he supervises both the business office and the production of the paper.

D. B. Abert, business manager of the Milwaukee *Journal*, has these dual duties. Writing in the brochure, "A Week in the Life of a Metropolitan Newspaper," here is what he says of the departmental line-up on his paper's business side:

In addition to the advertising department and the accounting office service, and credit, there are the purchasing department, which handles the procurement details on materials, supplies and services each year; the personnel department, which deals with employee procurement, policies, benefits, and kindred matters; and the building service department, which attends to plant and equipment maintenance. Our radio and television activities have grown to major proportions in our business structure. Our promotion department engages in important business building services ranging from market research to employee and public relations.

Commenting on the production side of a business manager's role, he writes:

We must remember that putting together a metropolitan paper is a complicated manufacturing process. We get out a new product every day, the equivalent of a large full-length novel. The timing of each phase of this tremendous undertaking must be as nearly perfect as we can make it. Minutes count. The team must click as a unit every hour of the day and every day of the year. This calls for careful planning, direction and control so that a constant flow of production is maintained.

Advertising's main divisions. The advertising manager has the job of selling the newspaper's advertising space, and the department he heads operates on most papers across the continent in much the same way. That is, the advertising department is usually broken down into three highly specialized divisions: local advertising; national advertising; and classified advertising.

On some papers the local advertising department is called retail advertising department, but under the different name it holds the same responsibility—securing the largest single volume of advertising. Its field covers department stores, women's and men's wear stores, drugstores, groceries, and the like.

The national advertising department deals with products which are sold across the country through many of the same outlets which we find listed under local advertising. Such products include automobiles, foods, cosmetics, beverages, medicines, et cetera.

The classified department often employs more personnel than the others, for its field consists of the thousands of small classified advertisements, lost and found, business opportunities, help wanted, houses for rent, and the like, which the papers publish each day.

Each of these divisions has a manager of its own, and each division is often subdivided into special types such as automobile advertising, travel advertising, financial advertising, and radio advertising.

In addition, some papers have a classified-display department for such categories as movies, hotels, and holiday resorts.

Advertising today has to do with selling beliefs, commodities, and services, and to the newspapers across the land it means a billion dollars in annual income.

Circulation and delivery. Newspapers place great emphasis on circulation, as papers base their advertising rates on the number of copies they can sell. The late Arthur Brisbane, whose contract with the Hearst papers was linked to circulation so that his income expanded as the readership grew, could state with conviction: "Circulation means to newspapers what the air we breathe and the circulating blood are to the human body."

Accordingly, the circulation manager's function is to sell as many papers as possible. In doing this, he tackles a two-fold problem, for his department has a traffic as well as a sales function. He has to see to it that his deliveries by newsboy, by truck, by train, or by airplane reach the purchasers of the paper while the news is still fresh and, if possible, before a rival paper can reach them. Under the circulation manager are minor managers who take care of city, suburban, and state circulation and delivery superintendents.

Apart from New York City, the upwards of 55 million newspapers which roll off the presses of the nation each day reach their readers through the home-delivery method. This system enlists the services of some 500,000 newspaper delivery boys, each of whom earns an average wage of nine dollars weekly for approximately eight hours of work. A paper with an average daily circulation of 350,000, 86 per cent of which goes direct to the homes, will employ as many as 5,500 delivery boys each day.

The newsboy has a long and honorable record in American journalism. Benjamin Day took the idea from London and introduced boys as street salesmen when he founded the New York *Sun* in 1833. Since then, hundreds of thousands of alert and ambitious youngsters, a cross section of their communities, have gained their initial business training by either selling or delivering papers. Their alumni include Thomas A. Edison, Henry Ford, Adolph S. Ochs, and Dwight D. Eisenhower.

The circulation department uses one of two methods with its delivery boy employees. Under the "office collect" plan, it employs a boy at a fixed rate which is based on the paper's price and the boy's route. Under the "little merchant" plan, it sells the paper at a wholesale price to the boy, who in turn retails them at the paper's regular price to the customer. Federal and state statutes exist to regulate the hours and conditions of employment of these young entrepreneurs.

In some cities newsstand sales rank high above home delivery as a circulation method. New Yorkers, for example, buy 90 per cent of their evening papers directly from newsstands, in many cases strategically placed at a subway entrance or exit.

William E. Robinson, when business manager of the New York *Herald Tribune*, compared the organization of a large city circulation department to the setup of a sales department of a manufacturing enterprise in which the product is sold in a large number of outlets having a rapid turnover.

The promotion department. The promotion department is a fairly recent development in American journalism, but its function is nowadays considered so important that the office of promotion manager in the business department's hierarchy is on a plane with those of the advertising and the circulation managers. His job and that of his department is threefold: to increase circulation, to sell more advertising space, and to build good will for the paper.

He tackles the first, that of sales promotion, by using the standard methods of publicity—advertisements in newspapers and magazines, streetcar and bus signs, billboards, and radio and television commercials. In addition, his paper may publish, as many newspapers do—notably the Chicago *Tribune*—illustrated pamphlets describing in an interesting way the procedures of editing and publishing a daily newspaper.

He tackles the second task by doing his best to help the advertisers already attracted to his paper. Much of this help comes under the head of research. He and his department make studies which analyze the markets served by the paper and point out the relation of the paper's circulation to these markets.

He builds good will for his paper in many and various ways. He organizes forums, introduces conducted tours through the newspaper plant, sponsors contests, promotes sports events such as the annual "Golden Gloves" boxing series. He has all the devices of expert public relations techniques from which to pick.

The Mechanical Division

The mechanical side of major papers consists today of six departments. These are:

1. The composing room.
2. The engraving room.
3. The stereotype room.
4. The press room.
5. The mailing room.
6. The service division.

Each of these six divisions has its own foreman who is responsible to the mechanical superintendent who is in charge of all mechanical operations. The responsibility of this superintendent is usually either to the business manager or to the chief executive.

Together, all these executives and the men and women who serve under them work as a team to produce each day's newspaper. This motivating sense of collaboration, this dominating *esprit de corps* has apparently always characterized workers in the Fourth Estate. Because of it they produce not a lifeless piece of merchandise but a vital entity. As Philip Gibbs has so memorably put it in his *Adventures in Journalism:*

A newspaper is a living organism, threaded through with the lives of men and women, inspired by their spirit, animated by their ideals and thought, the living vehicle of their own adventure of life.

12
Editing and Printing

The Copy Desk Takes Over—The Art of Copyreading—Art
of the Headline—Make-up—Composing Room Procedures—
Printing Methods and Types—The Teletypesetter—New
Developments in Printing—Growing Use of Color

All stories destined for the newspaper, whether they come from the typewriters of reporters and rewrite men or from the several wire services, require editing. This duty falls chiefly to the copyreader who sits on the rim of a horseshoe-shaped table—the copy desk. (Small papers do not have copy desks. The city editor and other editors read all the copy.)

The copy desk setup varies somewhat with individual papers, but most papers nowadays adopt one of two general procedures: the universal desk system or the independent desk system.

In the old days, the universal desk system actually was universal in the sense that it handled everything that came in. Nowadays, even on small dailies, the work is usually divided between the city desk and the telegraph desk. Between them they edit copy and write headlines for all "spot" news—everything except sports and financial coverage.

The independent or separate desk system, in operation on a large scale at the New York *Times*, allocates the news to different editors, each of whom has his own corps of copyreaders. At the *Times*, seven editors with a crew of from seventy to eighty men edit news designated as cable, telegraph, city, obits-amusement-society, finance-business, sports, and reserve news. The *Times* has also a separate desk for its International Edition.

Whether the system adopted be universal desk or separate desk, the process of editing runs along similar lines. In each case the story goes to a "slot man" who sits at the head but on the inside rim of the horseshoe desk. This editor or the news editor glances through the copy, quickly gauges its relative importance, determines the space it should occupy—200 words or a half or three-quarters of a column—and decides the type of headline it merits. He marks the desired length and headline type on the copy and passes it along to one of his copyreaders who sits on the rim of his horseshoe.

This copyreader, sometimes called desk man, rim man, or "mechanic of the editorial room," is the anonymous and frequently unappreciated collaborator of the writer. Newsmen who see his blue pencil flay their cherished prose have few good words to say for him, but Neil MacNeil in his book, *Without Fear or Favor*, indicates the newsman's true worth. He suggests that the reputation of many a star reporter rests partly on the work done by this man in the green eye-shade who combed out the reporter's clichés and made his clauses march.

Although the tradition persists that the copyreader is a former reporter driven to the horseshoe desk by middle age, this is rarely the case. As Chet Vonier comments in the *American Mercury*, "the good copyreader is captured young. The job is much too exacting and specialized to allow of any other method of recruitment. It requires more of a special sort of mental agility and resilience than an elderly brain can encompass."

Copyreaders generally are paid better than reporters. The work holds out attractions for men with editorial ability. The chances for advancement are good, as the copy desk is a recruiting ground for office executives.

This work is mainly twofold: the editing of the story and the construction of a suitable headline for it. The amount of this work varies on each paper and varies on each day. On a big desk, the copyreader may edit from five to ten columns. On a busy night the words he sets down in his headlines, if written as running matter, might total about two columns.

His editorial function is to bring each news item that comes to him up to par. As he picks up the copy and reads, he forms general conclusions about the story in hand. Has it news value? If it hasn't that, it's not worth printing.

Is it accurate and fair? Inaccurate items are not wanted by any newspaper. Unfair items are wanted by few papers, and their number is rapidly decreasing. The copyreader takes the repsonsibility for published inaccuracies.

Is it libelous? An item that contains words or implications that may get the paper into legal difficulties has to have the danger spots eliminated.

Is it complete? Is the treatment fragmentary and partial? Will it leave the reader up in the air? If so, its details must be rounded out.

If the item meets these qualifications, the copyreader starts his editing to fit his paper's requirements. These requirements may vary, but as a general rule, we may take it that the paper requires:

Clearness. The reader must have no difficulty in finding out just what the article means.

Condensation. The copyreader must cut and condense each story to the length assigned to it. As practiced in newspaper offices, condensation applies to words and not to ideas. Verbal frills may go but the meaning must remain. He frequently condenses by substituting short words for long ones. He writes "begin" instead of "commence"; he writes "try" in place of "endeavor." He knows that by careful condensation one quarter of the words can be omitted. One "and" is usually enough.

Arrangement. The copyreader's notion of logical arrangement differs from that of the literary man. It is based on the convention of the "lead" which puts the important part first and the least important part last.

Style. The copyreader's use of the word "style" has nothing to do with literary quality. As he uses the word it refers to particular rules which his paper has laid down for spelling, punctuation, capitalization, abbreviations, use of numerals, and the like. Such usages, along with a number of words and phrases to be avoided, vary from paper to paper.

He edits his copy along the foregoing lines by means of a set of standardized copyreading symbols which tell the typesetter what sections to omit, when to transpose, when to spell a word out and when to contract, et cetera. Some of the most frequently used symbols have been shown in an earlier chapter.

He then proceeds to check the copy's paragraphs and, if the story has sufficient length, supplies some subheads. The subhead is a line to be printed in a type which differs from the body type of the article and is used to break up the too solid look of a long column of type.

The best rule is to paragraph for ideas and not for mechanical reasons. Copyreaders also try to avoid being mechanical when it comes to the subhead. The look of the column demands a subhead every two sticks or a stick and a half at least, or say about every 300 to 350 words. The copyreader aims to have his subheads really mark divisions in the subject, and he tries to have them say something new and not merely repeat what has been already told.

The Fine Art of Copyreading

Here is an example of copyreading in action from an expert source—the general office of the United Press Associations. It is in the form of a memorandum sent to the Division Managers and Business Representatives of all bureaus of the former United Press, and it is reprinted here in full through the courtesy and with the permission of Merton T. Akers, editorial executive.

The story as originally written and filed read:

> Orangeburg, S.C., Jan. 4 (UP)—Juke Box Operator J. E. Hutto was driving peacefully into Orangeburg last night when he saw a car loaded with men careen to a halt in front of him.
>
> A man leaped out of the car, dragged another struggling man behind him, whipped out a pistol and fired twice. The second man stopped struggling and slumped to the ground. The gunman picked up the limp form and shoved it back into the car, which drove away.

Hutto gave chase but lost the "death car" in Orangeburg. He stopped and reported the shooting to Sheriff George Reed, giving him the car's Florida license number. Reed quickly notified the State Highway Patrol.

The Patrol flashed the report to all stations by radio. Roadblocks were set up all over the State.

Deputies meanwhile investigated the scene of the shooting. They found footprints but no blood.

Less than an hour later another flash came over the patrol radio network. Frightened witnesses reported another identical shooting at Summerton, S.C., 30 miles northeast of Orangeburg.

State troopers swifty charted the course of the car, and went into action. Minutes later they swooped down on the "death car" on the highway 15 miles south of Sumter, S.C.

Inside they found five laughing college students—all very much alive.

They told troopers they were on their way back to Duke University from their homes in Florida and only meant to enliven the auto trip a bit by staging a few fake murders.

The "murder weapon" turned out to be an antique pistol. The ammunition was firecrackers.

The troopers didn't think it was so funny. Neither did the students when the irate patrolmen notified Sheriff Reed in Orangeburg that they were holding the pranksters for him if he wanted them.

Reed answered that they were "just college boys having some fun" and told the troopers to let them go.

The patrolmen lectured the boys for a while at headquarters and sent them on their way. Troopers promised not to reveal their names. The students promised not to "shoot" anybody else.

Here is how the official UP memorandum edited this story, and in the accompanying reproduction we see the editor's pencil and copyreading symbols at work.

Orangeburg, S.C., Jan. 4 (UP)—Juke Box Operator J. E. Hutto was driving peacefully into Orangeburg last night when he saw an automobile full of men stop suddenly.

A man leaped from the car. He dragged out a struggling man and shot twice with a pistol. The second man quit struggling and fell. The gunman picked him up and shoved him back into the car, which was driven away.

Hutto chased the "death car" but lost it. He reported the shooting to Sheriff George Reed and gave him the car's Florida license number. Reed notified the State Highway Patrol.

The patrol called all stations by radio. Roadblocks were set up.

Deputies at the scene found footprints but no blood.

Less than an hour later another urgent call went over the radio. Witnesses reported an identical shooting at Summerton, S.C., 30 miles northeast of Orangeburg.

State troopers charted the course of the car. Minutes later they caught the "death car" 15 miles south of Sumter, S.C.

In it they found five laughing Duke University students —all very much alive.

The students said they were on their way back to school from Florida and only meant to enliven their trip with a few fake murders.

The "murder weapon" turned out to be an antique pistol, the ammunition—firecrackers.

State troopers didn't think the "murders" were funny but they let the students go when they promised not to "shoot" anybody else.

And the editorial reasoning that lay behind this expert copyreading? Here it is quoted verbatim from the official UP memo:

This news feature came off the day trunk wire and is an example of a loosely-written story. It is too long, full of adjectives and bromides, arrives at the climax too late and then wanters off into "just words."

The copy reader had three problems:
1. To tighten up the story and thereby speed up the action.
2. To cut out the excess words and bromides.

ORANGEBURG, S.C., JAN. 4--(UP)--JUKE BOX OPERATOR J. E. HUTTO WAS
DRIVING PEACEFULLY INTO ORANGEBURG LAST NIGHT WHEN HE SAW A CAR.
LOADED WITH MEN CAREEN TO A HALT IN FRONT OF HIM.

A MAN LEAPED OUT OF THE CAR, DRAGGED ANOTHER STRUGGLING MAN BEHIND
HIM, WHIPPED OUT A PISTOL, AND FIRED TWICE. THE SECOND MAN STOPPED
STRUGGLING AND SLUMPED TO THE GROUND. THE GUNMAN PICKED UP THE LIMP
FORM AND SHOVED IT BACK INTO THE CAR, WHICH ROARED AWAY.

HUTTO GAVE CHASE BUT LOST THE DEATH CAR IN ORANGEBURG. HE STOPPED
AND REPORTED THE SHOOTING TO SHERIFF GEORGE REED GIVING HIM THE CAR'S
FLORIDA LICENSE NUMBER. REED QUICKLY NOTIFIED THE STATE HIGHWAY PATROL.
THE PATROL FLASHED THE REPORT TO ALL STATIONS BY RADIO. ROADBLOCKS
WERE SET UP ALL OVER THE STATE.

DEPUTIES MEANWHILE INVESTIGATED THE SCENE OF THE SHOOTING. THEY
FOUND FOOTPRINTS BUT NO BLOOD.

LESS THAN AN HOUR LATER ANOTHER FLASH CAME OVER THE PATROL RADIO
NETWORK. FRIGHTENED WITNESSES REPORTED ANOTHER IDENTICAL SHOOTING AT
SUMMERTON, S.C., 30 MILES NORTHEAST OF ORANGEBURG.
STATE TROOPERS SWIFTLY CHARTED THE COURSE OF THE CAR AND WENT INTO
ACTION. MINUTES LATER THEY SWOOPED DOWN ON THE DEATH CAR ON THE
HIGHWAY 15 MILES SOUTH OF SUMTER, S.C.

INSIDE THEY FOUND FIVE LAUGHING COLLEGE STUDENTS--ALL VERY MUCH
ALIVE.

THEY TOLD TROOPERS THEY WERE ON THEIR WAY BACK TO DUKE UNIVERSITY
FROM THEIR HOMES IN FLORIDA AND ONLY MEANT TO ENLIVEN THE AUTO TRIP
A BIT BY STAGING A FEW FAKE MURDERS.

THE MURDER WEAPON TURNED OUT TO BE AN ANTIQUE PISTOL, THE
AMMUNITION WAS FIRECRACKERS.

THE TROOPERS DIDN'T THINK IT WAS SO FUNNY. NEITHER DID THE STUDENTS
WHEN THE IRATE PATROLMEN NOTIFIED SHERIFF REED IN ORANGEBURG THAT THEY
WERE HOLDING THE PRANKSTERS FOR HIM IF HE WANTED THEM.

REED ANSWERED THAT THEY WERE "JUST COLLEGE BOYS HAVING SOME FUN"
AND TOLD THE TROOPERS TO LET THEM GO.

THE PATROLMEN LECTURED THE BOYS FOR A WHILE AT HEADQUARTERS
AND SENT THEM ON THEIR WAY. TROOPERS PROMISED NOT TO REVEAL THEIR
NAMES. THE STUDENTS PROMISED NOT TO SHOOT ANYBODY ELSE.
UR+1SA

3. To reduce the story so a telegraph editor could splash it in a page one box if he chose to handle it that way.

Here in detail is why the corrections were made:

The first paragraph originally read that Hutto saw "a car loaded with men careen to a halt in front of him." It's simpler and faster to say he saw "an automobile full of men stop suddenly." Whether the automobile stopped in front of Hutto was immaterial—he saw it and that's the point; so out comes the last phrase of the first sentence. "Careen" was changed because the word means to tilt or tip, which the car probably did not do. "Loaded with men" is misleading. Presumably they were not loaded into the car but got in of their own accord.

In the second paragraph the writer took too long to set the scene and used too many words. He also wrote in four clichés—"whipped out a pistol," "slumped to the ground," "limp form" and "roared away." Note the substitute phrases and words. Breaking up the first sentence makes the paragraph more readable.

The third, fourth and fifth paragraphs suffer from the same trouble. By taking out the adjectives and inconsequential detail the copy reader came up with one paragraph in the place of three—a considerable word saving—and again quickened the tempo. There was no need to detail all the steps Hutto took to notify the authorities. Note the ones taken out.

Only minor changes are needed in the next paragraph. "Flash" is changed to "urgent call." Few persons outside our own business know what a flash is. The witnesses probably weren't "frightened." "Excited" probably would have been more explicit, but the situation doesn't necessarily call for an adjective. When in doubt about an adjective cut it out. "Another" is redundant in front of "identical."

The next paragraph about the activity of the state troopers contains two more bromides—"went into action" and "swooped down."

Now comes the climax paragraph. "Duke University" was moved up and substituted for "college"—two birds with one stone. The story actually ends after this paragraph but the reader will want to know at least three more details. Those are: why the students played the prank—for fun—and how they did it—with an old pistol and firecrackers—and how the case was disposed of—they went free. The rest is only excess wordage.

Art of the Headline

Although he works anonymously, the copyreader, when he constructs a good headline, joins the ranks of the creative artist. With short words and in short compass he can tell a whole story. He knows that the headline must fulfill two requirements: it must attract attention to the story; it must announce that story's main facts. He strives to see to it that each headline he concocts does both.

In his *American Mercury* article already noted, "Art of the Headline Writer," Chet Vonier indicates the restrictions under which the copyreader works.

The newspaper copyreader works within the narrowest of all literary limits. The style and size of type as well as the number of lines in the headline are determined by another editor before it reaches the copy desk. Each line of the headline will accommodate a limited number of characters—an average count for top-of-the-column headlines on most newspapers is eleven or twelve letters or spaces. Except on the most rural journals no word may be divided between one line and the next. As the paper progresses in size, other restrictions are imposed. On most newspapers it is regarded as sinful to end the first line of a headline with a preposition. On others a copyreader may not begin a headline with a verb, leaving the subject understood. On still other papers, an adjective or adverb has to be on the same line as the word it modifies.

Within such narrow limits, the headline writer contrives to write captions which are informative, intelligent, and occasionally droll. His vocabulary is highly selective and, if he is one of the experts of the trade, it is extensive too. He may borrow "nab" from thieves' argot, and "nuclear fission" from the physicists; he will pirate "knockout" from the sports page and "grand slam" from the bridge table. He has a high regard for words, but is not seriously hampered by a belief in their inviolability.

Fortunately for the headline writer the present-day trend veers away from the old strait-jacket style. Each year more and more papers adopt the "flush left" head. Here no effort is made at balance or filling out lines. The head writer tells all he has to, and the printer sets it all flush to the left.

The Present-Day Trend—Shorter "Heads"

The growing tendency today favors shorter and shorter heads. The short head boasts three advantages—it reads faster, it writes faster, and it sets faster.

Except in the more conservative papers, headlines have changed from all capitals to upper and lower case for the sake of greater readability. A popular innovation—again to make reading easier and speedier—is the "downstyle" head in which only the first word and proper names appear in "caps."

Another newcomer is the "kicker" head, favored for its typographical impact. Its frequent "gag" quality puts it along with the "teaser" head in the forefront of those devices used today to lure readers into the body type.

Again, only the more conservative papers retain the "jim dash." This, the short line which meticulously separates decks and stories, has generally gone by the board along with the decks or banks it once separated.

As Allan Holcomb writes in *Late City Edition* (Holt, Rinehart, and Winston, Inc.):

A newspaper may be judged pretty accurately by its headlines. If its aim is to amuse and shock its readers first, and inform them afterward, its heads will display an intensive repertory of shockers and thrillers. When a balanced news perspective is the idea, the head writer will endeavor to get the picture in focus, use just the right word and avoid the bromide, the shopworn phrase and the wisecrack.

The use of the banner line—that page-wide head in large type—illustrates Mr. Holcomb's contention. Daily it screams across the sensational press to chronicle a run-of-the-mill killing. It is reserved by the New York *Times* to announce the outbreak of a world war.

After a story has been duly edited and headlined, it goes to the composing room to be set in type. However, if it is a major or page one story, it requires a final "okay." For this final scrutiny, it goes

New Study
Links Cancer
To Smoking

British Report Says
Danger Increases in
Proportion to Habit

The Hartford *Courant*
Hartford, Conn.

ARMY CLEARS
INFANTRY UNIT
IN BRIBE CASE

Probers Fail to Find
Favoritism

The Chicago Daily *Tribune*
Chicago, Ill.

Ferry St. Bridge
To Be Dismantled
Unless City Buys It

Army Says It Will Be
Locked Unless Purchased
By June 30; Cites That
It Now Has Little Use.

The Buffalo Evening *News*
Buffalo, N.Y.

Drive Against
Underworld's
Leaders On

Deportation Is
Justice Dept. Goal

The Topeka Daily *Capital*
Topeka, Kan.

Chum Kills
Boy, 15, in
Accident

The Denver *Post*
Denver, Colo.

Across the land the headline grows shorter, less involved and restricted—a daily adventure in terse telling and swift announcement.

PROVINCIAL BANK HAS RECORD YEAR

Assets, Deposits, Loans
And Securities Reach
Peak Levels

The Telegraph-Journal
St. John, N.B., Canada

Old Year's Exit Due To Be Dry Weatherwise

The Atlanta Constitution
Atlanta, Ga.

'Most Vicious Strain Known'

Scientists Breeding 'Superbee' Get It, With 2000 Stings a Day

The Washington Post
Washington, D.C.

Wife Faints in Court as Druggist Gets Two-Year Sentence

The Boston Daily Globe
Boston, Mass.

Near-Zero Again Throughout Iowa

The Des Moines Register
Des Moines, Iowa

2 MEN ACCUSED OF HAVING $50,000 IN STOLEN WHISKY

Liquor Stolen in Hijack-
ing Nov. 10 Is Seized
by FBI Agents, Depu-
ties in Raid.

The St. Louis Post-Dispatch
St. Louis, Mo.

DRUG TESTED ON GIRL WHO QUIT GROWING

Doctors Hope Hormone
Will Bring Her To
Normal Height

The Sun
Baltimore, Md.

North, South, East, West—the headlines summarize the story.

to the desk of the night city editor or in the case of the New York *Times* to the "bull pen" where at least three assistant editors sit and pontificate. A make-up editor may also see the story, as well as a picture caption writer if any "art" is to accompany it on the page. Passed by this executive editorial desk and its place on the page's "dummy" duly noted, this story like its lesser *confrères* leaves the editorial side of the paper for the mechanical.

Making up the Paper

Although the managing editor has the final say with page one, it is the news editor who "dummies" the paper and guides the make-up man in his assembling of the diversified product.

If we take a standard size paper, we see that each page is divided off into eight columns and that the newspaper itself is sometimes divided into two sections. We find our attention caught by the front page, *page one*, and perhaps also by the *split page*—the "little front page" as it is sometimes called—which initiates the second section. If we take a tabloid-size paper, with its five-column width, its front page may even startle us.

This is natural enough, for the editors and publishers have planned those pages to do just that—to attract the reader's eye. This assemblage of headline, story, and picture is called the page's "make-up" and into it goes the best thought that the paper can muster. All types of newspapers—be they standard or tabloid in format, or conservative or sensational in policy—try to put their best foot foremost on their front pages. The conservative papers will aim at dignity and harmony, the more emotional will go in for a wild scramble of stories and headlines to fight for the reader's attention.

Three main theories of make-up dominate the country's front pages from coast to coast.

1. **The balanced make-up.** The very name here gives the clue to the product which exhibits a methodical arrangement of its stories and pictures, a symmetry in its design, and a harmony among its type styles.

2. The braced make-up. This style is sometimes called the "focus" make-up, a term more readily applicable to the method employed. Here the make-up editor arranges his material along diagonal lines from one corner of the page to the other—say, from the lower left-hand corner to the upper right—in such a way as to focus the attention on the story in the upper right-hand area where the day's chief story is usually placed.

3. The circus make-up. Here lack of any definite organization is the rule. Stories, heads, and pictures find themselves jumbled up in a diverting typographical hodge-podge with the blatancy of the three-ringed show which gives its name to the category.

The term "horizontal make-up" crops up frequently these days. This refers to the practice of setting headlines and body type in double columns. This method grows in popularity for it tends to counteract the narrower columns which newspapers are more and more adopting to reduce their newsprint bills. Editors know that reader interest increases as type is presented in wide blocks. Actually "horizontal make-up" is not a separate classification as the three just named. The use of heads or type in double columns can form part of any make-up pattern. The "horizontal make-up" occurs frequently on the braced or focus page as exemplified by New York's *Herald Tribune.*

In recent years a process dubbed "streamlining" has developed with the aim of making not only the front page but the whole paper more readable. It strives to give a more modern look to both type faces and make-up. Among its innovations are the use of larger body type and a still larger type for the opening paragraphs of the story; the elimination of rules between columns and the substitution of black dots for a story's date line, which normally proclaims the story's place of origin and its date.

Newspapers, like individuals, put great store on their physical appearance. Clothes do not make the man but they help. Type faces and their arrangement do not make the newspaper but they may reveal the quality of its contents. Each year the firm of N. W. Ayer and Son, Inc., of Philadelphia, which publishes the directory of newspapers in the United States and in Canada, awards a trophy known as the F. Wayland Ayer Cup for excellence in typography, make-up, and presswork. The fact that annually nearly half of the country's English language dailies hopefully enter the competition indicates the keen interest of their editors and publishers in presenting good-looking papers to their public.

In recent years, the winning papers in this Ayer competition have had front pages in which the various elements formed an attractive balance and over-all design. The use of headlines, body type, and white space created an effect of crisp authority. In addition, all worked to get an interesting below-the-fold appearance on the front page. Each year there seems to be a better handling of more photographs.

All winning papers avoided the tendency to cut down on the space between columns. Small space between the columns makes them appear squeezed together and therefore harder to read.

The most important new trend among newspapers is toward narrower pages with a resulting cut in the width of columns. Continuing trends include an increase in the number of papers dropping column rules to create more white space, more use of flush-left headlines, more use of front-page photos, and more use of Bodoni type for headlines.

The increase in white space—an increase that developed slowly— has now become as important and useful in news columns as it has long been in advertising space.

So much for the look of the front page. What of its contents? Each paper answers this question according to its type. The individual paper plays up what it considers will most interest its readers. In the case of the important paper such news will have significance; in the case of the less serious press, the front-page content may be merely divertissement or the "A B C's of Adultery, Banditry and Chiseling." In all types of papers, however, the effort is the same— to make the page a shop window, a showcase to attract customers. This tendency has lured many editors and publishers into giving front-page prominence to the sensational, into presenting a "daily disaster diet." A reader may well find himself depressed when he picks up the morning newspaper and surveys American life—that is, if he limits himself to the front page.

He may still feel depressed even when he hears an apologist for the press tell him that unfortunately news is concerned with the exceptional:

"People are not interested in a thousand husbands who do not beat their wives, but in the one husband who does. They will not read about ten thousand trains that arrive safely at their destination, but want all the details about one train that was derailed."

But what we tend to overlook is that the modern newspaper with very few exceptions does take note of the ordinary, routine, scheduled life. It does account for the normal husbands and trains—the life of a people is all there in the inside pages in columns devoted to "general" news. Many papers these days stress this element of comprehensiveness by placing indexes on their front pages to direct the reader to significant news beyond page one.

Theodore M. Bernstein, assistant managing editor of the New York *Times*, has called this absorption with page one a "fixation" which is a "national malady." He argues that the interrelation between page one and the rest of the paper is inescapable, and that the reader's field should be broadened to take in all sectors of the news whether they be on page one or page fifty-one.

The page 1 fixation is something that grips both newspapers and readers. From the angle of the reader it is the fallacious notion that all he need read to be well informed is the front page. From the newspaper's point of view the evil effect of such a belief is even more permeating because it leads not only to overplaying and exaggeration by less serious newspapers, but to sensationalizing in the writing of stories.

From all this we can see that the process of laying out the front page is complicated by such imponderables as varying standards of news judgment and varying editorial opinions. As qualities that page one stories may well possess, we can list importance, unusualness, interest, and readability.

The newspaper's managing editor outlines the "dummy" of the

page. This is the chart, the blueprint which allocates to each story, each picture, each map or cartoon its appointed position. Later, the make-up editor in the composing room approximates this charted layout in the finished page and tries to avoid such mechanical hazards as crowding and tight headlines. Editors nowadays give increased attention to the "below-the-fold" appearance of their front pages and no longer use this space as a catch-all for short news stories.

Some news stories begin and end on page one. Many others carry over or "jump" to the inside pages. For reader convenience the story in column eight, on the right-hand side of page one, is sometimes carried over to column one on page two. American editors usually reserve this position for the lead story of the day. Canadian editors tend to place their lead story in the left-hand column, acting on the theory that the reader's eye habitually travels from left to right.

The inside pages to which the longer front page stories jump contain the general news, the editorials, the regular newspaper departments, the "features," and the advertisements. Because advertising brings in by far the largest part of the paper's revenue—something like two-thirds of its income—the publishers allocate the greater part of their space to it. The usual proportion is 60 per cent advertising to 40 per cent news, but this proportion varies. Some days it may be 58 per cent advertising to 42 per cent news. When the proportion of advertising noticeably exceeds the standard 60 per cent and thus noticeably lessens the amount of space left for news and features, the issue is called a "tight" paper.

Because of advertising's importance to both revenue and content, the inside pages of the newspaper, with the exception of the editorial page and the "split page" which habitually contain no "ads," are first tentatively laid out by the advertising department. The editors then see how much space on each of the inside pages is left. To them, regardless of proportions, every issue is a "tight" paper, for they are always short of space. They have constantly to cut down some stories in order to find room for others. As Philip Gibbs made one of his characters remark in *Street of Adventure*: "If there was an earthquake at Tooting Bee, and if all the animals at the zoo broke loose and dined off the population round Regent's Park, you can't

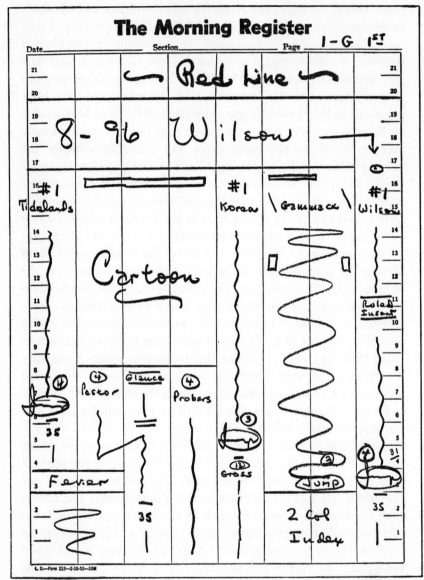

Front page "dummy." Newspapers regard the front page as so important that in most cases the managing editor himself decides its contents and makes out the "dummy" to guide the make-up editor. Here is an actual "dummy" or blueprint of the layout for page one of the Des Moines (Iowa) Sunday *Register*.

get more than 56 columns in an 8-page paper. That's simple arithmetic."

These inside pages, on most of which the advertisements have right of way because it is physically possible to make up news around advertising, are finally dummied with their quota of general news and syndicated features. In the case of departments such as society, sports, and the like, the dummy is made by the editor of the department.

Frequently the news and features, when set in type, fail to coincide exactly with the space allotted them on the dummied page. Stories have a way of running too long or too short. Differing amounts of space have to be filled. To meet these emergencies the make-up editor falls back on "fillers"—items of news and oddments of information set in type in assorted lengths more as an aid to last-minute make-up needs than for their inherent editorial value. Some of these fillers are labeled "time copy" which means that it is copy held for later use after it has been set. "When room copy" is similar in purpose, but much of the material labeled "when room" is already edited but not yet set in type. It has preceded the news stories through the pneumatic tube to the mechanical side of the paper, or it has been taken there by a copy boy.

Composing Room Processes

In the composing room a copy-cutter receives the story, and if it is a long one, he cuts it into short sections of a paragraph or two called "takes." These he allocates to individual linotype operators who set the story simultaneously to save time. When completed, all the "takes" are assembled in order in a tray called a "galley."

The linotype machine was one of the first of the great time-saving mechanisms to meet the speed requirements of modern journalism. Ottmar Mergenthaler invented it, and the New York *Tribune* first made use of it in 1886. It set type in a fraction of the time consumed by the old method of setting type by hand. Identical in principle is the Intertype machine. The mechanism of these two machines is as intricate as it is ingenious. The operator of the Intertype sits before a six-row keyboard somewhat resembling that of a typewriter. Here we will let the writer of the *World-Telegram and The Sun* Pamphlet, "Behind the Headlines," take over:

As the Intertype operator lightly touches the keys of his machine, "matrices" of letters drop from an overhead magazine into a line at his left. When the line is completed, he pushes a lever which moves the line against a mold into which molten lead is forced. The result is a "slug" or solid line of type, which quickly cools as it slides into a "galley" beside him.

For the setting up of large type such as that used in display headlines and in many advertisements, many newspapers use the Ludlow Typograph. Here the operation is not by keyboard. The Ludlow supplies matrices which the operator sets by hand in a special composing stick. This line is then cast in the Typograph unit. Line-casting machines are also widely used because of their speed. When the several "takes" of our story are in type and in the column length "galley" tray, a proof of it is "pulled." This simple process consists of inking lightly the type surface, placing a strip of paper over it and applying some slight pressure. This proof when pulled goes to the proofreader for correction.

The proofreader checks the story which has been set in type against the story in original "copy" form. Usually two people work at this; one reads, the other follows the proof. If the operator's fingers have hit the wrong key and misspelled a word, or inadvertently left out some punctuation mark, or put in upper case (capitals) when he should have put in lower (noncapital letters), then the proofreader uses his set of symbols to indicate the right correction. Some of these symbols coincide with those used by the copyreader, but not all. Perhaps because of this fact, confusion occasionally exists about the separate functions of copyreader and proofreader. Actually there should be no confusion, as their two roles are quite distinct. The copyreader is an important employee of the paper's editorial department. He edits the copy and is permitted on his own initiative to change, delete and even, on occasion, rewrite the story. He gives it its headline. The proofreader is an employee of the mechanical department whose sole duty is to see that the story in type coincides with the story in its original form. He corrects any printer's errors and sends his corrections back to the machines to be recast. He is not authorized to make any change in the story itself. If his trained eye catches something which he feels should be changed and which the eyes of the editors have missed, he brings it to the attention of the editorial department, and makes no alteration on his own initiative.

When the proof of the corrected story has passed the proofreader, the column of type is fitted into a page-size form called a "chase." This operation takes place on a table, called in some plants a "bank" and in others, a "stone." These tables are solid affairs, usually stone or metal topped. To insure the uniform surface of this type-filled chase, its contents are firmly locked in place and "planed," that is, a block of wood is placed over them and gently tapped with a mallet.

Our page-size, type-filled chase is a flat bed of type, and if our paper is a small, local sheet or a country weekly we can print our editions directly from these flat type forms. Nowadays, however, speed of news transmission urges speed in news publication, and all modern printing plants utilize one form or other of the rotary press idea. Accordingly our flat bed of type must become semicircular in form to fit the cylinders of these rotary presses. The process which turns the flat into the round we call stereotyping.

Let us follow our story along to the stereotyping department which adjoins the composing room. Securely locked in its chase, our story with the rest of the page is slipped off the bank or stone on to a special truck called a "turtle" which moves it smoothly along to the next step on its way into the paper.

In the stereotype room, a page-size papier-maché sheet is placed over the flat bed of type by a special machine which rolls it under tremendous pressure. The papier-maché sheet emerges from this steel press as a cardboard mold of our printed page, called a "mat." Here is our story as set in type, complete in every detail down to the smallest punctuation point. This mat or mold is now dried and then curved to a half-cylinder shape. It then goes into one of the autoplate machines which fills our mold with molten metal, and our page emerges as a cylindrical metal plate, the curved duplicate in every particular of our flat bed of type. When this finished plate is removed from the autotype machine, it is cooled with water and marked with its correct and identifying page number. It then goes on its way to the pressroom.

Here a pressman locks the curved plate with our story in its assigned place on one of the press cylinders. Each of these cylinders prints eight pages with each rotation. When every page of the edition reaches the press room in metal plate form and gets locked in place on a cylinder, light signals flash and the presses begin to roll. The ink, which comes from a fountain below the cylinders, is passed along by a number of soft composition rollers, two of which pass over the locked plates on the cylinders.

The paper is fed to the presses from a revolving reel which carries three rolls of newsprint. When one of these giant rolls of paper has unrolled itself almost to the end, one of two things may happen. In some press rooms an automatic device cuts off the sheet and glues to it the end of a new roll, and the press roars on without stopping. In other press rooms, when the roll is almost exhausted, a pressman smears the end of a fresh 1,600-pound roll with paste. Then just before the old roll is used up, the press is slowed down and the old and new rolls are fastened together.

The presses print, cut, and fold papers, and on the moving belts which convey them to the delivery room, every fiftieth is automatically pushed out of alignment, so in this way we can say that the presses count the papers too. In the delivery room the papers are tied into bundles for city delivery and carried to the loading platform where a fleet of trucks takes the bundles to the newsdealers, who in turn deliver the newspapers to the readers.

Summing up, we see that the typical newspaper story is written, edited, set in type, proofread, fitted into its allotted page, stereotyped, printed, delivered and, let us hope, read and enjoyed.

Printing Methods and Types

It's a far cry from Gutenberg's fifteenth-century hand press or the Cambridge Press first set up in the American colonies in 1638 to the great modern miracle presses which such firms as R. Hoe and Company, the Wood Newspaper Machinery Corporation, and Walter Scott and Company nowadays develop. Yet the medieval and the up-to-date both operate on the same principle: both print by the heavy impact of inked plates against paper.

Today, thanks to the many mechanical refinements which have speeded up production, great multicolor presses can roll out the many-hued pages of our mass circulation magazines at a rate of 1,000 feet of paper a minute. Printing itself has developed into a three-billion-dollar industry which engages, according to the Bureau of Census reports, some 13,000 plants, which number would be more than doubled if such allied processes as duplication were added to the tabulation.

The three major divisions of this ancient craft are defined by the three major printing processes: letterpress, lithography, and gravure.

Each process has special virtues and drawbacks. Here is *Fortune* magazine to describe them:

Letterpress. Letterpress is the oldest form of printing. It stems from the old art of wood-cutting in which the artist gouged out the surface areas of his woodblock not meant to print, leaving the printing design raised in relief. The Chinese began printing books from woodblocks as early as 868 A.D. With the European invention of movable type in the fifteenth century, the same principle was carried over. Even with the introduction of metal type, type-setting machines, halftone production of pictures, and huge rotary presses, the principle remains the same. Raised type inked on its surface is pressed onto paper with pressures up to 1,200 pounds per square inch. Halftone plates, etched into thousands of *raised* dots per square inch, varying in size to produce gradations of tone, print in the same way.

Lithography. Lithographic printing images, instead of being raised, simply rest on the surface of the plate as an ink-attracting film or surface area. The term for this type of plate is planographic. Its principle was discovered in 1798 by Aloys Senefelder, a poor German artisan, who found that by drawing in greasy crayon on a certain type of limestone, and flushing with water, a new kind of printing was made possible, which became widely used for color reproductions. The greasy areas took oily ink, wetted areas repelled it.

At about the time of World War I, as the supply of stone neared exhaustion, the industry turned more completely to the use of thin, grained zinc plates, the ink-attracting image being fixed on by photographic means, the surrounding grained areas taking water. About the same time, an offset method of printing came into wider use. The inked plate first prints against a rubber-blanketed cylinder, which then transfers the inked image to the paper. Offset halftones employ dots of varying size, like letterpress, but the dots are not raised as they are in letterpress.

Gravure. Gravure, the youngest of the established forms of printing, is the exact opposite of letterpress. Its printing image is sucked into the plate. It derives from the old art of metal engraving or etching (intaglio), in which the artist, with a sharp tool or acid, dug out the lines he wished to print, leaving the surface as the nonprinting area. A stiff ink was then forced into the design, the surface cleaned and a print made by pressing paper on the plate under such pressures as literally to pluck out the ink. Since no fast commercial process could work with such stiff inks, in modern gravure all lines and tones including type, are broken up into a cross hatch of tiny wells to hold highly fluid ink. A "doctor" blade attached to the press scrapes the "plate" or printing cylinder surface clean after each inking. Gravure halftone "dots" or cells are deep-etched into the plate and *vary in depth, not size*, thus building up tones by actually varying the thickness of ink on paper.

Fortune Magazine sums up by deciding: Letterpress is the most stable; Offset is the most economical; and Gravure has the widest tonal range.

Types of Type

Journalism in all its forms—books, magazines, pamphlets, newspapers—has a variety of type sizes and faces from which to choose. Although the actual work of printing belongs to the mechanical side, the decision as to which type to use rests with the editorial side.

Printers measure their work not by the inch but by the *pica*, which is one-sixth of an inch; and the *nonpareil*, which is half a pica. They measure advertising matter by the *agate line*, which is one-fourteenth of an inch.

Type size is designated in units of one seventy-second of an inch, called *points*. Point size refers to the height of the type measured from top to bottom in its tray.

Type width is measured in units called *ems*. The standard or 12-point em measures one-sixth of an inch. Accordingly we call a newspaper column that is two inches wide a 12-em column. The em of any size type is the square of the body of that type.

The type in which a book, magazine, or paper is mainly set is called the *body type* of that publication.

For newspapers, the most important typographical development has been the increase in the size of body type. This increase has been gradual. At the turn of the century, six-point type was the rule, with nondescript design the rule too. By 1926, scientifically designed type, devised to counteract the distortion caused by stereotyping, came on the market. It set the standard at six and one-half point. Early in the 1930's the popular size became seven point. Today the standard is eight point with a rapidly growing trend to nine point.

This trend reflects the current tendency to make newspaper reading both easier and pleasanter. Editors realize that their product competes not only with other print media, but with radio and television, for the reader's leisure time. They strive to keep him in the body type as long as possible. Accordingly they use shorter headlines to lure him into it and more readable type to keep him there.

Type faces vary more in name than they do in origin. Each is based on one or other of the five main type classifications. These, in the order in which they appeared in printing history, are *Text*, *Gothic*, *Script*, *Roman* and *Italic*.

𝕿𝖊𝖝𝖙, which most of us call "Old English," dates from the hand-inscribed manuscripts of medieval monks. We use it now on announcements, Christmas cards or in advertisements when we wish to give an impression of sanctity, formality or quaintness.

Gothic, which we associate with headlines, is square and black. We can associate its name in our memory with the massiveness of a cathedral.

Script is well named because it appears as based on handwriting.

Roman forms the basis of the largest group and the most widely used. It developed as a compromise between Text and Gothic.

Italic, which we use when we want to give a word or phrase some special emphasis, is a delicate sloping type based usually on Roman.

Advent of the Teletypesetter

The greatest innovation in the whole printing business in recent years has been that of the teletypesetter—or TTS as it has come to be known. In fact it has been the biggest innovation since the linotype machine was invented by Ottmar Mergenthaler, and like the linotype, the teletypesetter cuts both time and cost.

Actually the invention is hardly new. It has been used by some papers in the United Kingdom for over thirty years, and it was introduced into the United States in 1932. Its present spectacular growth on this continent dates from 1950 when the Associated Press opened in the Carolinas the first teletypesetter circuit run anywhere by a news agency. This introduction proved so successful that by 1952, the AP was delivering its news by teletypesetter circuit to more than four hundred newspapers in more than forty cities. In Canada, the newspapers were just as quick to see the advantages of this new method, and today its operation in the provinces has been absorbed into the Canadian Press.

First, as we have seen, the printers set type by hand, letter by letter. Then in 1885 in Baltimore, Mergenthaler took out patents on a machine to set type line by line. This was the foreunner of the line-casting machines now in general use. An operator uses a keyboard to release from a storage magazine the proper matrices—thin strips of metal with letters cut into their edges—to make words. The matrices fall on a moving belt and travel into the assembly box in order.

Spacebands in the form of double wedges face to face (the thickness varies as the wedges slide against each other's slanting sides) are dropped between the words. When the line is almost full, the operator pushes on a lever and the matrices and spacebands take position before a mold. The line is "justified" to fit the exact width of a newspaper column by pushing the spacebands from below. Molten metal then is forced into the mold.

The result is a metal bar or slug, with letters in relief, automatically trimmed to the right height and thickness and pushed out into a tray with other slugs ready for use in the news page. The matrices and spacebands are returned automatically to their channels in the storage magazine.

This cheaper, man-saving method revolutionized newspaper production everywhere.

Now the new revolutionary agent, the teletypesetter, takes the operator away from the line-casting machine. Through its use, more lines of type can be produced without more equipment. The cost per line of type is lower. Then, when the teletypesetter is used at the end of wire circuits, one operator working in a central office can set type simultaneously in ten or a hundred other offices with which his only connection is a flimsy telegraph line.

A Development of Teletype

The teletypesetter is a development from the widely used teletype, the machine which transforms electrical impulses, which may be sent thousands of miles, into a printed message.

An operator using a "perforator"—which resembles an oversize typewriter keyboard—types the newspaper story as he would on a typewriter. But instead of typing letters he is punching tiny holes in a narrow strip of paper tape, each group of holes representing one letter, punctuation mark or operating function of a line-casting machine. The tape is run through an attachment called an "operating unit" which can be used to run almost any line-casting machine but which works most efficiently on high-powered equipment planned especially for it.

Any newspaper can adopt this local operation to set news and advertising copy at a twofold saving of cost. With some intensive training, the perforator can be operated by any typist who uses the "touch" system, and costly line-casting equipment run by teletypesetter operating units turns out type two or three times as fast as the average manually operated machine.

When the teletypesetter is extended to circuit operation, the scope for saving is greater. One or two operators in a central office—operators who have to be infinitely more efficient than those on local operation—make the original teletypesetter tape. A compact little machine called a "transmitter" sends over telegraph wires the same electrical impulses that locally would run a linotype.

Theoretically these impulses would be fed directly into an operating unit on a line-casting machine in each newspaper office served on the circuit. In practice, however, a "reperforator" is used to reproduce at each newspaper the original punched paper tape. This new tape is fed through one or more operating units at whatever time and in whatever order the newspaper staff decides.

Definite drawbacks to the expanding scope of TTS, however, are already noted. It is felt that the country's newspapers may become even more standardized than ever, and that in all probability the style of the future will be determined in large measure by the press associations because of the teletypesetter. This will leave little or no opportunity for a newspaper to have its own style.

New Developments in Printing

Except for changes in typography and make-up, the newspaper has had few changes mechanically. However, since the end of World War II, the commercial printing industry has seen some fast developments which foreshadow application to newspaper printing.

A recent development in typesetting is the Electro-Typesetter. This typesetter, originated for the *Wall Street Journal* and its country-wide editions, is an adaptation of the Linotype. The keyboard has been removed and the mats are released by means of electrically operated solenoids actuated by means of pre-punched paper tape in a central control room. The machine delivers body type, a newspaper column wide, at about twelve lines a minute. Automatic devices shut down the machine if anything goes wrong.

The Intertype Company's new Monarch model has no keyboard and is operated by pre-punched tape. The company claims that it can deliver fourteen lines a minute.

Another Intertype development, the Fotosetter, sets type by film. Using the circulating matrix principle, the Fotosetter utilizes mats which carry negative images and are exposed, one at a time, in a camera-like device. The product is a roll of film bearing line after line of type face images in either negative or positive form on either film or paper. The film may be used to make regular letterpress plates, offset plates, or gravure plates and cylinders.

The American Type Founders' typesetter puts type images on film by means of two devices which resemble typewriters. One cuts a tape which actuates the camera device. This is less costly than other film typesetters.

According to Wayne V. Harsha, editor of *The Inland Printer*, the impact of photo typesetting on the newspaper industry may be considerable within the next quarter century. Writing in *The Quill* (March 1960) he says: "Film typesetters may eventually displace many hot metal machines in the preparation of display advertising type forms. The film may be used for making conventional letterpress engravings in full page size from which mats may be rolled and curved stereotype plates cast, or even further—curved original plates which may be put directly on the press, by-passing the stereotyping process altogether."

Growing Use of Color

The current popularity of "color" in news stories has a present-day counterpart in the popularity of color in news photographs. In fact, a recent major development in American journalism has been the growing use of color in news pictures—in "run-of-press" color, that is, in regular press runs as opposed to specially prepared color. This popularity, while greatest in the Western states, has grown rapidly from coast to coast. Statistics show that in the East, 52 per cent of newspaper readers get multi-color dailies, in the Midwest, 87 per cent, and in the far West, 96 per cent.

Although the Milwaukee *Journal* used run-of-press color as far back as 1891, the bill ran into prohibitive figures, and apart from isolated instances, newspaper readers got their news pictures, as the majority of them get them still, in black and white. Since World War II however, technical improvements in the process have brought color down to a cost level that most newspapers—at least 800 of them—feel able to afford. In fact the number of American dailies using run-of-press color has increased 25 per cent since 1956.

The Minneapolis *Star* ranks as one of the outstanding users of fast and timely color with its news. The *Star* prints news and news-related color pictures five times a week—such as a four column picture of an American Legion parade across page one just five hours and nineteen minutes after the news photographer had snapped the shot—and while the parade was still marching on!

Despite this marked and growing emphasis on color, the seven big dailies in New York City have shown little intention to follow suit. Their reasons? The high cost and poor quality of newspaper color, and reader indifference. Actually, color equipment may require an investment of as much as $500,000.

13
Industrial and Business Journalism

The Company Publication—Its Distinctive Categories—Its Format and Content—Development of the Business Press— Its Character and Importance—The Farm Press

Despite growing pains still evident in some quarters, industrial journalism has steadily matured since World War II. Today with an enhanced professional status it is expanding in the number of its publications and developing in its technical skill.

Although some industrial publications began in the nineteenth century, no formal survey took place before 1928. This disclosed some 575 "house organs" as they then termed them. By 1933—four years after the market crash which precipitated the depression period—the total had shrunk to 280. As business conditions improved, the number of company publications again mounted and by 1941 reached 4,000. The war years added still more, but the postwar period showed the greatest growth of all. Today their combined circulation reaches the impressive figure of 160 million per issue—two and one-half times the per issue total of daily newspapers. The gross circulation figure just quoted includes the press runs of 1,000 or less per issue of smaller ogans as well as press runs in excess of a million. Some of the giants in the field include: *Ford Times* (1,320,000); U.S. Gypsum's *Business of Farming* (1,250,000); Mutual of Omaha's *Mutual Moments*

(1,500,000); Industrial Harvester's *Tractor Farming* (1,200,000); Chevrolet's *Friends Magazine* (1,500,000); and the Dodge *Job Rater* (1,250,000).

Just here a definition is in order. Let us consider an "industrial' or "corporate" or "company" publication as one that is sent free to its readers and which in one way or another frankly promotes the interests of its sponsor.

Although the title "house organ" has lost popularity with the practitioners, who now prefer the terms used in the definition, the name "house organ" retains its own descriptive value. But by whatever name we call the publication, it falls into one of three distinctive categories. It is either an *Internal*, an *External* or a *Combination*.

1. Internal: This type of company publication is directed primarily to employes and stockholders, such as "WE" sponsored by Western Electric.

2. External: This type goes to salesmen, sales prospects, agents, dealers, wholesalers, customers, and others, like Standard Oil's (N.J.) *Lamp*.

3. Combination: Here, as the name suggests, editorial aims are joined to reach several groups. Usually, in practice, the company expands the Internal type to interest outside readers in the manner of General Foods *G F News*.

The readership area pin-pointed by these three types many serve to indicate why American management willingly spends the millions allocated to their publication. They enable management to establish communication with the specific publics which an industry or a company wants to reach—employes, stockholders, dealers, customers, and people considered "thought leaders." As John Earl Davis, editor of *Shell Progress* points out, "The industrial publication has two proper functions: to *inform* and to *persuade* on behalf of the company that pays the bills."

In the internal type of journal—that directed toward employes— the management wants to persuade employes to certain lines of action: good work habits, reduction of waste, regard for safety rules, honest workmanship to protect the product's standard and integrity, and to think well and speak well of the company. To achieve this the good internal type will tell the workers what they want to know about their company—its policies, its products, its manufacturing operations, its outlook for the months ahead and the longer years ahead. Fully one half of the publications listed belong to the internal or employe journal type.

In the external publication—the one that goes outside the company to dealers, distributors, salesmen, and prospective customers, the magazine's message concentrates on sales. If it is a marketing publication, for instance, it will tell what the product is, what it will do for the customer (often in terms of what it has done for other customers), and how the company's service makes the product more effective. As it is directed toward dealers, the publication also suggests to them how to sell it, how to treat customers, how to run their places of business more profitably. About one quarter of the industrial magazines fall within this group, most of them expertly edited and smartly turned out with colorful "copy" and covers.

C. H. Dykeman, editor-in-chief of the Ford Motor Company's dealer publications, has underlined the effectiveness of this type of paper. Some external magazines, he says, have grown to be so accepted and necessary a part of the dealer's operation that they are looked upon as one of the company's most important expenditures, because these skillfully edited publications never appear to "push"; instead they serve the dealer by providing him with new ideas and new techniques successfully used by other dealers. He feels that the chief reason this new kind of dealer publication is so successful is that it is a direct link between factory and dealer. "In this day of larger and larger organizations, with necessary and important field organizations, this link can be vitally important. The editor with skill, courage and persistence can so win the respect and trust of a dealer organization that he actually becomes a key executive in his organization. What he puts into print can actually be the chief medium for informing the dealer organization of company policy . . . this is pretty potent stuff." (*The Quill*, April 1955.)

The combination type—also an external in the sense that it goes outside the company, has the widest appeal of all. Here management adapts the internal, or more rarely the marketing publication, to reach and interest more of the general public. Through it management seeks to persuade all kinds of people to think well and to speak well of the company and of the industry and of Industry in general. It would like to persuade voters and their representatives in government to reject unfriendly legislation. It wants to assure stockholders that they have invested wisely in a well-managed company. Frequently these consumer magazines are dubbed "soft sell" or "low pressure" or "long range"—terms indicative of their role as good will builders. One quarter of the total number of industrial publications rank as combination magazines. As both these external type publications enjoy budgets larger as a rule than those allotted to the employe type, many emerge each month as fine examples of the graphic arts.

Because the combination type reaches a general leadership, more stress is laid on appearance, on "art" and entertainment. Nevertheless the editor sees to it that the reader gets the latest information about the company, the industry, and the economic system. He inserts features on how people connected with the company live and work; about how society is benefited by the products and skills and activities of the company.

Format and Style

The majority of these three types listed (58 per cent) come out as monthlies. In the case of the employe journal which may sometimes contain "spot" news, the publication may be more frequent—sometimes bi-monthly, sometimes weekly. Although they have no set rules for the format, the majority (63 per cent) favor the magazine style and the 8½" × 11" size. This has been found a convenient size which lends itself to flexible layout. Of the minority appearing in other sizes, some prefer a smaller format which separates them from the vast majority, and some go in expensively and expansively for a larger size aiming at prestige publication. About 25 per cent publish more than twenty-five pages with some going beyond sixty pages. Some 40 per cent use color, often four colors, and the majority (62 per cent) are printed by letterpress; thirty-one per cent use offset. According to Con Gebbie, a specialist in the field, "In general the trend today is toward sizes and formats which more nearly reflect the purpose of the publication involved."

From all the foregoing it can be seen that these industrial publications with their formula of out-and-out promotion plus a variety of general information are more than just propaganda organs and more than sales brochures. Broken down, a typical issue might contain one-third material of direct company interest; one-third material of indirect company interest; and one-third material with no conceivable company interest or direction. The inevitable inference is that such publications require editorial abilities of a highly specialized kind.

Naturally enough the good industrial editor uses in his publications the identical skills that hold and influence the readers of newspapers and general circulation magazines—good planning, good reporting, good writing, good "art," and good design. But in addition to these tried and trusted journalistic techniques he needs a background of precise knowledge in his unique field and an attitude of mind in general sympathy with his employer's aims.

Training for Industrial Editors

Because of the growing importance of industrial journalism, a training program is developing based on the experience of successful editors in the field. Some colleges include training for industrial journalism in their curricula. For such courses the International Council of Industrial Editors have outlined what it believes such academic training should include.

Professor Clement E. Trout, who has pioneered classroom training in journalistic specialties at Oklahoma A & M, feels that college training for work on industrial publications should include "the usual journalistic skills of writing, editing, reporting and production with a supporting background in the field of commerce. Such topics as business organization and finance are fundamental."

Such college training, however, is largely preparatory and should be followed, he says, by some type of practice to give the individual experience in practical work and to develop individual responsibility. Professor Trout describes newspaper experience as "good"; practical experience in some phase of business as "excellent," but experience on the staff of an industrial publication as "best of all." Summing up his conclusions (*The Quill*, April 1955) he says:

Training for industrial editing then includes first an understanding of industry and a favorable attitude toward its activities. Then, command of the skills of communication through the printed page. College or other types of study of commerce courses and journalistic skills linked with experience to learn how to use the knowledge seems to be the most favored program.

Business Magazines and Newspapers

Although both take the business world as their parish, the company publications and business journalism differ fundamentally. Business magazines and newspapers serve an entire industry or field. They are business ventures and make money from subscriptions and advertising. "House" journals on the other hand serve one organization only and are turned out by companies whose interest is not publishing as a business.

The vast majority of these trade publications take the magazine format. The Standard Rates and Data Service, Incorporated, lists some 2,270 of them in its directory and classifies most of them as monthly publications. Few claim a monopoly in their fields, and the majority face keen competition in both circulation and advertising. A prevailing practice is for one publishing firm or center to sponsor a variety of publications covering diversified interests—as for example the thirty-three business magazines with their 1.3 million subscribers turned out by the McGraw-Hill Publishing Company of New York. This firm, by the way, has the world's largest editorial staff—622 full time editors. The Butterheim Company, also of New York, illustrates in its four main publications the diversity tendency: *The American City* features articles and advertising aimed at municipal governments; *Contractors and Engineers* pinpoints the construction industry; *Mart Magazine* as its name suggests has in view the needs of the appliance and retailing fields; while *Overview* with a subscription list bristling with the names of school board members and deans appeals to the nationwide education market.

In commenting on the growth of business journalism, the magazine *Industrial Marketing* (1960 MDB) points out that "while business papers had their start in the United States more than a hundred years ago, their greatest development has come in the past fifty. Since 1900 trade publications have had their greatest development both in numbers and influence. At present there are about 2,000 journals of this character, plus 270 in Canada. In addition there are over 340 business reference books which play an important part in the sales plans of manufacturers whose specific market is industry or trade."

CLASSIFICATION AS TO PURPOSE

A foreword to Julien Elfenbein's authoritative textbook, *Business Journalism*, now in its second revised edition, gives an idea of the field's comprehensiveness in noting that there are "at least one and frequently two or more papers devoted to each and every important phase of agriculture, mining, manufacture, transportation, and marketing. There are professional business papers in the hotel, school, hospital, and restaurant fields, specialized papers in the fields of sales, advertising, and marketing; and industrial papers covering every important phase of manufacturing activity."

Each in this broad survey of monthly or daily business journalism falls into one of three main divisions and can be classified by its editorial purpose. One type of publication deals with the interests of those engaged in *production*, and in the allied fields of construction, public utility operation, transportation and other activities where the use of mechanical power and equipment is important. Another type serves the function of *distribution*, supplying business information to wholesale and retail merchants who buy for resale. Still another group of papers serves *vocational activities* (though the element of resale is sometimes present, as in the restaurant field). Then there are some business publications which perform more than a single function. For example, a paper may supply information for wholesalers and distributors as well as for producers and processors.

In studying this whole field, students encounter two terms which need clarification—the *horizontal papers* and *vertical papers*. Horizontal papers circulate broadly through industry, or deal with a single function common throughout industry. Vertical papers serve but a single industry through covering that special field. For example, *Purchasing Week*—a horizontal trade publication—is directed toward the interests of the purchasing function (generally the purchasing agent) throughout virtually all industries; *American Machinist*, on the other hand, is classified as vertical. It serves a specific field of industry, metalworking, but deals with the interests of various operational functions in such plants, from top management through several levels of production responsibility.

Trade Newspapers

According to *Editor & Publisher's* listing, there are some thirty-five daily trade newspapers, if we stretch the term "trade" to include three sport dailies, chiefly racing forms. In addition some fifty-six dailies appear listed under the comprehensive grouping of "Court, Commercial, Financial, Legal." This authoritative directory breaks down the trade entries into Agriculture (5); Apparel (3); Building and Construction (6); Entertainment (5); House Furnishing (1); Labor (1); Metal (2); Petroleum (2); Resorts (1) and Sports (3).

With years of authority and prestige to its credit, *Women's Wear Daily* (circulation 47,215) may well stand as an example of a successful trade newspaper. It is the best known of five Fairchild publications —all published under the slogan "Our Salvation Depends upon Our Printing the News."

Because *Women's Wear* prints the news with accuracy and impartiality, it has become required reading for all those who design or make or sell clothes for the American woman. To insure a comprehensive news coverage its publishers spend four million dollars annually on a network of twenty-five American and foreign news bureaus, plus 405 correspondents and "stringers."

Take up an average issue of this paper and run through its pages. Even if in no way concerned with the apparel industry, the reader will find that this well written and well planned daily has much to attract and hold the interest. Its balanced front page gives the chief spot to date-line Paris. Here, John B. Fairchild, regarded highly as a fashion reporter, files his story on the Paris "openings" through Wireless Fairchild News Service. His copy is straight news. On page two, in a box headed "Today in Paris" he relaxes into gossip about a "snobbish showing" from which buyers and manufacturers are excluded. "Too bad," he says, and notes that a glamorous film star has been invited. Passing through full page advertisements, the reader finds that Paris crops up again on page five opposite a "Letter from Madrid." Several pages are given to "columns"—one, "Today and Yesterday in Retailing," wonders what has happened to the "art of sales promotion." Although most of the advertisements deal with the women's wear field, some are aimed at buyers such as those for airlines, liquor, and restaurants. Among headlines like the one which proclaims "Prints and Stripes Newest in Woolens" there crop up provocative ones like "New Dog House Now Has World by the Tail," topping a story from Philadelphia where a recent firm burst into prosperity on dog garments. The bulk of the paper deals with its chosen field under such department headings as Fabrics, Furs, Millinery. But the reader encounters as well such standard newspaper departments as financial, television report, a theatre page with a well conceived and amusingly written play review, and even a comic strip in form if not exactly in content. However, there is one standard feature that *Women's Wear* does not have—an editorial page.

The information which business publications provide boasts wide variety. Its presentation employs all the standard print media techniques developed through journalistic practice. Recruits for this specialized field will find that they need skill in the basis arts of communication, and an ever increasing knowledge of their subject. They will soon develop some comprehension of the importance of business journalism to the nation. What is this importance? Some measure of it may be gained from the growing belief that the economic pre-eminence of the nation is in no small measure due to the services in the past and in the present rendered to industry by its business press.

The Farm Press

Although agriculture as a pursuit continues to seem to most people a way of life rather than an industry, the nation-wide farm press falls legitimately within the scope of this chapter. As noted previously, agricultural journalism boasts five daily newspapers, but in addition there are 230 farm publications in the United States with a combined circulation of 27,349,749 subscribers. Each year the farm press grows in importance as a national force and is being regarded more and more as a career field which rewards the writer both in interesting and worthwhile work and in interesting and worthwhile income. The present-day enhanced importance of farm journalism springs in no small measure from the fact that American agriculture is now undergoing its third major revolution. The first came in the mid-nineteenth century when the farmer substituted animal power for manpower, the second in the 1920's when mechanical power took the place of animal power. Today agriculture is engaged in the third great revolution—the substitution of capital and technology for manpower, horsepower, and mechanical power. To cover all this adequately the successful farm editor and reporter needs not only a sympathy with rural people and their problems, not only a proficiency in the conventional journalistic skills, but technical knowledge of a high order.

Leading publications in this field are: *National Live Stock Producer, The Prairie Farmer, Successful Farming, The Farmer-Stockman,* and *Western Livestock Journal.* The *Rural New Yorker* is one of the great farm papers of the East and has exerted a profound influence in the dairy industry. Because of its militant editorial policy, thousands of farm families regard it as the dairyman's bible, and as an equally important guide for other branches of agriculture.

In Canada the farm press, with fifty-one periodicals and 2.5 million readers, represents an important segment of the Canadian technical press. Among the leaders are *Free Press Weekly, Prairie Farmer, Country Guide,* and *Family Herald.* Along with their farm news and features, these periodicals provide popular appeal material as well.

14
The Editorial and the Editorial Page

The Editorial's Development, Purposes and Ethics--Its Structure and Range—The Cartoon—The Editorial Page: Its Features and Make-up—"Opposite Editorials"

On every page except one, the newspaper reports and records the actions, the ideas and the opinions of the world at large. It reserves only one page and sometimes only one column to voice its own ideas, its own thoughts, its own opinions. For the paper to express opinion concerning the news it prints is a perfectly natural procedure. News and opinion have a way of going hand in hand. The first question which springs to our tongue whenever a person brings information of interest is, "Well, what do you think of it?"

In the early days, journalism published news and opinions separately, the one in newsletters, the other in pamphlets. Daniel Defoe first united these two journalistic streams in one publication in *The Review* which he published in London in 1704.

This special page, the editorial page, consists usually of the paper's own opinions, expressed verbally in its editorials and graphically in its cartoons, and also the opinions of others. These outside opinions may be the ideas of the paper's readers, the familiar "Letters to the Editor," or short excerpts from the opinion column of other papers under some such head as "What the Press Is Saying."

211

In the early days here, the newspapers had no separate editorial page. Opinion they did have, but it took the form of observations tacked on to the end of the news or more usually of letters to the editor signed by some pseudonym. To Noah Webster goes the credit for first placing his editorials under the masthead of his paper.

During the era of colonial journalism and for a full century after, most of the editorials in any American paper were written by one man, the editor. Today, except on very small papers or those which publish syndicate-supplied editorials, the work engages the talents of several individuals. This editorial staff may consist of two or three editorial writers or, in the case of large metropolitan papers, as many as ten or twelve.

The men and women who write editorials bear a heavy responsibility to the public. They have the obligation to be well informed, to make themselves specialists on the particular subjects on which they write, and to be fair in the opinions which they form and express. No one man, these days, can emulate Francis Bacon and "take all knowledge for his province," but as Geoffrey Parsons, when chief editorial advisor of the New York *Herald Tribune*, said:

> The richer the writer's background, the larger his ability to stimulate thought about anything. A good editorial writer addresses the largest classes ever reached by a teacher, philosopher, or critic. . . . He cannot know too much, if he is to hold their attention.

Editorial Code of Ethics

That editorial writers both individually and collectively realize their responsibility as molders of public opinion is evidenced by the tone of the Code of Ethics which the National Conference of Editorial Writers has compiled and adopted. The preamble to this code points out that "the editorial writer, like the scientist, must pursue Truth no matter where it leads if he is to be faithful to his craft and to his society."

The basic points of the code are these:

1. The editorial writer should present facts honestly and fully.
2. He should draw objective conclusions from stated facts, basing

them upon the weight of evidence and upon the considered concept of the greatest good.

3. He should never be motivated by personal interest.
4. He should realize that he is not infallible and should give voice to those who disagree with him in a public letters column and by other suitable devices.
5. He should review his own conclusions and correct them should he find them based on previous misconceptions.
6. He should have the courage of well-founded conviction and never write anything that goes against his conscience. Where editorial pages are more than the product of one mind, sound collective judgment can be achieved only through sound individual judgments. Therefore thoughtful individual opinions should be respected.
7. He should support his colleagues in their adherence to the highest standards of professional integrity.

Editorial Purpose, Structure, and Range

No individual editorial writer knows the exact percentage of his readers, but he feels safe in presuming the type of reader he is reaching. He regards this reader as a person possessing background and education who has an interest in the result of reflective thinking, desires more information than the news reports offer and seeks some interpretation of their meaning and import. Accordingly, the editor sees to it that editorials are written in a style and with a content worthy of such a readership.

The present-day newspaper editorial has emerged as a distinctive journalistic form. Its closest literary cousin is the essay. But the editorial differs from the essay in its brevity and its contemporary nature. An essay written in the eighteenth century remains as fresh and readable today as when Joseph Addison or Richard Steele first penned it, for it deals as a rule with some subject of abiding value. An editorial written in the eighteenth century holds interest today merely for the antiquarian, for it dealt with a subject pertinent only to its immediate moment.

We can define an editorial then as a short essay steeped in the sense of timeliness.

The purpose of this "timely essay" is to set forth what the newspaper itself thinks. It makes known these ideas and opinions in various ways. The late Arthur Brisbane, who had a vast following in his time, believed that the editorial writer's opportunity was four-fold: he could teach, attack, defend, and praise.

Teaching is the most important and the most difficult.

Attacking is the easiest and most unpleasant though sometimes necessary.

The defending of good causes, of the weak against the strong, of the new idea against ridicule, is important and usually neglected by editorial writers.

Praise also is neglected, except in a partisan sense without meaning. . . .

First have something to say. Then say it so that people will see it, read it, understand it, and believe it.

Ideally the function of the editorial is to inform and lead public opinion. It interprets the current news to the reader and points out its significance. "If from time to time and in some places its leadership should be in the wrong direction," says the New York *Times*, "the dependable corrective is always close at hand if the news columns present the facts honestly."

The editorial's structure is simple. It consists of its caption or title; of the "news peg"—the information on which the editorial is based; of the opinions stimulated by this news peg; and sometimes an editorial explains the reasons for these opinions. We can call these three units the informative, the reactional, and the deliberative. As many editorials run to just three paragraphs, we frequently see these divisions set down in the foregoing order.

The caption often has real editorial value in itself and can express opinion or set the tone for the whole editorial. Sometimes it is merely a label or an attention-getter.

Today's tendency is toward shorter and shorter editorials. The average length of editorials across the land is but 300 words. This trend toward brevity limits the editorial writer to a compass smaller than that employed by the professional in any other field. The clergyman can exhort at length; the lawyer can plead to the extent of the judge's patience; but the editorial writer must condense fact and argument to a few short paragraphs.

The range of subject matter for editorial comment is almost limitless. The editorial writer can find his inspiration in the past, in the present, and in the future, so long as he is able to give his editorial that timely slant or twist which the editorial recipe requires.

Certain news events naturally demand editorial comment. Outstanding political topics, important legislation, the death of prominent individuals, inventions and discoveries, record-breaking feats of various kinds, sporting events, and questions of general social interest all serve as grist for the editorial mill. In addition, the editor encourages his writers to turn out what he calls the "light" editorial. He knows that his readers always enjoy the humorous approach. Such editorials sometimes tease a current social foible or fashion or pick up for comment some amusing situation which the news of the day happens to present. A rule similar to that which governs the news columns applies to the editorial page as well—an article on local affairs draws more interested readers than one on an occurrence hundreds of miles away. There is a marked trend today toward brightening editorial comment. The heavy encyclopedic type of article has lost favor.

An analysis of editorials printed in six daily papers over a two-week period showed that the editors gave the bulk of their space to national, international, state, and municipal topics, while the balance was made up of welfare, health, social subjects, economics and labor, obituaries, appeals, congratulations and other personal references, religion, science, and odds and ends.

Style and the Editorial

Although newspapers generally devote something less than two per cent of their space to their own opinions and their own special pleading, they regard this material as far more important than the space allotted would seem to indicate. Accordingly, much care is given to the expression of the paper's opinion, to the actual writing of the editorial, and to its content and style.

Frequently the editorial stands as the one piece of really creative writing in the whole paper. The editorial writer then, denied the ballyhoo of headlines and the attention allure of crime, lust, and raw conflict which the news pages exhibit, must develop interest compulsion in the ideas he provides and in his method of presenting them. He devotes thought to his choice and use of words; he aims to write with authority, and in this way he tends to counteract the effect of a too hurried and sometimes slipshod reporting and headlining of the news; he embellishes his own style with apt quotation from his background reading, and he takes the time to give his copy the benefit of careful and precise revision. As a result he frequently achieves a piece of contemporary prose which is at once graceful, cogent, informed, and stimulating.

Let it not be assumed, however, that an editor or an editorial writer must conform to fixed and rigid rules. He remains free to influence his reader in any manner he sees fit. The one thing that editorials claim to have in common is that they usually appear under the masthead on the opinion page of their journals. The late William Allen White and many another small-town editor has effectively talked to "Main Street" in that local thoroughfare's own idiom, and they have made plain to Main Street the meaning of problems and events not only at home but in far-off places. Henry L. Mencken on February 10, 1938, filled six full editorial columns of the Baltimore *Evening Sun* with black dots—some 1,000,725 of them—to dramatize the number of federal employees. The late Rollo Ogden, when editor of the New York *Evening Post*, commented on Theodore Roosevelt's early procedure in Panama by reprinting from Kings 1:21, the story of King Ahab's seizure of Naboth's vineyard under the caption, "Panama, 899 B.C." Originality kowtows to no formula.

Actually the editor's function remains what it always has been: to interpret the news, to guide opinion, and to crusade for good causes. But the area in which he operates has been extended.

Former Governor Charles A. Sprague, who is editor of the *Oregon Statesman*, reiterates these functions and indicates the wider field of action when he says:

Today's editor should throw himself zestfully into his job, multiplying what talents he has and employing them freely and fearlessly in the fight against ignorance, fear, hypocrisy, kluxism, and fuzzy think-ing. He should not hesitate to tackle dragons abroad and crackpots and rascals at home. He should aim at the mass audience and not fire till he sees the whites of their eyes—then let them have it. If he does this he will have a place in whatever Valhalla is reserved for good ex-editors, and have a heap of fun as he goes along.

Not least of the editorial's functions is to entertain. The editorial writer frequently finds this assignment more difficult than merely to argue a cause or set forth a political dogma. The present-day trend, however, is increasingly toward brightening the editorial page with what are called "change-of-pace" editorials. Here is such a one from the Richmond, Va., *Times-Dispatch* which is at once entertaining, a "change of pace" and also a skillful *tour de force*:

PUT THOSE PREPOSITIONS
WHERE THEY BELONG AT

Columnist Robert Ruark made some strong statements Monday concerning the rule against using a preposition to end a sentence with. He said there was no logical reason why you shouldn't put one of those "lousy, skimpy little words" at the tail end of a sentence if you wanted to.

There's really nothing for Columnist Ruark to get excited about. Prepositions always are supposed to govern other words, called their "relatives," and only the laziest writer should find it difficult to arrange the sequence of his words so that the relative is last and the preposition is before.

Sometimes, with all the belittling of the old tried and standard rules, we wonder what modern literature is coming to. Instead of polishing their sentences, as did the old masters of the language, many of today's writers sit down and simply dash something off. Prepositions are left dangling naked at the end of sentences, and you can't tell where they're going to or where they came from. These unclad words, tied onto nothing, appear about to take off.

In the speaking art, too, conformity with standard rules of grammar should be striven after. Here, errors are easier to fall into. A person who wishes to leave a good impression with his listeners should use the very best grammar he is capable of. With anything less, he should refuse to put up.

It is a sad commentary on the literary world today that fundamental rules of grammar are laughed at. This is the age of skepticism when there's little left to cling to. Fortunately, however, there are a few purists in the writing and speaking arts who refuse to cut corners and whose work can be depended on.

Yes, Ruark, end your sentences with prepositions if you want to. But don't try to influence other writers, who to such a flagrant violation of rules of grammar will never give into!

The Editorial Cartoon

Side by side with the written editorial goes the pictured one—the cartoon. Here we get the newspaper's views in graphic form. In this picture-minded age, many readers who feel they lack the time to read a conventional editorial will gladly pause long enough to glance at the cartoon and catch its editorial meaning. It is claimed that more than three readers out of five take in the editorial cartoon.

For years the cartoon has proved a potent force in molding public opinion. Benjamin Franklin, that journalistic innovator, published the first one here in his famous "Join or Die" sketch. This woodcut pictures a snake cut into eight sections, each section representing one of the seaboard colonies. His Pennsylvania *Gazette* published it in 1754 to unite the colonists in the French and Indian campaign. Later editors reprinted this disjointed reptile as propaganda in the American Revolution. Thomas Nast in *Harper's Weekly* made the cartoon an agent of reform in 1870–71 when his drawings played a major part in breaking up the notorious Tammany Tweed Ring. Contemporary cartoonists such as David Lowe in the United Kingdom and Bill Mauldin in the United States show that the cartoon still retains its power as an effective editorial agent.

Annually a Pulitzer Prize in journalism goes to reward the country's outstanding cartoon. The criteria which the Committee of Awards uses read: "The cartoon shall embody an idea made clearly

Freedom's Defenders. The cartoonist in his individual paper or syndicated across the land makes an editorial point in graphic form. It is claimed that three readers out of five take in the editorial cartoon.

The Real Skid Row. This cartoon from *The Courier Journal* of Louisville, Kentucky, makes its editorial point readily apparent.

apparent, shall show good drawing and striking pictorial effect, and shall be helpful in some commendable cause of public importance." These standards of judgment will form for us an adequate definition of a worth-while editorial cartoon. Most papers place the cartoon on the editorial page. The Chicago *Tribune* makes it a frontpage feature.

Courtesy of Chicago Sun-Times

Cartoonist Burck of the Chicago *Sun-Times* makes an editorial comment on the college commencement season.

Other Editorial Page Features

Letters to the Editor. Among the prized contributions to the newspaper are letters to the editor, and the best of them usually find their way into print on the editorial page under some such caption as

"The People's Forum" or "Vox Populi." The weeks when concise well-written letters on current topics pour into the editor are considered periods of growth. Some of these letters glow with praise; others drip with censure. The editor is glad to receive both types, and nowadays both find their way into print on the editorial page. Here is what a veteran editor-in-chief, the late Rollo Ogden, thought of letters from readers:

One of the features of the editorial page which I prize very highly is letters sent in from the outside. We do like to get the views and opinions of our readers although they may be quite contrary to those of the paper. I think that such a section in any paper is of great importance and interest. It refutes the impression that the editor prints only his own opinions, and will not give a fair hearing to those who differ from him. This [the printing of contrary views] is comparatively a novelty in journalism in this country. The old idea was to shut out everything that did not agree with the policy of the paper. The reading public likes to feel that a newspaper is not confined to printing the judgments of its editors, but wishes to open a forum for all kinds of opinions and political views. Nothing pleases me more than to get a letter taking issue with the position of the paper. It should be brief and not insulting, but we are willing to go to great lengths to give the outsider the chance to express himself freely.

From early days the reader's letter has been ranked as an important feature. Today in England, the letters to *The Times* (London) are as widely read as the newspaper articles and are signed often by authoritative names.

"Press Digest." A staff member, usually known as the exchange editor, looks after the copies of newspapers published across the country which come to his office in exchange for his own paper. Frequently he places in a special binder the editorial pages from the nation's outstanding journals. From these he can select and reprint in his own paper pertinent paragraphs, each with the appropriate credit line, and in this way show how the editors in various parts of the country are reacting to the news. Such exchange columns make an interesting and valuable editorial page feature.

Miscellaneous Features. Many newspapers choose from their own files outstanding bits of news which appeared in the paper ten, twenty, or fifty years ago on the same day of the month and compile for the editorial page an individual feature which many of the older readers find thought-provoking.

Sometimes the "Poem for the Day" will round out the opinion columns. These adventures in verse are frequently contributed to and paid for by the paper itself; sometimes syndicates supply them; sometimes they are "lifted" from volumes of minor verse which have outlived their copyright and reached "public domain." Occasionally these poems have editorial force; frequently they can claim merit; even more frequently they strike the sophisticated reader as banal or sentimental. The make-up editor has a way of regarding them all—good, bad and indifferent—as "filler material."

Editorial Page Make-up

The editor-in-chief usually outlines a "dummy" to indicate the general make-up of the page. He is guided by such considerations as the importance of the subject matter, the need for a variety of topics, and by the length of the editorials. However, it is the make-up editor in the composing room—where mechanical exigencies have right of way—who usually decides the final appearance of the page.

Frank E. Raschig of the Indianapolis *Star* has made some valuable generalizations on this question of putting the page together:

Certain well-defined ideas of make-up have come to be accepted by the majority of leading newspapers, principally dealing with the physical appearance of the editorials as a means of attracting the attention of the reader casually turning over the pages in his progress through the paper. An editorial page which resembles the classified advertisements for dullness is not likely to be read by the individual pressed for time, which in this amusement-seeking generation includes almost everybody. Larger type than the non-pareil of the news columns is necessary to avoid a heavy appearance and to make hurried reading easier on the eye.

A newspaper's story content may be gleaned from the headlines or the first few paragraphs, but the editorial, if interesting at all, requires time enough to complete the article. For this reason, 8-point or 10-point type is preferable.

A point in psychology also enters into the make-up of the editorials in the effort to avoid the appearance of undue length. A long editorial is usually only half as valuable as two shorter ones, and in order to give the appearance of greater brevity, as well as to provide a variation from the standardized width of the news columns, editorials set in wider column measure make a more attractive appearance.

Opinions differ as to the amount of space which should be devoted daily to editorial comment. Some papers use three or four columns for this purpose on the theory that the average reader should find sufficient variety to interest himself in a minimum of one or two of the editorials. Four or five average length articles should cover the important news of the day without sacrificing quality to quantity production.

Opinions differ too in so far as the position of editorials is concerned. Some editors place the leading editorial immediately below the paper's masthead. Others put their leading article at the top of the second column which they consider the right position for the day's leader, just as the last column on the front page is reserved for the day's most important news event.

In this matter of editorial page make-up, the late William Randolph Hearst contributed typographical innovations. He was the first publisher to print wide-column editorials. He removed the editorials from the conventional and traditional inside pages to the back page—a practice which some other editors later followed. Many editors were influenced by the large type, short paragraphs, simple style, and illustrations which the Hearst editorial page exhibited.

In recent years, few innovations of any moment have been introduced into the make-up of the newspaper's page of opinion.

"Opposite Editorials"

The page "opposite editorials" has an importance because of its position. For this reason many papers give it a distinctive character which sets it apart from the usual news-plus-advertisement content.

One metropolitan paper, for instance, reserves this page for its obituaries. Preferring the quick to the dead, another journal in the same city devotes its "opposite edits" to photographs of debutantes, prospective brides and to news of the goings-on of Society.

The famous old New York *World* filled it with "columns" bearing such by-lines as those of Heywood Broun, Alexander Woollcott and Franklin P. Adams and made the pages so arresting that many readers who might have normally skipped over the editorials were attracted to them by the brilliance of this "opposite edits" assemblage. Similarly, today editors throughout the country use this page for their commentators, their book reviews, and features of a like nature.

15
Columns, Columnists, and Commentators

The Appeal of the Personal—Types of Columns—The Columnist's
Freedom—Criticism of Columns—Columnists on the Air

Although the newspaper column today ranks as a standard feature of the press from coast to coast, and although its readership far outnumbers that of the
anonymous editorial, both its ubiquity and its popularity
are comparatively recent. It began almost simultaneously in various parts of the country during the last
quarter of the last century. The Springfield *Republican*
had something like a column in 1872; Eugene Field
sired a somewhat different type with his "Sharps and
Flats" in the Chicago *Daily News* in the 1890's; and at
the same time on the West coast, Ambrose Bierce was
compiling "Prattle" for the San Francisco *Examiner*.

Today some columns are indigenous to the papers
which publish them—compiled and written by the paper's own staff—but the most famous and, of course,
the most widely read come to the nation's press through
syndicates.

It is interesting to note here that the practice of the
syndicates differs fundamentally from that of the news
agencies. The agencies have a way of playing up their
own credit line and playing down or omitting the name
of the writer. The syndicates on the other hand play up
the name of the writer and soft pedal that of the syndicate. The reason here is that the syndicates are first

and foremost sales organizations, and they wish to handle writers with salable bylines.

To find the reason for the column's drawing power we must take a backward glance into newspaper history. Up to the 1870's, the American newspaper was very largely the mouthpiece of one individual—its editor. Readers turned the pages to see what Benjamin Franklin had to say or what William Cullen Bryant, Horace Greeley, or Henry J. Raymond had to say and not what the Pennsylvania *Gazette*, the New York *Evening Post*, the *Tribune*, or the *Times* thought about public affairs. Journalism was personal in the sense that the individual editor rather than the paper voiced the ideas and opinions. But when the newspaper became "big business" and its organization grew complex and the field for editorial comment expanded, the individual editor found himself multiplied into an editorial staff which contributed to an anonymous page. No longer could the reader tell the individual source of the opinions. He read what the *Sun* or the *News* or the *Star* had to say. The old familiar "I" had given place to the editorial "We."

We all prefer personality to anonymity. Readers of those early anonymous sheets probably felt them to be cold and impersonal; they missed the warmth and vigor of the individual. Accordingly, they welcomed the return of the "personal" in the columnist, even though at first he indicated authorship merely by initials. Oddly enough the definitely personal came into the column fairly late in its history and more or less by accident. Franklin P. Adams, the "F.P.A." of "The Conning Tower," introduced it when he initiated in his column his burlesque of Pepys' Diary. Quite naturally the diary form injects the personal, for it deals with what the diarist sees, does, feels, and thinks.

Although the word "column" might indicate that the contents run to the conventional 1,000 words or so of the usual newspaper column measurement, the length frequently varies. Some columnists turn out a daily stint of 800 words or more; some put the end mark to their outpourings after 500 words or less. The late Will Rogers wrote a famous column which averaged but one paragraph.

Types of Columns

We have today some eight or so popular types of columns:

1. The signed editorial column. Here we find what resembles an editorial in form, but an editorial palpitating with the personal element, for it voices the opinions and the ideas which the columnist himself holds and thinks at the time. These pundit paragraphs have frequently an oracular air to them. In many cases they exhibit good writing and sound reasoning. Thousands of readers turn to the signed editorial column for stimulation and for guidance. The best known column of this type carries the by-line of Walter Lippmann.

2. The standard column. This type of column handles editorial subjects of lesser importance and deals with each in a paragraph or so. Characteristically it uses a light touch. An early compiler of this type of column—"Gleanings"—in the Springfield *Republican* called the process "raking after the cart." The standard column is frequently unsigned and may be the work of one individual or the combined output of a staff.

Outstanding columns in this category are "Topics of the Times," in the New York *Times* and "The Talk of the Town" in *The New Yorker.*

3. The hodge-podge column. Here the columnist presents to his readers a little of this and a little of that. He takes variety as his guiding principle and sees to it that his column's contents illustrate that motif. Accordingly, in the hodge-podge column verse may follow a pointed paragraph, or a burlesque advertisement may rub shoulders with a modernized proverb or parody. The column conductor strives for variety also in the typography he uses, and he employs many eye-catching type faces and patterns in presenting his wares. Many of the early columns came under this head.

4. The contributor's column. Here the amateur poets and satirists and inventors of "nifties" do the work and the conductor sits back and draws the pay. Of course the conductor also selects the material, frequently edits it, and quite as frequently becomes a contributor himself. Everyone seems happy with this arrangement.

The amateur feels repaid by having his stuff published and by the publicity which publication gives him. The conductor feels that he is encouraging new writers. Some well-known authors got their start in contributors' columns. The most famous was Edna St. Vincent Millay who made her debut as a poet with verses in F.P.A.'s "The Conning Tower."

5. **The essay column.** This type of column is rare today because the essay type of writer is rare. Christopher Morley when he wrote "The Bowling Green" for the old New York *Evening Post* demonstrated day by day the fascination of the essay column. The light familiar essay, the prose equivalent of the old *vers de société*, has distinguished exponents in such writers as Joseph Addison, Charles Lamb, Oliver Goldsmith, and more recently in G. K. Chesterton and A. A. Milne. It can be all things to all men; it can mock and chatter or beguile and charm. It has an unlimited range of subject matter, but a rigid rule—it must never be didactic or dull. In form such a column may consist of several short little essays on as many subjects or one essay on one subject. At its whimsical and graceful best it adds distinction to journalism.

6. **The gossip column.** Interest in human beings—in their virtues and more often in their vices—makes us prick up our ears at the mere mention of gossip. The editors of the country weeklies have long known the potency of this appeal and fill their papers with little items about the goings and comings of neighbors and their friends. The metropolitan papers give their sophisticated sheets something of this small-town flavor by printing the gossip columns. Here the reader finds out about the foibles and follies of the great and near-great and the would-be great—the so-called celebrities whom he knows by name because he has read about them frequently and seen their pictures in the paper. Walter Winchell, an ex-"hoofer," brought notoriety as well as popularity to the gossip column by specializing in intimate revelations. For a time it was a wise woman indeed who knew she was going to have a baby before Mr. Winchell knew it. This column, which first appeared in Bernarr Macfadden's tabloid, *The Evening Graphic*, and now appears in hundreds of newspapers throughout the land, has inspired the

phrase "keyhole journalism" as a description of this whole class of newspaper work.

The gossip column quickly became the happy hunting ground of the personal press agent who by fair means or foul aimed to get the singer, dancer, actor, writer, or politician he was publicizing mentioned by this or that gossip columnist. Akin to the general classification, we have the specialized gossip column which deals with the personalities of Broadway, Hollywood, radio, and sports.

Among the most popular columnists in these categories, we can list Ed Sullivan, Hedda Hopper, Louella Parsons and "Red" Smith.

7. **The jingle column.** The newspaper which uses prose as its chief medium has always had a corner here and there to spare for verse. The jingle column, as its name implies, consists of adventures in rhyme. Widely syndicated journalistic versifiers have been Walt Mason and Edgar Guest who have in their time turned out miles of verses. Readers throughout the country have come to know their by-lines and many have found pleasure and inspiration in their work. Some newspaper verse boasts quality and style. The smartest has cropped up in such show windows as F.P.A.'s "The Conning Tower." The usual jingle column consists of but one poem; some, however, present several short pieces each by a different writer. For the most part the subjects chosen for newspaper verse are those which have wide reader appeal such as nature, its trees and flowers; the seasons; infancy, childhood, and adolescence; young love, mother love, the love of home; and kindred human interest topics.

8. **The dopester's column.** We all like to be taken behind the scenes to get a peek at the show from an angle denied the ordinary mortal. This is particularly so where the show is an important one, such as statecraft. In its way the dopester's column has much the same technique as the gossip column and much the same appeal, but it transcends that chatterbox in significance. In the dopester's column the trivial names give place to those of government leaders, politicians, Congressmen and Senators, and the "gossip" concerns national and international affairs. It draws the reader through its implied promise of "inside stuff." When conducted by men who

have pipe lines to sources of valid information, the dopester's column frequently amazes readers by the accuracy with which it forecasts the news of as yet unannounced appointments and other governmental tidbits. Drew Pearson's name leads all the rest in this category, and his *Washington Merry-Go-Round* published from coast to coast attracts more readers than any other syndicated column. Another field in which the dopester's column flourishes is sports. The sports dopester's column presents a similar bill of fare of gossip, inside stuff, and prophecy.

The advice and service to reader columns which cover a variety of topics are considered in another chapter.

Although we find it easy enough to set down types of columns, we run into difficulty if we attempt to classify the men and women who write them. To the business office the "best" columnist is the one who attracts the largest readership and so acts as a circulation builder. The intelligent reader and the student of journalism prefer another scale of values. Fortunately we have had and have now some columnists who satisfy both the business manager and the discriminating reader.

Heywood Broun stood out as an early example. Academically educated at Harvard and journalistically educated through sports writing, general reporting, and dramatic criticism, Broun brought to column writing the requisite background and the requisite style. In addition, he brought a great love of humanity, a capacity for righteous indignation and a shining honesty. Of his own work, he said: "I've been wrong, I've eaten words and whole columns. But I never wrote anything I didn't believe when I wrote it."

Walter Lippmann has the educational background and the newspaper experience which together enable him to write with authority. In addition, he has the unusual knack of clear and simple exposition. The product of private education, early and frequent trips to Europe and also of Harvard, Walter Lippmann at an early age became a practical student and soon a specialist in the fields of government and economics. His journalistic training includes the early experience as one of the initial editors of *The New Republic* and later editor-in-chief of the old New York *World* when it was the country's leading liberal daily. After the end of the *World* in 1931, Walter Lippmann turned columnist and has reached a vast public through his column "Today and Tomorrow." In it he frequently manages to bring light to the average citizen and to make the rough places smooth in that difficult terrain where politics and economics meet.

The Columnist's Freedom

Nowadays the columnist who signs his wares may express himself with the utmost freedom so long as he steers clear of libel and obscenity. He may, in fact, voice a point of view contrary to that held tenaciously by the newspaper's own editorials. He may even take pot shots at the publisher's "sacred cows." In fact, newspapers today sometimes go out of their way to select columnists who hold views diametrically opposed to the policy of the papers themselves. They do this because they feel that the reader seeing the editorial readiness to exhibit both sides will regard their papers as broadminded and fair. Such a happy state of affairs did not always exist. It came into being in the middle and later 1920's and largely through the efforts of Heywood Broun. Broun regarded the journalistic field with what his critics considered naive idealism. He believed the newspaper to be an institution dedicated to public service and an instrument designed to combat injustice and to preserve civil liberties. He felt that opinions expressed under his column's heading, "It Seems to Me" should quite naturally reflect what seemed to him. Accordingly, he took leave in season and often out to differ in his column with views which his paper, the *World*, expounded on its editorial page. This difference came to a head when Broun attacked the prosecutors of Sacco and Vanzetti. The owners of the *World* did not forbid him to write further on this subject; they merely spiked his columns. Similarly, after the sale of the *World* when his column moved to the *World-Telegram*, he continued his nonconformist stints, and when his contract came to an end it was not renewed. Heywood Broun pioneered for the principle of a columnist's right to express his own opinion, whether it happened to coincide with the paper's opinion or not.

Although apparently losing his fight to gain freedom of expression in a signed column, Heywood Broun was actually winning it. Perhaps it was the outbreaks of divergence of opinion on the less serious subjects which led publishers and editors to see how interesting to readers such divergence could be.

After Heywood Broun, other columnists began to chafe at editorial restrictions and started to write what they really felt and thought. By then editors had come to see the value of diverging views. When columnists disagreed with the editorial page on which they frequently appeared, the earth no longer trembled and shook. Today the freedom of the columnist to write what he wants under his own by-line is recognized, but so also is the publisher's freedom to delete, censor, or drop when he feels the occasion demands such action.

Criticism of Columnists

When the columnist has developed a specialty and sticks to it, and when he writes on a subject to which he has given study and thought, all is well and good. The trouble through the years has been that some columnists come to consider themselves as specialists on everything in the heaven above, on the earth beneath, and in the water under the earth. They develop inflated egos and traits of omniscience. They begin to speak like the Oracle from his tripod.

Westbrook Pegler, with unusual candor, has commented in the *World-Telegram* on this tendency of his craft under the caption "Myriad-Minded Us."

Of all the fantastic fog shapes that have risen off the swamp of confusion since the big war, the most futile and, at the same time, the most pretentious, is the deep-thinking, hair-trigger columnist or commentator who knows all the answers just offhand and can settle great affairs with absolute finality three days or even six days a week. . . .

What causes us? Well, as nearly as I can figure it out, this trade began as a sort of journalistic vaudeville intended to entertain the customers and exert a little circulation pull of a slightly higher tone than that of the comics. Actually even now at our grimmest, we aren't one, two, six with a real good strip in which some man is plotting to put out a little girl's eyes or throw a little boy into a blast furnace, a reassuring fact if you are considering the good sense of the nation, as the syndicate managers, in their nasty way, are always reminding us.

Columnists on the Air

Radio and television have a way of giving oral duplicates of the more popular forms of written journalism. News bulletins duplicate the paper's headlines; commentator programs resemble vocal facsimiles of the newspaper's "columns."

Many of the types of columns familiar to readers have now become a commonplace to listeners—editorial columns, "hodge-podge" columns, jingle columns, dopester's columns, and gossip columns.

The "big name" commentator takes over on the air the part played by the "big name" columnist in the newspaper.

In the case of the "gossip column" several practitioners from Hollywood are ambidextrous and operate in both media. Drew Pearson heads the "dopester's" column on the air as he does in newsprint.

Sports as a subject also inspires on the air its editorial commentators, its "gossip" dispensers, and its "dopester" forecasters.

Similarly the service-to-readers phase of journalism becomes the service to listeners on the air, and radio sees to it that its specialists are there to tell its audience how to do this and that, from winning a mate to cooking a dinner.

16
Journalism Reviews the Arts

Standards of Journalistic Appraisal—The Book Review and Its Structure—Criticism of the Drama, Music and Ballet—Problems of Radio and Television Criticism

Journalism includes as news the whole range of the serious as well as the lively arts. Accordingly, it gives space and care and often talent to the reviewing of books, plays, motion pictures, ballets, concerts, exhibitions of painting and sculpture, radio programs, and television shows. But a basic difference exists between the function of the reviewer sent to cover a new play and of the reporter sent to cover a new fire. True, each must include the news facts in his story, but in the case of the reviewer the reader expects appraisal as well. As Brooks Atkinson, when dramatic reviewer of the New York *Times*, pointed out, "The news of a play is not a terse statement of facts, like a stock market table, but an expression of opinion. Readers are concerned less with 'what' than 'how well.' "

Because this element of evaluation in itself becomes part of the news of a new book, motion picture, or orchestral performance, a reviewer often finds himself dubbed with the title of "critic." This is chiefly a courtesy title, for true criticism lies poles apart from journalistic appraisal. The characteristics of criticism ordain that it be an art form in itself—expressive, creative, and communicative; that it be directed at readers whose chief interests are literary, musical, dramatic, or artistic as the case may be; and that it

235

keep in line with the established tradition of criticism as both learned and humane, journalistic and dense, versatile and strongly centered—the tradition of writers like Jules Lemaître in France, George Saintsbury in England, or Edmund Wilson in the United States.

But whether he call himself "critic" or "reviewer," the journalist who surveys the arts adopts one of several existing methods for his evaluation:

1. **The classical method.** Here the reviewer judically considers the new work of art in relation to the standards established by authority or tradition in that particular field into which the new work falls.

2. **The reportorial method.** This is largely descriptive. The reviewer describes the book, the picture, the play, the program and conveys his opinion through both the details he selects and the ones he omits.

3. **The panoramic method.** This calls for historical perspective as the reviewer considers the book, play, or symphony he is discussing against the whole pageant of books in the same general category, plays of a similar type, or music of a like school or class. We might also call this the *organic method*, for it judges a work not by some rigid set of standards or by subjectively recording the amount of excitement it generates, but by its own structure, its idea and reason for being, and gives it a place among other works, superior or inferior to it, judged in the same manner.

4. **The impressionistic method.** Here we hark back to Anatole France's famous concept of criticism as "the adventure of the soul among masterpieces." The reviewer of the impressionistic bent considers the book, play, painting, music, or motion picture in the light of the effect which it makes upon him as a sensitive human being. The value of such criticism depends on the value of the critic as an individual. It can be no better than he is.

To become a competent reviewer of any of the arts the writer must secure as complete a comprehension as possible of that art's history, scope, techniques, and development. Reading still maketh a full man, and the embryo reviewer will find countless books in each of the art fields from which to fill his personal reservoir of information and understanding. The work of reviewing calls for several basic qualifications in the individual who would successfully embark upon it; these are listed below:

1. A definite liking for the branch of the arts selected—books, music, theatre, cinema, painting, or the dance. One could hardly expect a tone-deaf reporter who frankly disliked music to give a satisfactory report on a symphony orchestra's most important concert.

2. An adequate background of knowledge in the given field, be it literature, drama, music, the graphic arts, the motion picture, or ballet.

Take the case of a book reviewer. In order adequately to appraise contemporary work in literature he must possess the necessary frames of reference—a firsthand knowledge of the best that has been written in fiction, biography, or general literature not only in his own country but abroad.

3. A well-defined point of view. All criticism is personal opinion. No matter how impersonally a reviewer may appear to be writing, the opinion is his own. The value of his opinion depends on the extent of his knowledge of his subject. A play reviewer, for instance, might describe an actor's playing of a scene from *Richard III* as "highly inventive" and "original." This would be a well-defined point of view, all right, but it would lack value because the young reporter did not know that the acting he described as "original" had been traditional stage business for the part of the hunchback Richard since the days of David Garrick. There were kings before Agamemnon.

Let us take up the chief types of newspaper reviewing more or less in the order of their introduction in American journalism.

Book Reviewing

Notes on books and reading appeared early in colonial papers. Sometimes these comments were homegrown; more often they were "lifted" from the more literate *Spectator* or *Tatler* of the mother country. Today book publishing has become a great industry, and the interest in books increases each year as education spreads. The country's great newspapers do a major service in reporting and commenting on the hundreds of titles which each month come from the book publishers.

Statistics would indicate that upwards of 250 newspapers across the land regularly give space to book reviews. In many cases these reviews are not staff written but come from syndicates, some 23 of which offer this service. It is encouraging to note, however, that more local newspapers than before, some 140, are writing their own reviews. And for the first time many medium-sized dailies—as in Aberdeen, South Dakota; Danville, Illinois; and La Porte, Indiana—are carrying local reviews. A majority of the syndicated material is written in New York where the literary climate is untypical of the country as a whole. However, without the syndicated columns, some of which originate with the wire services, many smaller papers would carry no reviews at all. This forms the strongest argument which the syndicates advance in their own defense. They also claim that they have not replaced out-of-town reviewers so much as supplemented them.

The major newspapers maintain regular book departments which provide their readers with well-written comments in each daily issue, and some papers such as the New York *Times*, the New York *Herald Tribune*, and the Chicago Sunday *Tribune* come out with a special book review section on Sundays.

Of what does a good book review consist? The American newspaper regards the new book as news; therefore the good book review consists first and foremost of information. In a line or two at the head or foot of the review appears the title of the book, the author's name, the number of pages, the publisher, place of publication, and the price. In his first paragraph the reviewer usually mentions the title and author again and usually indicates whether the book is a novel, a biography, a book of travel, a collection of essays, a treatise on one of the sciences, or a volume of verse. He quickly gives news of the book's type.

This demand for information is basic. The first question a reader asks is, "What is the book about?" The second is, "How good is it?" and the third, "Will I like it?"

The reviewer answers the first question through the adequacy of his reporting. In his opening paragraphs he manages to describe the book. If he is reviewing fiction, he indicates the type of story the author has written and the time in history in which it takes place; he tells something about the main characters and indicates the type of complication in which the author involves them. Only bad reviewers give a rehash of the plot. Good reviewers leave the story and its surprises to the author to tell in his own way.

The reviewer answers the question, "How good is it?" by setting down his own judgment of the book in relation to his knowledge of other books he has read in a similar category. He gives his own personal opinion, influenced by his own taste, preferences, and knowledge. This indication of the book's worth is no more than an extension of the reporter's function and is not in the true sense criticism. But when, as J. Donald Adams has pointed out, "a review passes judgment on a book against a clearly perceptible background of standards of value, reviewing becomes criticism at least on its simplest and least ambitious level."

If our reviewer succeeds in answering the first and second questions satisfactorily, he will already have provided his reader with the answer to the third, "Will I like it?" Any reader with gumption who grasps what the reviewer has said about the type of book, the materials of the book, and how the author has handled them will have gauged fairly accurately whether or not the book is one that will interest him. No reviewer can be "all things to all men" without ending up by being nothing to himself. However, he knows general reading tastes. He knows that many readers read books in order that they may chatter about them. This class prefers "best sellers"—the books that are in the news or books that have some eyebrow-lifting qualities either in their contents or through their author's reputation. Many readers read to inform themselves; they want to learn; they want books that will help them in their careers. Others read for inspiration. Still more read for amusement. Our reviewer then, in the very act of keeping his own judgment strictly personal, can tell his reader to which particular taste the book in hand caters.

Summing up, we can say that a competent review of a book of fiction reports to the reader along six lines:

1. It gives an understanding of the nature, but not the surprises, of the plot.
2. It tells of its type or class—historical novel, psychological novel, mystery story, et cetera.
3. It indicates the locale in which the story moves.
4. It gives a hint of the book's tang and flavor chiefly through short "quotes."
5. It introduces the chief characters.
6. It expresses an opinion as to how the author has handled his material.

When the reviewer turns to a work of nonfiction, other ingredients enter into the recipe of his review. In these days, many biographies, books of travel and so-called "inspirational" books—all nonfiction—rank as high as novels on the best seller lists. In many cases these books are genuinely important books into which much care, research and thought have gone. They cannot be commented on as blithely as a mere adventure story. Here are several phases which a good nonfiction review covers:

A. It gives some orientation on the author, answering such reader questions as these:
   1. What other books has this author written?
   2. Is the present book in line with his previous work?
   3. Is it a new departure for the author?
B. It gives some orientation on the subject, answering such reader questions as these:
   1. Is this the result of new research in this line?
   2. Is it a new departure in the field?
   3. Is it an advance on the author's previous work?
   4. Is it old stuff dished up in a popular form?

Even the experienced reviewer tackles his work with a sense of adventure. He is perhaps the first person besides author and publisher to see the book. He opens it with expectancy. As he goes along, he notes a page here and a paragraph there to which he may refer. He writes down an apt phrase which the author has used, as he knows that quoting is a good way to give the reader an indication of the book's flavor. If he has to review a book of verse, he uses quotes extensively, for he has found it next to impossible to indicate the quality of poetry by telling about it in prose.

Play Reviewing

Unfortunately the first-class living theatre is no longer available to the public outside of a few of the larger cities. However, even the demands of the craft unions cannot completely stifle the dramatic impulse, and in very many centers, what Broadway calls the "tributary theatre"—little theatre groups, drama clubs, and the like—has sprung up and in some cases does outstanding work. In addition, universities and colleges augment their classes in drama and play-writing with competent productions of classic and contemporary plays, so that play reviewing is at least an occasional if not a constant assignment with most papers. Newspapers in cities which boast a regular theatrical season, such as New York, Boston, Chicago, Philadelphia, Los Angeles, and San Francisco, have experienced dramatic reviewers on their staffs, and in the chief centers the papers maintain drama departments. In many cities the task of "covering a show" may fall to any reporter who happens to be free for an assignment. This job of dramatic reviewer is the one which many embryo journalists would pick if they had the chance.

Play reviewing boasts a long history and a roster of eminent practitioners. Much of it has been ephemeral and has died as soon as it fulfilled its function, but Aristotle is still read though he covered shows in 322 B.C. So is Charles Dickens, Eugene Field, A. B. Walkley, Alexander Woollcott, James Agate, and George Bernard Shaw. William Coleman, editor of the New York *Evening Post* under Alexander Hamilton, began play reviewing in America. Up to that time the actors themselves had penned the not-too-objective appraisals of their work which the papers carried.

Like the book reviewer, the play reviewer is essentially a reporter. He feels that his individual reader wants to know what kind of a play it is and whether he or she will like it, and he tries in his review to tell just that.

The late Alexander Woollcott was an excellent play reviewer, and he has left on record a definition of the job that is both fair and clear. He argues that the reviewer's function is not, as many seem to suspect, to teach actors and dramatists and producers the rudiments of their craft—he may do that in passing, but his review is not primarily aimed at them.

The review of a play, as it appears in the morning newspapers, is addressed not to the actors nor to the playwright, but to the potential playgoer. The dramatic critic's function is somewhat akin to that of an attendant at some Florentine court whose uneasy business it was to taste each dish before it was fed to anyone who mattered. He is an ink-stained wretch, invited to each play and expected in the little hour that is left after the fall of the curtain, to transmit something of that play's flavor, to write with whatever of fond tribute, sharp invective, or amiable badinage will best express it, a description of the play as performed, in terms of the impression it made upon himself. . . . If he be skillful at his task, the interested playgoer ought to be able to guess pretty shrewdly from his report whether or not the new play in town is of the kind he or she would enjoy.

In addition to a knack for communicating the play's "flavor," the expert dramatic reviewer must have other attributes:

1. He must write easily and rapidly. In that "little hour" after the fall of the curtain, he must organize his ideas and set them down with no opportunity for revision. Frequently his copy is fed page by page to the machines as each page leaves the reviewer's typewriter. He hammers out his epigrams at white heat.

2. He must have an adequate working knowledge of the theatre, of its history, its traditions, its temperament, its resources, and its limitations.

3. He must have an appreciation of the dramatist's problem—the job of getting both story and ideas across to the audience in sound and action, in words and pantomime.

4. He must understand all that the attendant skills contribute to the finished production—the art of the directors, scene and costume designers, and electricians.

5. He must detach himself from the magic of the theatre. Although the fun of playgoing is to enjoy the illusion of reality, the

Photo Courtesy of N. Y. Daily News

THE CAMERA AS REPORTER

The picture coverage of news events stands out as one of the distinct trends in present-day journalism. Newspapers great and small across the land have discovered the reader attraction which vivid news pictures exert. The New York *Daily News*, "New York's Picture Newspaper," ranks as a pioneer in the field of news photography. In 1919, when the *Daily News* was first published, there were few news photographers. As a result the *News* had to develop and train cameramen who could not only get a picture, but could get *the* picture, who could report with their cameras instead of with words. The result has been the increasing appearance of photographs in almost every newspaper in the country, the development of the weekly picture magazines and the growth of great news picture syndicates.

The above photograph, taken from a *News* airplane by cameraman Gordon Rynders, shows the severed bow of the tanker "Pendleton" wallowing off Cape Cod in a raging storm which split the tanker in two.

The camera covers sports. *Daily News* photographer Tom Watson snaps his fellow cameraman Charlie Hoff and his long-range "Big Bertha" camera ready to pinpoint for the fans the high spots of the game. Each year, newspapers across the country carry more striking action shots of sports than of any other phase of pictorial news coverage. The *News* may cover an important sports championship with as many as ten cameramen.

Fire and flood. Disaster whenever and wherever it strikes makes news. Here Charles Payne's photo from the air tells the grim story of Connecticut River flood damage, while *Daily News* photographer Ed Clarity has snapped the shutter in that split second when the walls of a Brooklyn warehouse started to topple.

Photos Courtesy of N. Y. Daily News

Air view and land view. As in the case of this railway wreck, the *Daily News* sometimes finds that its airborne cameramen can achieve an over-all impression of an event's scope, while ground photographers pick out specific details that are missed from the air. *News* photographer Gordon Rynders shoots the comprehensive over-all picture, while his fellow photographer Charles Payne catches a close-up phase of the catastrophe.

Associated Press Radio Photo from London

Another shipwreck. The first picture in this sequence shows the tanker "Pendleton" wrecked off Cape Cod. Here we see a Norwegian tanker after a collision. Similar news pictures these and yet with a vast difference. The first picture was developed in the office of the *Daily News* in New York. The second travelled by radio across the Atlantic. Compare the two for distinctness. These news pictures are now transmitted daily around the world by radio. Color pictures can also be transmitted by radio or wire by means of color separation—each color is sent as a separate transmission.

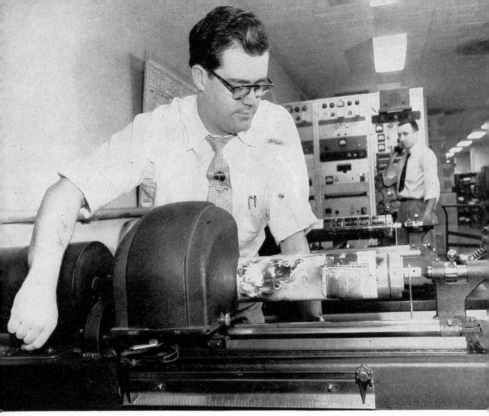

The miracle of present-day photo transmission. Today, news and pictures ride the wires side by side for simultaneous publication in newspapers across the continent.

Prior to 1935 news pictures would lag days behind the events they portrayed. Since then, thanks to the development of the Associated Press Wirephoto which did pioneer work in this field, newspapers in California, for example, can receive finished prints exactly like the ones at the sending stations on the Atlantic seaboard. The time taken up in the transmission of a picture is only five to eight minutes.

Today both of the two great wire services operate similar systems of news photo transmission—the AP with its Wirephoto, the UPI with its Telephoto. Both AP and UPI operate coast to coast circuits for rapid transmission of news photographs. Major newspapers have direct communication with these circuits and receive the photos simultaneously with their transmission.

Not only photographs, but maps, graphs, weather charts, diagrams and even finger prints can be sent and received in the same way as a picture. At the basis of it all is the photoelectric cell. The accompanying photographs illustrate the process and they are published with the permission of Associated Press Wirephotos. Above wirephoto operator Cleland Emerson, with hand on starting button, prepares to "roll" a picture from the New York AP office.

Photos Courtesy of Associated Press

A picture is mounted on a cylinder, complete with caption, for transmission by AP Wirephoto. These impulses travel over the wires at the rate of 100,000 per minute. So perfect is the synchronization that each of these impulses is recorded on the revolving film at exactly the same fraction of a second in every one of the cities on the wire network. In the bottom picture the photoelectric eye "looks" at the photo on the sending apparatus and transforms what it "sees" in light and dark portions of the photograph into electrical impulses of varying intensity.

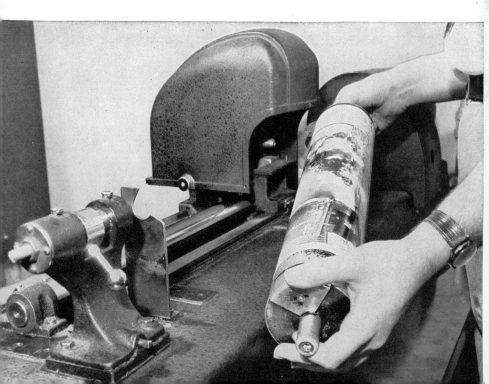

Photo Courtesy of Associated Press

And across the continent, the paper gets the picture. The negative is taken to a darkroom, a few steps from the receiving machine, where it is developed. The finished print given to the editor is exactly like the one at the sending station. This fight picture, taken in Madison Square Garden, New York, shows a Californian boxer on the receiving end of a punch.

The identification or "caption" material is typed at the sending station on a strip of gummed paper and pasted to one end of the photograph being sent. This caption rides along the wires in the same manner as the picture itself and is reproduced as shown here in the received picture.

reviewer has to break that illusion for himself because of the analytical nature of his job and in order to gain a right understanding of the odd blend of the arts he is covering.

In addition to these assets, many critics have brought to their job an urbane wit which gives their writing an endurable as well as an enjoyable quality. Shaw's printed play reviews, written when he was a young reviewer in London, make excellent reading today. The late Percy Hammond of the New York *Herald Tribune* had, as Brooks Atkinson has pointed out, a flair for phrases. "Bulging with lust," "a rancid vagabond," "Mr. So and So wore his tights competently"—phrases that carried much more meaning than the individual words which composed them.

Alexander Woollcott was adept himself at giving what he called the play's flavor. To him the quality of *Cradle Song*, the chaste, serene drama of a foundling baby girl left on the steps of a convent, was "like the chime of bells on a clear frosty night." Robert Littell had probably more than badinage in his mind when he reported that a play called *The Tyrant* "went through all the deliberations of chess for the excitements of tiddlywinks," and the late A. B. Walkley of *The Times* of London showed a mastery of succinct as well as sharp invective when his critical review of a play entitled *A Dreadful Evening* consisted of the one word, "Exactly."

The effect of adverse newspaper comment on a new play is nowadays so disastrous that drama reviewers come frequently under critical fire themselves. Few reviewers are in a better position to answer such attacks than Brooks Atkinson, and few can do it better. Such criticism of critics, Mr. Atkinson says, is based on the assumption "that in some inscrutable fashion, they [the reviewers] should be business agents of the theatre. Sometimes they are abused for their artistic myopia. But usually they are accused of destroying a producer's financial investment, of damaging business property, and of throwing actors out of employment. Broadway persists in regarding them as business forecasters, or as property appraisers." He acknowledges, of course, that "it is almost impossible for a play to succeed when the critics are unanimous in expressing unfavorable opinion," and that even a "divided press," as it is called, is considered a terrific obstacle to business success. To this extent, Mr. Atkinson says (New York *Times*), the critic is, through no fault of his own, related to the business of the theatre.

If his opinion is to have the slightest value to his readers, however, it behooves him to ignore the business of the theatre completely. The continued health of the theatre depends to a considerable degree on his being an independent agent—as independent and disinterested, for example, as the theatregoer whom supposedly he represents. . . . The only loyalties he can recognize are to his readers, to the theatre and to himself. To his readers he owes an accurate report and an independent expression of opinion. To the theatre he owes a sense of informed responsibility. By virtue of his office he is the theatre's champion. Like everyone who is sincere and enlightened, he wants to throw what influence he has into the development of a finer theatre, since he knows what has often been proved, that no theatre can be much better than its critics. To himself he owes the greatest responsibility of all. Before he can be honest with his readers or the theatre, he must be honest with himself. In fact, his responsibility to himself is of such supreme importance that every other part of the question is comparatively trivial. Criticism is the man; it can be no better than he is.

The Reviewer and Music

Music, long called the universal language, stands today as the universal art experience. Radio, records, and television bring the best music as well as the worst to metropolis and hinterland alike, and village band and choir play as important a role as the symphony orchestras and the opera companies in communicating to their communities what the critic Olin Downes termed "the most moving, subtly articulate, swiftly expressive of all the arts man has created." Because of this universality, most people know a little at least about music; very many have studied it for years, and many are amateur and professional artists in the field.

Accordingly, the newspaperman who essays to comment on music needs a background and training in his subject more extensive and more profound than newspaper reviewers of any of the other arts. He writes for a select, informed, and musically cultivated public as well as for the casual reader. Important American music critics have had this background. Some of them, like Virgil Thomson formerly of the New York *Herald Tribune* and Deems Taylor, formerly with the New York *World*, are able musicians in their own right and composers of note. The major papers make it a point to cover with news and comment the many musical events which in the season form part of each metropolitan day. This calls for a sizeable staff of trained reviewers who sift the new performers, evaluate the new works offered, and in this way make selective listening possible for the music lover and the general reader.

Motion Picture Reviewing

Although music forms the most universal of all art experiences, the motion picture stands out as the most universal of all art exhibits. "Whereas the drama," as Eric Bentley has pointed out, "has today no roots in the life of the community as a whole, the film is the most popular art of this or perhaps any age. Since, moreover, the mass audience is so calculatingly considered in the actual making of film, since any one film is put together by so large a number of people, the films reveal more about society as a whole than any other works of art except literary masterpieces."

Despite the fact that until recently there has been little first-rate art in the movies, the impact of the films on the mass audience has consistently been tremendous. Again to quote Mr. Bentley: "In the movies are to be found the dreams and yearnings of average modern man, dreams and yearnings that take many complex shapes. If today the ties of religion are weaker than they were, superstition is the stronger for it. Thus, while a movie may as art be crude and spurious, it may as magic and myth be diverse and profound."

Accordingly, editors throughout the land, knowing the widespread interest in the films which exists, try to satisfy that interest by devoting space in each issue of their papers to gossip and comment on Hollywood personalities and to increasingly competent reviews of the Hollywood product. In fact, the history of motion picture reviewing parallels the history of the screen itself and dates from the reporting of the knockabout film comedies of the early days of this century when custard pies were young.

These first reviews did little except report the film's story and strew adjectives at the feet of the early players. As the writers gained perspective and experience, they began to establish sound criteria. By the time silent films gave way to talking pictures, recognized standards for judgment existed which needed only slight adjustment to include the added dimension.

What are the aspects of a film which the critic considers in his review? First and foremost are the story and the director's handling of it. Does it maintain pace and mobility? Does it act, or is it static? Picture reviewers usually frown upon an obvious photograph with appropriate gestures of a three-act Broadway play. The story, of course, must not be trash.

Experienced critics recognize and applaud technical skill in this matter of story action. As a substitute for movement of story we frequently have movement of camera. Diversity of camera angles and occasional roving of camera "eye" together with intellectual suspense will neatly conceal, if effectively done, a story's stand-pattishness. Occasionally, these mobile cinematics save a worth-while but static story. The reason for this emphasis on story movement is because shadows do not hold public attention like flesh and blood on the stage. The audience at a stage play is content to listen to actors saying bright or dramatic things. When the actors are not in-the-flesh, the audience wants more to look at to compensate for the deficiencies of this synthetic immateriality.

As far as consideration of the acting goes, practically the same standards apply to the films as to the stage—good diction and intelligent characterization. With the silent films, actors had, of course, to get their meaning across with pantomime. With the talking pictures, they have dialogue to aid them as have actors on the stage.

This film dialogue is judged for its intelligence and general literateness. Triteness is always bad. The dialogue in the movies must further the story more quickly than in a stage play, because the film must unreel its plot in a playing time of an hour and a half.

Critics welcome originality in the material of a film. Hollywood practice tends to repeat and repeat any once-successful picture *genre*. This results in a deluge of crook plays, Broadway and night club plays, G-men or prize-ring pictures, as well as stereotyped plots.

Along technical lines the critic usually notes the quality of the camera work and the recording. Pictorial and camera effects should be a part of every good picture, and in color films the naturalness of the color is the criterion, except, of course, in cartoons and other fantastic excursions in the spectrum. The sound track must be clear and audible but not too loud.

In addition, the direction of the film naturally comes in for comment. In the days of the silent films, Hollywood was filled with directors who possessed definite personal styles in film-making. One preferred sets that were ornate and lavish; another sent forth films characterized by a sly, slightly sardonic urbanity and by deft, sparkling pictorial epigrams; a third might have a penchant for shrewdly lighted pictorial symbols and so on. The chief cause of the submergence of the director's personality is, no doubt, dialogue. As Richard Watts, Jr., has pointed out, "The director remains the most important figure in screen manufacture, but despite his comparative dictatorship, he is not as omnipotent as he once was. He may check up on the dialogue, but he seldom writes it, and it is obvious that unless the speech is in the mood of the picture style it will tend to throw it out of focus."

It is the director who gives each picture its structural style. There are many types of motion pictures, and each must be judged in accordance with its purpose and functional design. There are serious dramatic expositions, nimble romantic comedies, musical spectacles, factual surveys, western "horse operas" and many more. Each has its artistic pattern—and that's what the critic judges.

Like the drama reviewer, the film critic holds the potential patron in mind and uses his influence to better the type of entertainment he covers.

However, film reviews, unlike play reviews—which have considerable box office influence—have an immediate commercial effect only on foreign films and "art" pictures. For these pictures, usually seen by more discriminating audiences, attendance is in direct ratio to critics' reviews.

Ballet, Painting, and Sculpture

As in the case of music criticism, the newspaper writer who would helpfully and intelligently cover the art of the dance and graphic arts like painting and sculpture needs in addition to his news sense and his reportorial flair for expression a genuine understanding of the art he reviews and as exhaustive a background as possible in its history and techniques. His limited readership is also a highly informed readership. It consists in many cases of professional exponents and trained amateurs in these arts, all of whom expect an informed approach on the part of the newspaper.

Covering Radio and Television

Although the posts of radio and of television commentators are the most recent in the newspapers' review of the arts, they grow daily in importance. With the advent of radio in the 1920's, the majority of newspapers contented themselves with printing program listings and publicity agents' items about popular performers. Intelligent journalistic criticism of radio developed slowly. As Jack Gould puts it in the New York *Times*:

For all its influence on American life, broadcasting has received only intermittent study as a cultural and social force. Over the years, radio has rocked along its own sweet way, comparatively free from thoughtful and discerning evaluation of its role in daily living. This probably is a principal reason why so much broadcasting is as bad as it is.

Fortunately today the leading papers across the land have awakened to their critical responsibility toward the programs that come out of the loud-speaker and to the multitudes who listen. They have assigned as monitors men and women capable of reviewing the merits or demerits of the radio's presentations.

In line with reviewers of the other arts, the best radio critics regard themselves primarily as reporters and give the news facts of the programs they discuss. They measure what they listen to by their own standards and beliefs and their appraisals act as guides to the worth-while and as warnings against the shoddy and meretricious.

The best radio critics have come to make effective use of ridicule. This device has already cleared the airwaves of much unworthy stuff and some unworthy practices on the part of sponsors and performers. Individuals who can stand any number of conventional critical attacks usually crumple up the moment they are laughed at.

Critics in giving applause to outstanding achievements and unbiased appraisals of new departures are more than mere guides to good listening. They benefit the public by encouraging fresh and more imaginative programs.

When it comes to television, with its added dimensions of sight and color, the critic can call into play many of the criteria developed in drama and motion picture reviewing.

One school of thought believes that reviewers should judge television programs within the content of the TV medium. However, a broader attitude holds that television cannot be judged only by its own rules. This point of view argues that as television claims the attention of and makes its influence felt on millions of viewers daily, it is not a static or passive force but must be considered in the light of contemporary life as a whole in the same way as the theatre, movies, and books are judged. And as in the case of the theatre, movies, and books, the television reviewer sets himself to answer two inevitable questions:

1. What is this program trying to do?
2. How well is it doing it?

Although the program may be over and done with before the viewer reads the review, the phases of the performance which the reviewer praises or damns have nevertheless an impact on each reader and therefore on the mass taste. Presumably the immediate effect of the review is felt chiefly by the sponsors and producers of the show.

For example, Jack Gould of the New York *Times* admires the real achievement of the Columbia network's program, its sponsor Westinghouse, its adapter Worthington Minor, and its director Paul

Nickell for bringing Shakespeare's *Coriolanus* from the Appian Way to the television screen, but he goes acutely and constructively to the point of the production's weakness when he says:

> Basically, "Coriolanus" is the study of a brilliant soldier who ultimately is the victim of his own uncontrollable pride. He has scorn for the common people and cannot bring himself to pay them court. He even is impatient with honors because he accepts them as a matter of course and doubts whether they are worthy of his greatness.
>
> But through a combination of circumstances it is to be feared that Mr. Minor, who did the adaptation, and Paul Nickell, who directed, never quite caught the full measure of their man. On the screen there was seen a type rather than a dominant personality and there was lost that sense of dramatic unity built around a forceful, mature and arresting figure.

The television critic as a "stand in" for the public has from time to time performed a real service in drawing attention to important sessions of the United Nations or other outstanding public events which should be covered by television. In notable instances such comment has had real effect, and networks and stations have cancelled their profitable trivia to use the medium, as they are pledged to do, in the public interest.

With sagacious and acute newspaper critics on the job, perhaps television may eventually attain the "intellectual destiny" which Niles Traummel, formerly chairman of the board of the National Broadcasting Company, foresaw for it in *Variety*, when "the television screen is lit in the homes of America with the type of programs that will create an intellectual miracle in the minds of our people"!

Already this still growing medium has influenced the social and economic habits of the nation to a degree unparalleled since the advent of the automobile. Its impact on the nation's cultural development and political thinking and action is, we can presume, equally impressive. Accordingly, it may easily come to pass that the newspaper's most recent critical post—that of television reviewer—may in a short time become its most important.

17
Journalism as Entertainment

Journalistic Uses of Fiction, Humor, and Puzzles—The Comic
Strip: Its History, Technique, and Economic Importance

Journalism has long regarded the providing of entertainment as one of its legitimate functions. Early newspapers and magazines vied with one another to amuse their "gentle readers." Daniel Defoe, in his paper *The Review*, introduced fiction in the form of news and later inaugurated the first serial with his own classic story, *Robinson Crusoe*. Richard Steele in *The Tatler* and Joseph Addison in *The Spectator* won the affection of the public with the pleasant humor of their familiar essays. In colonial America, James Franklin tried to achieve something of a *Spectator* quality in his *New England Courant*, but his urbane and ubiquitous brother, Benjamin, proved more successful as he had humor in his make-up and the wit to realize its value as an interest stimulant.

Probably it was Richard Adams Locke's pseudoscientific fiction—the famous "Moon Hoax" series in the *Sun* in 1835—which first impressed American editors with the circulation-building qualities of entertainment. Up to then the penny papers which served up police court tidbits to the semiliterate "citizens and mechanics," as Ben Day's *Sun* did, and the respectable six-penny journals which chronicled political and financial news for their sedate and respectable clientele had never come into competition. But the "Moon Hoax," fanciful tale though it was, proved that some types of stories have attractions for the sophisticated as well as for the simple. Succeeding editors frankly used the circulation pull of fiction. Moses Y. Beach, when he acquired the *Sun,* ran Horatio Alger's sagas as serials. Horace Greeley made constant use of fiction in his *Tribune* and *Weekly Tribune,* and later Charles A. Dana on the *Sun* published the short stories of Bret Harte and Robert Louis Stevenson.

Today fiction as short story, short-short story, and as serial forms a standard entertainment feature of both the newspaper and the magazine. Publishers of papers in smaller cities find their surveys show that romantic fiction serials attract at least 50 per cent of women readers to their papers.

Occasionally, individual papers run short story contests and publish as free-lance contributions the winning entries and sometimes the stories of the runners-up. Usually they depend on syndicates, some of which specialize solely in stories, to supply all their fiction needs.

The contest also has an entertainment value although papers consider it chiefly as a circulation builder. Occasionally, as with the short story, these contests inspire a competitive interest. Readers submit photographs, "bright sayings," and the like for a definite prize. More frequently newspaper contests run to the guessing game or out-and-out quizzes. The late Captain Joseph Medill Patterson used contests from the start to aid in building the largest newspaper circulation in the United States, as well as to provide amusement to his growing horde of customers.

Allied to the newspaper quiz is the puzzle, and newspapers for years have used anagrams and the like to divert the reader. Impressed by the sudden rebirth of interest in the crossword puzzle in the 1920's, most papers nowadays include one or more in each of their issues. Even the conservative New York *Times* succumbed to the pull of the crossword puzzle to the extent of initiating one in its Sunday issues in 1942 and finally to presenting one each day in 1950. Crossword puzzle fans, of course, regard this feature as one of their favorite paper's greatest assets. England's poet laureate, John Masefield, has gone even further—he regards them as the only solace in the press. Writing to *The Times,* London, to thank that newspaper for its crossword puzzles, he said that for a good many years the puzzles were about the only things in any paper that gave him and his wife any solace.

"Doctor Johnson," Mr. Masefield wrote, "whose virtuous life you would have lengthened, would have praised you in some such words as these: 'You seldom move either pity or terror, but you often elevate the sentiments; you seldom pierce the breast but always delight and often improve the understanding.' "

The Value of Jingles and Jokes

Jingles and rhymes have delighted mankind through the ages. The deftness with which they call up a comic image to the mind and the flip way they have with words and syllables, taken together with their easily understood message, commend them to a wide readership. Probably "Mother Goose" and other nursery rhymes formed the taste, but the flavor lasts. A succession of competent versifiers seems always to be at hand to supply the jingle type of divertissement. Millions of newspaper readers over the years would look for the by-lines of Walt Mason and Edgar A. Guest. True, many of their verses told human interest stories or propounded homespun wisdom, but readers probably turned to them each day more for their fun than for their philosophy, and editors usually classify the rhyme-a-day contribution as an entertainment feature.

Astute editors value humor as a stimulant to reader interest quite as much as they regard it as an entertainment asset. Few things attract attention quicker than a laugh, as writers and particularly speakers well know, and it is the prospect of another laugh ahead which frequently keeps readers reading and listeners listening. Accordingly, editors prize the humorous twist in features, human interest stories, in pictures, cartoons, and even in editorials. The earliest "columns" were composed largely of funny lines and quips under such captions as "Wise and Otherwise" and the like. Editors frequently embellish their editorial pages not only with "Golden Texts," but with amusing anecdotes, suitably boxed and labeled.

But the entertainment feature which leads all the rest by unmeasured miles is the comic strip. Dr. Gallup and other pollsters give these strips a readership which leaves straight news and other features of the paper far behind. The latest published statistics proclaim that 82 per cent of men readers and 78 per cent of women readers daily devour the comics. Allowing for the 20 per cent of readers who skip them, the total readership exceeds 70 million and approaches 100 million. Among our media of mass communication, only the movies come anywhere near this figure with perhaps one movie-goer for every five or six followers of the strips. Some of the more popular strips are Blondie, Dick Tracy, Gasoline Alley, Nancy, Little Abner, Peanuts, and Pogo.

Publishers are not blind to the economics of this popularity. All major papers with the exception of the New York *Times* take advantage of their circulation-building value. Even *The Christian Science Monitor* has its own brand of comic strip. Today publishers can choose from about 500 so-called "comics," funny and unfunny, which they can buy from syndicates like those of the Chicago *Tribune*, New York *Daily News*, and King Features, or from one-man ventures.

The Comic Strip

Of course comedy in the graphic arts is no new thing. Caricature, for instance, cropped up in Pompeii, in Athens, and in ancient China, and humorous sketches and illustrations had long been a feature of European and American publications. But the newspaper "comics," either in panel or strips, are something else again. They have become the most avidly consumed art form yet produced in the civilized world.

Journalistic historians give February 16, 1896, as the date of their birth, naming Richard F. Outcault of Joseph Pulitzer's *World* as their creator and the "Yellow Kid" which first appeared on that Sunday morning as the progenitor of a vast and varied line. This Yellow Kid, "a grinning, ugly, abortive child in a gaudy night-shirt of light yellow" was an immediate success. So great was his popularity that when William R. Hearst effectively used his checkbook to induce Mr. Outcault to bring his gaudy child to the New York *Journal*, Mr. Pulitzer engaged another artist, G. B. Luks, to keep a twin Yellow Kid cavorting on his native heath—the Sunday *World*. This battle of colored inks in which the shade of the Kid's nightgown figured so prominently gave the public the clue to refer to the goings-on of the uninhibited sensational press as "yellow journalism." The Yellow Kid appeared in single panels, and his popularity led to other single picture series.

The comic strip continuity as we now know it came with the "Katzenjammer Kids," Hans and Fritz, now well over half a century old. Their originator was Rudolph Black, one of the editors of the New York *Journal*. He suggested to one of his young artists, Rudolph Dirks, that he draw the characters in strip form and gave him the plot idea. This first strip consisted of six colored panels and occupied half a page. On the heels of the success of this first sequence, other strips soon appeared. R. F. Outcault branched out with "Buster Brown," and George McManus started his long-lived "Bringing Up Father." As a possible forerunner of the later adventure strips, Charles W. Kahles began his "Hairbreadth Harry" in the Philadelphia *Press* in 1906.

Most of these strips appeared only once a week as Sunday features. James Gordon Bennett, Jr.'s New York *Evening Telegram*, which had a penchant for cartoons, was the first paper to use strips in daily editions. It ran them a few times a week in black and white. The first comic strip to appear six days a week was "Mutt and Jeff" by Bud Fisher. The San Francisco *Chronicle*, which initiated this famous strip in 1907, ran it opposite the sports page. Presumably because of this association, the strip began giving tips on the races. This practice earned a reputation for Mutt and the strip itself and a fortune for its creator.

Children began calling these features "the funnies." This was apt enough when they coined the name, for at first humor predominated. Each sequence aimed to end on some laugh line or laughter-provoking incident. Then humor gave place to a story element based on adventure, mystery, crime. Edgar Rice Burroughs' famous character "Tarzan" was taken over by the comic strip artists and idea men and began the first adventure strip in which a story was continued every day. Frequently these continuities were anything but funny, but their serial-narrative characteristics fascinated the public, and the strips grew into a new art form of unprecedented vitality and popularity. "Andy Gump," "Gasoline Alley," and many others first began their careers in the 1920's. Humor began to reappear in the 1940's, and single panels with a humorous twist gained a new popularity. During World War II the GI cartoonists, notably William H. Mauldin, developed a flair for satire in the army publications. His "GI Joe" became as well-known as the nation's generals, and United Features took it over as a syndicated item for civilian consumption. Somewhat to his surprise, Bill Mauldin discovered that while civilians appreciated his pot shots at army "brass," they showed a ready resentment when his satire hit nearer home.

As commentators have pointed out, the comics themselves would not merit a critical thought were it not for their immense popularity which makes them an economic asset to the newspaper. They are a contrived product—neither "folk art" on the one hand nor truly "primitive" on the other. Coulton Waugh in his book *The Comics* has gone into their evolution and impact with a wealth of detail, and William Laas in the *Saturday Review* (March 20, 1948) has made an acute analysis of their basic technique.

Comic Strip Technique

To Mr. Laas, the art work in the comics is in the same class as "doodling," but an element of craft is applied to this raw material. The fast sketch, he writes, is developed with imagination and design until it is clear, active, vivid, and concise, but at the point beyond which it would lose this appearance of spontaneity, the development is arrested. Stripped to its basic function, comic art emerges as "the *delineation* of characters and the *narration* of their adventures." Mr. Laas stresses the importance of character as the foundation of a strip's pattern and as the reason for its ultimate success or failure. Actually the art work, he says, is subordinate to the story it tells, and the story in turn is subordinate to the character whose story it is. The central character of a comic strip must win the fans. It is the one element that cannot be manufactured but must be *created*.

He feels that the best comics all have one quality in common, that of earthiness. And he notes that few of the men behind these strips come from the college-bred class. Instead, they have a background in colorful trades, vaudeville, the sea, the circus, or adolescent reporting—"just very ordinary Joes, blessed with humor or perception." Perhaps it is because of this fact that writers and artists in other fields seldom succeed when they attempt strips. The late Booth Tarkington failed when he tried to put *Penrod* into the "funnies."

Popularity has given to some strip characters an extraordinary longevity. People have been born, have lived and have died within the lifespan of a cartoon character. The continuing top favorites like "Li'l Abner," "Gasoline Alley," "Blondie," "Nancy" and "Dick Tracy" all saw the light before World War II.

As in the case of the first comic strip—"The Katzenjammer Kids"—idea men rather than the artist who actually draws them still create both character and story. The late Captain Joseph Medill Patterson, when co-publisher of the Chicago *Tribune*, is credited with originating several of that paper's most successful comics. Later, on his own paper, the New York *Daily News*, he proved equally inventive. The injection of anti-New Deal propaganda in the strip "Little Orphan Annie" marked the first attempt to influence public opinion through this medium.

Has the comic strip an artistic future? Many people feel that it has. They point out that in advertising, in propaganda, and in education—as used, for example, in the armed forces—the strip technique has shown itself as a fast medium for communicating ideas. Critics of the strips have contended that they degrade the fan's taste and retard his ability to read and to think. Publishing history, as illustrated by the success of the tabloids, indicates that pictorial journalism in any form tends to create new readers out of ex-illiterates.

Again to quote William Laas, "The critics of the comic strips have now come to concede that to enjoy the comic strips one is not required to be either a child or a dolt, but conceivably it helps."

Ways of utilizing and presenting comics vary across the continent.

When used as separate sections—as on Sundays or as inserts—many papers purchase them in actual printed form from syndicates. Larger papers frequently turn out their own colored comics in their own plants. With daily strips the habit for years was to run them on a definite page or on definite pages, day in and day out. The Chicago *Tribune*, however, which owns, originates and syndicates many famous strips, has never segregated its comics, but has sprinkled them through all parts of the paper. This method, of course, compels the addicts to scan a variety of pages with their reading matter and advertisements. An increasing number of editors are now following this *Tribune* method. Picking up a midweek copy of the Boston *Herald*, for instance, one found the first comic—the panel "Everyday Movies"—on page four. Page twelve, the editorial page, presented a comic cartoon. On the top of page twenty, "Caesar" appeared in three panels. The picture page, twenty-six, had a double column layout of four comic cartoons, and page twenty-seven had nine separate and distinct strips.

Advertisers quickly noted the potentialities of the comic strip technique and just as quickly utilized it. Today, advertisements in the format of the comics proclaim the virtues of a multitude of products and crop up in the pages of a multitude of publications.

18
Journalism Serves Its Public

Advice Columns, Hobby Columns, and Kindred Features—An
Outlet to Reader Opinion—The Support of Worth-while
Campaigns—The Newspaper's Extramural Service

The idea of serving the public lies deep in journalism's
precept and practice. First and foremost it strives to
alert its readers and listeners to the vital meaning of
events. It does this by providing them with information
in the form of its own considered editorial judgments.
In addition to this fundamental usefulness, journalism
in all its forms provides a manifold list of special aids
to its clients to make their lives fuller, safer, richer,
healthier, and in many ways more rewarding.

Some of these service features bear close relationship
to news itself; some have none. Among the typical service activities in the first category we can list such useful
items as news of the arrival and departure of ships,
planes, trains, and buses; the printing of tide tables
daily in coastal cities; and the listing of the times of
arrival and departure of mails for foreign countries.
Also, through printing letters sent in by readers, which
are often inspired by the news, the newspaper serves
these individuals by giving them a chance to blow off
steam, to express a contrary opinion, or to initiate projects of public importance. Among the services which
bear no relation to the news come the varied multitude
of features which we can classify generally as advice
columns. There seem to be as many of these columns
as there are general needs among the readers. They

cover everything from how to "burp" the baby to how to judge a genuine antique.

Typical Advice Columns

The magic lure of the advice column lies presumably in the prestige of print itself. Anything handwritten or typewritten, no matter how important, lacks in the eyes of the average individual the authority of the printed word. Accordingly, readers who in many instances could find more expert advice nearer home from friends, teachers, or ministers choose to write to some syndicated seer who knows nothing of their background or circumstances, and presumably they follow that seer's printed words of wisdom as they would the utterances of an oracle.

As indicated, by far the greater part of these service-to-reader advice columns which papers large or small make a point of using come from syndicates. In isolated instances a paper will conduct an advice department along some specific line, but such adventures in helpfulness usually prove expensive and time-consuming. Papers have found it both easier and more economical to rely on what the syndicates supply.

The personal problem column. The cynic may suggest here that "Advice to the Lovelorn" columns should more appropriately be considered along with the newspaper's entertainment features. Nevertheless, if at times the questions asked and the advice given read like a burlesque, there is no doubt that this feature fills a definite reader need. Fortunately most syndicates employ for this purpose the talents of capable newspaper people who under widely known pen names strive to unsnarl the reader's emotional problems and perplexities with a genial mixture of shrewdness and common sense. The amiable lady who advised under the pseudonym of Dorothy Dix received the widest syndication and made it a point to select for comment the questions with the widest appeal. This practice has been followed by her chief successor in the field, "Dear Abby," who likewise dispenses common sense seasoned with humor. The most popular format across the land in this type of column is to print the advice-seeker's letter in full and follow it with the colum-nist's reply. Two such letters and two such replies make up the average daily stint. A typical column, for instance—and one which shows the wide age range attracted—starts off with a letter signed by "A Reader" which praises the columnist's stand in urging fathers and mothers to keep their own homes instead of going to live with their married children. The writer tells of her own happy experience in living independently in her own apartment. The commentator, in a somewhat longer space than the original letter, expands the idea with further illustration.

Advice-seeker number two, who signs herself "Jane" and gives her age as fourteen, complains about having to wear one of her elder sister's hand-me-down frocks at her graduation from the eighth grade and the prospect of having to wear another of her sister's "formals" when the time comes to graduate from the twelfth. The sympathetic and constructive answer given suggests that in three or four years' time Jane might, through baby-sitting and other chores, earn enough herself to pay for her twelfth grade graduation finery.

The child care column. The care, training, discipline, and home education of children form the chief concerns of a large segment of the paper's women readers. While many of these would not dream of bringing their own problems to a newspaper, they read with interest the replies given to less reticent parents and frequently find in those replies answers to their own particular perplexities. Specialists in various phases of child welfare at times pool their erudition under an all-embracing syndicated by-line and use the question and answer format for the most part, though this method gives place on occasion to short articles on some specific subject, such as the over-indulgence of the young in television.

The health column. Health and legal problems, like death and taxes, confront at some time or other every reader of a newspaper. To tackle reader queries along these lines, the syndicates employ professionals in the several fields—a physician to deal with health, a lawyer to lay down the law. The best columns of this type are the ones where the specialist has also had journalistic training and is able to translate the technical terms of his science into plain and simple English. King Features' widely read column "About Your Health," conducted by Dr. Herman N. Bundesen, usually starts off with a short dissertation on some such subject as high blood pressure and concludes with questions and answers.

The homemaking column. The general subject of homemaking breaks down into a wide range of topics. Columns under this head span the area between "What's Wrong With the Ailing House" to "Today's Tested Recipe." They deal in turn with interior decoration, food, furniture styles, gadgets, and labor-saving devices. Some papers run home forum departments and aim at a comprehensive coverage as a daily or weekly feature.

Other popular and widely read advice columns deal with beauty and styles and fashions. In fact, a survey made by the National Newspaper Promotion Association showed that patterns drew more ready response than any other service feature, and this despite the fact that patterns were the only feature which involved a payment by the reader, anywhere from ten to twenty-five cents a pattern. The survey covered replies from ninety United States and Canadian newspapers with a combined circulation of 13,408,636 and tabulated reader response over a thirty-day period. Among other things the survey showed that reader response followed a decidedly local pattern. For instance, one midwestern city got only three beauty inquiries during the month while a New England newspaper with comparable circulation got 3,654.

Another midwestern newspaper pulled 1,400 lovelorn inquiries while a New York newspaper with several times the circulation pulled only 474.

Typical Hobby Columns

The shortening of the work week for most people has brought with it a greater leisure and quite naturally inspired a greater reader interest in pastimes and hobbies. To many readers, a column on a favorite hobby stands out as the pleasantest service that their newspaper provides. Columns on bridge, canasta, gardening, photography, stamp collecting, and motor travel bristle with hints and comments which readers find useful, and they undoubtedly create good will for the papers which publish them.

The bridge column. Bridge figures as a year-round pastime, and each of its millions of devotees seeks constantly to improve his game. The purpose of the newspaper bridge columns is to satisfy this desire. They consist mainly of clear exposition and acute analysis. The columns are either staff-written by an expert or are supplied by syndicates. Large papers frequently produce their own individual bridge column—that of the New York *Herald Tribune* has long been famous. The New York *Times* started in with a staff-written Sunday column, but now makes bridge a daily feature with the by-line of Albert H. Morehead. Also in this field the Jacoby column is justly famous, and Shepard Barclay's widely syndicated feature "Barclay on Bridge" daily analyzes specific problems with diagrams of hands and plays, in papers across the land.

The garden column. Gardens, too, provide a year-round interest. Even when snow covers the ground, the avid gardener dreams of next year's blooms and vegetables, and the columns which cater to him fill their space with preparatory information leading to next season's labors and triumphs. This whole field of garden coverage runs far beyond mere horticulture. It takes in landscape gardening, tools and equipment, garden furniture, fences, flower foods, watering gadgets and the like. Newspapers have found that garden columns have a real economic value as they stimulate advertising by seed producers, plant and shrub nurseries, and the manufacturers of the mowers and equipment used for lawns and terraces. An illustrated article on day lilies, for instance, inspired no less than four growers equipped to supply that flower to advertise alongside the column. Metropolitan papers, despite their large gardenless readership, run Sunday garden pages throughout the year and frequently expand into seasonal garden supplements and departments.

Other hobby columns. Collecting remains a deeply rooted human passion, and columns devoted to this hobby attract a large, if specialized, readership. Stamps are probably the most universally collected item and stamp columns outnumber the others in this field, though columns devoted to rare coins and antique china and furniture appear with fair regularity. From time to time some collector's items, like ship models, for instance, have a vogue for a season or so and inspire columns during the length of their popularity.

New developments in photography, such as the growing perfection of color films and the increased delight in home movie-making, have brought about an intense new interest in the field of photography. Camera columns and notes crop up with increasing frequency in daily papers, and few Sunday issues come out without a section devoted to camera trends and interests. As with gardening features, newspapers have found that articles on photography attract advertising from manufacturers and retailers in that field.

Americans have always loved to travel, and the universality of the motor car today makes travel readily available to almost everyone. Although advertisements of steamship companies, railroads, and resort hotels appear daily, newspapers generally seem inclined to treat travel as a week-end feature. Most large papers go in for Sunday travel pages which swell to full departments when the vacation season opens, and frequently to lavishly illustrated supplements.

Whether the pseudoscience of astrology is a service, a hobby, or an obsession can remain an open question. Newspapers believe that many of their readers hold an interest in its claims and publish syndicated columns such as "Your Stars Today" to satisfy it. A typical column, under the subhead "If It's Your Birthday," hits a wide mark with generalizations such as "The coming year can be somewhat trying for you if you will allow yourself to be easily discouraged by people who enjoy a negative attitude," and "You are in the midst of making some important decisions about your future and these cannot be hurried—take plenty of time." It takes all sorts to make a readership.

Some Seasonal Services

Journalism, and in particular the newspaper, aids the public with a number of seasonal services which year in and year out have proved of perennial value. First in this list come the various safety campaigns. Newspapers effectively get behind such campaigns as

Fire Prevention Week with their editorials, news features, pictures and cartoons. Similarly they advocate saner Fourth of July celebrations, more careful supervision of bathing beaches, and, most frequently of all, safe driving procedures. The Newark *News*, for instance, got staunchly behind New Jersey's Highway Safety Program and made wide use of pictures showing automobile accidents. The *News* found these a "great cautioning influence."

In election periods the newspapers provide an important service to voters when they print comprehensive biographies of all candidates seeking votes with records of their public activity. The Milwaukee *Journal*, for example, runs such a "Who's Who" of candidates as a service to voters shortly before elections.

As taxes rise and forms multiply, many a baffled wage-earner appreciates the help in making out income tax returns which newspapers big and small seek to offer. Tax experts who write these features bring to light exemptions and other savings which the unknowing might overlook, and frequently aid the labor of compiling the tax return which is on occasion more painful to the individual than the actual parting with his cash.

All articles and illustrations which swing open cultural doors, whether they be regular or occasional features, must rank among the outstanding of journalism's services to mankind. In these days of expert color printing, some papers make a point of reproducing masterpieces from the great American and European collections. As a regular feature *The Christian Science Monitor* uses a halftone cut of some recognized work of art to dominate the center of its Home Forum page. It accompanies the picture with a brief expert description which, that paper feels, has given many readers the equivalent of a standard course in the fine arts. Certainly such features tend to keep readers in touch with the timeless standards of beauty.

The publishing of advertising ranks as a newspaper service to readers, although the newspaper happens to be well paid for performing it. Even the late publication *PM*, which came out for some years without benefit of advertising, felt that the listing of bargains was a duty it owed to its public. Each day it ran an unpaid-for shopping guide in which it picked out the best buys in town. As the veteran editor of the Milwaukee *Journal*, J. D. Ferguson, has pointed out, if there were no advertisements and a newspaper could be supported by subscription alone, it would have to include in its news of the day what was available in the stores and at what range of prices. The paper would not say where. That's what the advertiser spends his money on—telling customers where.

Journalism's Extramural Services

All those activities outside of publishing its news and views and features may be termed the newspaper's extramural activities. Particularly is that term applicable to all those service activities which build good will. Outstanding in this category are the benevolent funds for charitable purposes which newspapers from early days have sponsored with success. The old New York *Evenng Post* started the ball rolling in 1878 with the first Fresh Air Fund. Today there is hardly a paper of any size that does not have its regular appeals for the unfortunate—Thanksgiving and Christmas aid, the support of rest homes for the aged, and the like. Famous along this line is the New York *Times'* "Hundred Neediest Cases" fund which that paper appeals for annually in its December issues and which through the years has raised millions of dollars and distributed them through recognized social agencies.

Probably because of its wide human interest value, newspapers have a marked fondness for child welfare work. Activities such as the New York *Herald Tribune's* Fresh Air Fund, the *Journal-American's* Milk for Babies crusades arouse generous public support, provide far-reaching benefits, and reflect most favorably on their journalistic sponsorship. Some papers conduct or raise money to support summer camps, life-saving teaching, health clinics, playgrounds and supervised games.

Serving an older youth group, newspapers sponsor dramatic contests and athletic events. The Chicago *Tribune's* annual "Golden Glove" fistic festivals would seem to lead the field here.

While the awarding of prizes and the presentation of premiums originate as part of the promotion department's work, with the object of increasing circulation, many readers regard such prizes and premiums as services. There is something in this attitude, for the distribution of good phonograph records, dictionaries, sets of standard authors' and other worth-while books at low cost to a wide public can well rank as a journalistic service.

In addition to bringing benefits to their readers, most papers nowadays make a point of serving their immediate personnel. Few modern newspaper plants have neglected to include cafeterias for employes in their plans. Such cafeterias, run by the paper itself without the overhead of rent, separate insurance, and other charges, can operate without the profit motive and can provide the men and women employed in all departments of the paper food at a reasonable cost and at all hours.

Other employe benefits include participation in group insurance and in hospitalization plans. Large papers maintain a hospital department in their buildings where employes can obtain medical, nursing, and sometimes dental care. Recreational facilities which some papers have provided include game rooms and gymnasia. Popular among the social activities organized for employes are athletic teams and musical clubs.

Above and beyond the call of duty have been the long-range programs of constructive aid with which some American newspapers have benefited their communities and their states. Not content with beautifying its own city with boulevards and parks and even an art museum, the Kansas City *Star* built up the economic condition of its reader group with its campaigns for and establishment of purebred cattle farms in Missouri and Kansas. Parallel in its nature and effect have been the efforts of the Dallas *News* to make scientific farming the rule in north Texas. The Detroit *News* sponsored the building of model homes in its city. And it must not be overlooked that many a weekly paper with a tiny circulation has lent its weight to sponsor a local band or a local ball team. The idea of service to the community remains the same.

19
Journalism in Pictures

Development of Pictorial Journalism—How the "Cut" Is Made—
Picture Editors and Departments—Present-day Uses of Pictures—
Miracles of Picture Transmission—Picture Preferences of Readers

Journalism began with pictures. Thousands of centuries before recorded history, primitive man sketched and painted on his cave walls the story of his days. If we visit the recently discovered caves of Lascaux, France, we can see for ourselves his graphic reporting—the tales of his hunts, his battles, the animals he chased, the clothes he wore or didn't wear, the weapons he handled. Pictures made up the first written language, and from them the alphabet we now use developed.

Today we live again in an era of pictures. They confront us from newspapers, from magazines, from books—many of them frankly picture books—from the films and from television. Each year their impact on our culture increases, for the social scientists tell us that the dent on our consciousness inflicted by a picture is more lasting than that left by the printed word.

The present-day emphasis on pictorial journalism stands out as a phenomenon of the twentieth century. It had to wait not only for developments in photography itself but for the invention of swift and adequate processes of reproduction such as that of "halftone" engraving. Probably the first pictures in books were the "illuminations" which the monks of medieval times drew and painted by hand in their missals and prayer books. Later the woodcut came into use, and by means of these wooden blocks carved in relief, line drawing and maps could be reproduced in quantity. Woodcuts crop up from time to time in the early American colonial newspapers. In fact, the first illustration in an American paper was from a woodcut of the flag of the United Kingdom of England and Scotland, and it appeared in the Boston *News-Letter* in 1707. Benjamin Franklin's famous "Join or Die" snake cartoon was reproduced by means of a woodcut in his Pennsylvania *Gazette* in 1754. Coming to the nineteenth century we find American newspapers making increasing use of woodcuts for drawings and maps. The New York *Sun* was the first of the penny papers to embellish its text with pictures when it showed a sketch of "Herschel's Forty-Foot Telescope" in connection with its famous "Moon Hoax" series in 1835. Later, during the Civil War, the New York *Herald* utilized wood engravings to reproduce the many maps, some of them half a page in size, by means of which it kept its readers abreast of the conflict.

These woodcuts were based on line drawings made from sketches or early photographs, and it was not until the country's premier "tabloid," the New York *Daily Graphic*, devised a process known as "granulating photography" in 1872 that actual photographic reproductions appeared in the press. Both the *Graphic* and the process were short-lived. Actually, photography itself and photoengraving had to become established sciences before realistic pictures were possible at a cost that most papers could afford.

Photography developed through the nineteenth century. Two Frenchmen, J. N. Niepce as initiator in 1814 and later J. M. Daguerre as collaborator, did pioneer work in the field. In 1839 they invented a process of making permanent pictures on brightly polished silver plates which went by the name of "daguerreotypes." The daguerreotype was the aristocratic cousin of the more popular "tintype."

An independent step and one in a forward direction came in 1839 when William H. F. Talbot came along with a process which utilized sensitized paper instead of metal plates. In 1840, John W. Draper, a professor at New York University, made the first successful picture of the human face, that of his sister, and the exposure took five minutes. In 1851, Frederick Scott Archer invented the collodion process, and after that, reproduction on a metal base became outmoded. Since Archer's day, photography has progressed amazingly in speed and efficiency.

In recent years, in fact, equipment quality outranks in many cases photographic ability. The great advance came after World War II, when new films made by Kodak in the United States and Ilford in Germany gave to the news photographer high speed with little or no grain. Film speed indexes began to soar. Both Germany's Leica and Japan's Nikon produced new models in 35-mm cameras which proved a real boon to the news photographer, who in existing light, without flashbulbs, can now make 36 exposures in less than a minute. The 35-mm camera has made a marked impact on metropolitan picture-journalism and may in time take over the journalistic photograph field.

The process of photoengraving developed from the 1870's on, but it was not until 1897 that S. H. Horgan made the first halftone stereotyped successfully for a newspaper using a web-perfecting press. This picture appeared that year in the January 21 issue of the New York *Tribune*.

In the newspaper we call all illustrations "cuts" which are engraved reproductions on zinc or copper of photographs or drawings. We divide this general term more specifically into *halftones* and *line cuts*.

Newspapers and magazines use the *halftone* for photographs. Here the image is reproduced by thousands of closely packed light and dark dots (approximately 4,200 to the square inch). Take a magnifying glass to any newspaper photograph and discover this optical illusion.

Newspapers and magazines use *line cuts* to reproduce maps, cartoons, pen-and-ink sketches, and the like. These are engravings etched in line on zinc. Through a process known as the Ben Day process, based on the use of screens, the printer can enhance these line cuts with a variety of shadings.

Making the "Cut"

Up to a few years ago, this was the standard procedure:

Photographing the picture to be printed was the first step in making a "cut." If the picture is itself a photograph, it must be rephotographed through a "halftone screen" which breaks it into tiny dots. (In most newspaper engravings these dots number about 4,200 to the square inch.) The camera which does this rephotographing also automatically scales the picture to the desired dimensions. The film is immediately developed in an adjacent darkroom.

After it has been developed, the film is stripped from its paper backing and carefully mounted on glass.

The picture, now mounted on glass, is next transferred to a sheet of sensitized zinc which will be etched with acid so that all parts of the plate that should not print are eaten away.

An engraver coats this plate with a reddish-brown powder, sometimes nicknamed "dragon's blood," preparatory to its actual etching in nitric acid. This powder adheres to those parts of the picture which are not to be etched away.

Next the etched plate or "flat" is carefully inspected for flaws and then passed to the "router" who will rout away unneeded metal, cut the sections apart if necessary and send them along to the "finisher." After the finisher has tooled away minor imperfections, the cut or cuts go to the composing room to be tacked on a metal type-high base by a "blocker."

The halftone was made originally of zinc for newspaper use. Nowadays it may be made of aluminum, copper, brass, or any one of a number of alloys. Lightweight magnesium halftones have proved popular.

In recent years "rapid-etch" and powderless etch processes have been developed. This means that halftones, line plates, or combination plates can be produced rapidly and made ready for page forms in just a few minutes.

Another sensational development in the engraving industry is the photopolymer plate, the product of the Dupont Company. With the trademark "Dycril" this photosensitive flexible plate may be etched without an acid solution in fifteen minutes and mounted either for flat or curved press equipment.

Both halftones and line cuts as finished products reach the compositor in the composing room and he places them in the spaces which await them on the made-up page of type.

As natural outgrowths of these technical advances, there followed in logical succession a number of newspaper developments. First, from the beginning of this century on, came the increasing use of illustrations under the blanket term "art" in newspapers, magazines and books. Then emerged the picture editor as an entity, followed by his multiplication into a picture or art department. A definite impetus to this trend came when the New York *Times* introduced in April, 1914, its famous rotogravure section, a supplement to its Sunday edition in which page after page of photographs were reproduced by intaglio printing on rotary presses. This set a fashion across the country and increased the picture consciousness of the reading public. Coincident with this demand for pictures, agencies to furnish them came into being, called picture syndicates. Then came picture papers usually in tabloid form and finally the picture magazine. Recent developments include that of the reporter-photographer and embrace the miracle of speed—speed in securing, speed in processing, speed in transmitting. Picture transmission these days has become, like news transmission itself, almost an instantaneous job. A picture taken in New York reaches California in a matter of minutes. Let us trace the more important of these developments in sequence.

The Picture Editor

Because of the increasing importance of picture news coverage, alert city editors find it good practice to put the picture editor as close to the city desk as possible. On some papers even the chief photographer has his desk near the city desk. This close liaison makes it possible for those responsible for picture coverage to be "in" on city desk activity, so no time is lost getting cameramen into action.

This proximity also enables the city editor to brief the photographer on the story he is going out to cover.

From this we can see that the picture editor's job is one more of organization and selection than of actual assignment. On metropolitan papers he has perhaps as many as twenty men under him. He knows each of these men as an individual as well as a technician, or in some cases an artist. Accordingly, he can send a man to do a job for which he is temperamentally as well as professionally best suited. While the cameraman's importance to the newspaper grows appreciably each year, editors still regard him, as Al E. Davies puts it in *Late City Edition*, as "the madcap of the newspaper business." Because he knows his men personally the picture editor can size up the photographer's qualifications for a particular job. He knows whether his man reads merely the comics and the race results or whether he has a comprehensive idea of the flow of the day's news. He can augment the city editor's briefing, when necessary, with newspaper clippings and even a carbon copy of the story to be "shot." He can urge his photographers to help on the captions, giving other data than just the "left to right."

The picture editor of a major newspaper goes through a day's grist of some two hundred pictures. From these he selects some twenty to thirty. Where does he get these pictures? What are his criteria of selection?

Pictures come from the paper's own cameramen. They come from the many picture syndicates such as Acme and Underwood & Underwood, and, of course, from the Associated Press and United Press International. UPI, for instance, has a stock news photograph service with a library of some five million stock news photographs. Some pictures come from trigger-happy amateurs who just happen to have a camera handy when pictorial news breaks in their vicinity. Many pictures come from public relations departments and publicity men. And the alert picture editor never forgets the picture resources of his paper's own morgue.

The picture editor selects his pictures from this welter of photography much as the city editor selects his stories from the mass of "copy"—first and foremost on the basis of newsworthiness. These include pictures that record "spot news"—a train wreck, a devastating fire, a White House marriage or funeral; pictures of people in the news. He next considers pictures that come in after the event but that are still newsworthy. In most cases because his paper subscribes to several agencies, he has several shots of the same happening from which to choose. He selects the one he wants for pictorial excellence and its potential qualities for clear and distinct reproduction in the paper.

In addition to newsworthy pictures, other types have come in to him. Few picture editors can resist a good "human interest" photograph—an eight-year-old youngster weeping over the dead fox terrier in his arms—a mother welcoming home her long-lost son—the pictures that record the humor and the pathos of ordinary humanity's daily drama. Then there are what he calls "feature" pictures —babies, pets, oddities. He winnows the "publicity" pictures from theatres, motion picture companies, travel and resort agencies, charitable organizations, and the multitudinous government departments of his own state and of Washington. His paper's policy helps him decide when he comes to "cheesecake," also known as "leg art." It tells him what and how much to use. He knows as well as the next one how many readers would like to look at the picture of a pretty girl, and how many more would like to look at the picture of a pretty girl with legs. Last in importance to him come the purely pictorial offerings, the "salon" studies of nature and still life.

In addition to his paper's policies, the picture editor has had to learn his paper's pictorial "taboos." Some papers, for instance, will not permit pictures of dead bodies to appear. In the case of war and catastrophe pictures this taboo eliminates many effective layouts.

Once he has made his selection, the picture editor starts on the "captions." Caption is a blanket term that covers all writing which accompanies a cut, both title and descriptive text, but a more precise usage makes caption refer to that written material which is printed *above* the picture. The term "underlines" or "cut line" denotes the more detailed copy that is to be printed *below* it. A good picture editor sidesteps coyness in this matter of captions and underlines and the tendency to play on words which finds acclaim in some quarters. A sane rule makes the text which accompanies the cut conform to the same standards that govern all other copy in the paper. He sees to it that a slug identical to the one on the picture accompanies each caption.

Before his work for the day ends, the picture editor checks up the schedule which the engraving department sends along to indicate the total column width and depth of the pictures to be used that day. He passes this on to the make-up man along with notations as to which cuts must run and which can be left out in a pinch.

The Use of Pictures

Today, even what we call conservative papers use a great deal of "art," and in the case of the picture papers, the tabloids, the space allotted to pictures greatly exceeds that devoted to text. In a standard size newspaper these days we encounter illustrations of some sort or other on every page from the front page to the last with the sole exception of the classified ad section. On page one, we find our spot news picture. If this illustrates a tremendous story, the chances are that the conservative paper because it has more space will devote more space to pictorial coverage than a tabloid will. Each department has its pictures—obit, society, motion picture, radio, real estate, financial, and of course sports.

The newspaper uses "art" to supply variety to its type columns and in this way attract the reader's eye. It uses pictures and, in particular, diagrams, because often pictures and diagrams will convey the required information more clearly than can be done with words. It uses pictures to satisfy its readers' curiosity about the appearance of persons, places and objects. Perhaps a State Capitol has been remodelled. An illustration of the new portico will show the country the Capitol's new look more quickly and more clearly than will a thousand words.

The Picture Papers

America has known weekly illustrated papers such as the *Police Gazette* for many years, but the popularity of the daily picture paper belongs to this century. Papers of this type had proved successful in England where they received the name "tabloid" because of their compact form, and some of them, including the London *Daily Mirror*, owned by the energetic and iconoclastic publisher, Alfred Harmsworth, Viscount Northcliffe, had achieved vast circulations.

Encouraged by Lord Northcliffe's example, Captain Joseph Medill Patterson and his cousin, Colonel Robert R. McCormick, co-publishers of the Chicago *Tribune*, launched a picture tabloid, the *Daily News*, in New York in 1919. After a halting start it quickly caught on and soon won the largest circulation of any daily in the country. It specialized in pictures, many frankly "cheesecake," and comics. Imitators sprang up across the land, and the most successful were those which unabashedly copied the *Daily News* in format and content. The *News'* chief home-town competitor, Hearst's New York *Mirror* established in 1924, was aptly named. The impact of these tabloids on the average reader is to make him look for a picture with every important story; the impact of the tabloids on the standard size papers is to make them increasingly eager to supply the pictures that the reader looks for.

The Picture Magazines

For years America had nothing in the illustrated weekly field to compare with the European picture periodicals such as *The Illustrated London News*, founded in 1842, and the Paris *L'Illustration*, started about the same time. Although the mid-nineteenth century saw the advent of *Leslie's Weekly* and *Harper's*, these magazines were as much literary as pictorial. With the advent of *Life* in November 1936, Henry R. Luce, its publisher, changed the scene and gave the greatest impetus to date to the use of photographs to convey information. *Life* was followed in two months' time by *Look*, and other picture magazines began to appear shortly after.

The impact of these magazines on the reader increased his growing appetite for pictures, and the wealth which the huge circulations soon amassed saw to it that with each succeeding issue he got better and better ones.

The new element in these picture magazines, of course, is the great advance in camera technique which began in Germany around 1925 and spread rather gradually to the rest of the world. Its most highly skilled practitioners today are the men who take pictures for American magazines. As Roger Butterworth says in the *Saturday Review*, "During the war these men together with some of their colleagues in the armed forces and the news services, lifted the profession of photo-journalism to new heights of expertness, daring and art. We owe our most vivid impressions and our most important record of the war to them."

Life, alone of the large circulation picture magazines, puts its emphasis on picture coverage of news, and, as much as a weekly can, on "spot" news. Other magazines such as *Look* go in for what they call the "picture story." There is nothing particularly new about this picture story idea, as Hearst's *American Weekly* has been running much the same thing for years. The basis of the picture story in its present-day form is the formula. This formula has been set down in exact and scientific terms by Daniel D. Mich and Edwin Eberman, both editors of *Look* magazine, in their book, *The Technique of the Picture Story*.

The first step, they report, is to do "preliminary, basic research," on the story subject. The next and apparently most important is to be "sure of your 'angle.'" To be sure of the "angle" one has to think in terms of either title or headline. The title, the authors say, often comes before anything else. Many stories are selcted because someone thought up a "selling title." Next comes the preparation of a "shooting script," shaped carefully in line with the selected "angle" and title.

The defect in this formula lies in the fact that it allows little leeway for the photographer's own ingenuity and inventiveness and ignores him completely in the editorial preparation of it for the public.

What kind of stories do picture magazine editors prefer? Messrs. Mich and Eberman list as the first requirement "an interest that transcends spot news"—in which news value is unimportant. (This rule, of course, does not apply to *Life*, which does publish "news picture stories.") Other high-ranking requirements are "universal interest" and "focus on people rather than things." "The story of a boy and girl in love is still the most appealing that can be told pictorially or otherwise."

With the picture story so "saleably manufactured" as they put it, it comes as no surprise when they state that "many of the problems involved in constructing picture stories are similar to those involved in making movies."

Today, picture content looms as more important than technical proficiency. Editors nowadays look less for technically perfect exhibits of camera work and more for pictures that illustrate the news story, bring out the nuances of the situation, and answer the viewer's questions—pictures that communicate. As William B. Dickinson, managing editor of the Philadelphia *Bulletin* puts it: "Photographers need to regard themselves less as specialists, more as members of a team seeking to provide a product that will interest and inform the reader."

The Reporter-Photographer

A new field may be opening up for the young man who has two strings to his bow—journalism and photography. The paper which has to send two employees, a reporter and a cameraman, to cover an event would much prefer having merely to send one. The reporter has trained himself to set down "word pictures." The cameraman, though he may be an expert technician and even an artist, may have no journalistic sense. The perfect combination for this era of picture journalism is, of course, the alert newsman who is at one and the same time a skilled photographer. To aid him in his work, he has today the miraculous advances in photography and in photo transmission. However, the Newspaper Guild has so far seen fit to forbid reporter-photographers.

Miracles of Transmission

Nowadays the radio-telephone and the radio-sound-photo process unite to speed up with miraculous efficiency the covering of a pictorial news event, the processing of the picture itself, and its forwarding to the picture editor for publication.

In *News Workshop*, the paper published by New York University's Department of Journalism, Jay M. Steinberg tells how both these devices help papers do a better job of getting the news. Consider, for instance, the use of the radio-telephone:

. . . Frank Cushing, a photographer for the Boston *Herald-Traveler* was driving his car, which was equipped with an experimental radio-telephone unit, when he heard a police call about a hold-up. A fifteen-year-old boy had robbed a store.

When Cushing got to the scene, he had to crawl along the roof of a nearby house to get his picture. It showed the youth brandishing a revolver and holding a school boy in front of him as a shield. The *Traveler* ran it with the caption, "Boy Gunman at Bay."

That picture was reprinted in 500 newspapers throughout the country and won the Pulitzer Prize.

The *Traveler* was one of the few papers making use of telephone-equipped cars at that time. Since then, however, many other papers have recognized that they are a valuable tool in gathering the news.

Next we come to the radio-sound-photo process which John Reidy, chief photographer of the New York *Daily Mirror*, calls "the most revolutionary and progressive step ever taken in news picture coverage since the advent of press photography." Here is Mr. Steinberg again with an illustration of how this radio-sound-photo operates:

Suppose that a staff photographer was covering a spot news story at some place within twenty-five miles of the *Mirror* office. It is just fifteen minutes before page one deadline. He takes his picture and steps into a special darkroom-equipped station wagon. He develops, fixes, and dries his shot in two minutes and places it on the sound-photo drum for transmission. That process takes one minute per inch, so that a 5 x 7 negative would reach the office five minutes later. A little more work is needed at the office, but ten minutes after the photographer started developing his picture twenty miles away, it is handed to the picture editor.

Not only do devices speed the work of the paper's own staff photographers, they also serve to speed up the reception of pictures from anywhere on the globe. The Associated Press' Wirephoto service has pioneered in this field since 1935. Through this invention of the Bell Laboratories, which the Associated Press took over and developed, news and pictures ride the wires side by side to tell the reader a quick story of a busy, ever-changing world. By means of Wirephoto both text and illustration can cross the American continent in a matter of minutes, and in the case of photographs from Europe, Wirephoto has helped move a picture to Associated Press papers faster than the earth spins around the sun. A Louisville, Kentucky, newspaper was on the street at 11:30 A.M. with a picture that had been made in London at 12:30 P.M. the same day. Between Louisville and London there was, of course, a six-hour difference in time, but the picture had moved to Louisville faster than the earth moves around the sun despite the time consumed in preparing for transmission.

At the heart of Wirephoto and similar systems which have revolutionized modern newsgathering is the photo-electric cell. It provides the solution to the problem of how to get pictures from one place to another along with the news. Just how it does all this, we will let the Associated Press' own pamphlet, "AP Wirephoto: Miracle of Modern News Gathering," explain:

How Wirephoto Works

The photo-electric eye "looks" at the photo on the sending apparatus, transforms what it "sees" in light and dark portions of the photograph into electrical impulses of varying intensity. These travel over the wires at the rate of 100,000 impulses per minute. So perfect is the synchronization that each of these impulses is recorded on the revolving film at exactly the same fraction of a second in every one of the thirty-two cities on the 10,000-mile wire network. No such precision of operation and control is to be found in other mechanical equipment in the world.

An ordinary positive photo print is wrapped around a cylinder on the sending machine while an unexposed negative is placed on an enclosed cylinder of the receiving machine. Attendants along the leased wire network make 20-second tests to make sure the proper amount of current is being applied. Then the attendant at the sending point presses a button on his machine that starts, at the same instant, every receiving machine along the line from a dozen to thousands of miles away.

As the cylinder on the sending machine rotates, the scanning equipment containing the photo-electric eye moves on a carriage similar to a machine shop lathe horizontally alongside the picture on the cylinder. A beam of light is thrown on the picture through a tiny aperture one hundredth of an inch square while the cylinder bearing the picture revolves. This beam of light reflects off the photographic print into the photo-electric eye where the reflected light rays—strong or weak as the light or dark portions of the picture rotate past—are transformed into electrical impulses.

These electrical impulses are "built up" by means of amplifiers to travel the thousands of miles that may be necessary to reach the receiving point. Here they are adjusted to suitable strength for feeding into the receiving machine.

On the receiving machine is the light-proof or light-sealed cylinder mounted on a lathe-like arrangement similar to the cylinder on the sending machine.

Inside this lightproof cylinder is the unexposed film. The electrical impulses coming from the sending machine pass off the line to an electric bulb which is lighted to a degree of brightness varying in proportion to the strength of the current received. The strength of this current which lights the bulb in turn depends upon the shades of light and dark found on the original print at the sending end.

The light from this bulb, located near the negative, is focused through a lens to less than pin point size so that it strikes the negative on the receiving cylinder as it revolves in perfect synchrony with the picture on the other end of the wire. The negative or film is thus exposed in exact proportion to the amount of light reflected from the original picture on the sending cylinder. The machines stop automatically when the transmission is completed.

The negative is taken to a dark room a few steps from the machine where it is developed and a print made. The finished print, to be given to the editor, is exactly like the one at the sending station.

And the time thus taken up in the transmission of a picture is only eight minutes.

The identification or "caption" material accompanying the picture is typed by an editor at the sending station on a strip of gummed paper and pasted to one end of the photographic print being sent. The typewritten caption rides along the wires in the same manner as the picture itself and is reproduced in the received picture.

Wirephoto thus is not limited solely to transmission of pictures. It can carry all manner of graphic material which will tell the news more completely. Maps, graphs, weather charts, letters that become exhibits in court trials or at government hearings, diagrams or even finger prints can be sent and received the same as a picture. All stations on the network can receive the same picture at the same time from the one original print at the sending station.

Before United Press and International News Service merged to become United Press International, each had its own electronic photo transmission system similar to the AP's *Wirephoto*. These systems were named respectively UP Telephoto and International News Pictures. In addition INS was operating in 1953 a new transmission development, called International News Fascimile, whereby pictures could be sent anywhere by wire or by radio and received on special electrolytic paper requiring no photographic processing. This fascimile transmission proved a boon to television newscasting, as both news and picture could be transmitted over the same wire or radio channel for instant use by the receiver.

The merged companies, combining their photo transmission facilities—now called UPI Telephoto—provide, in addition to news pictures, a commercial and industrial photo service, announcing, "Anything that can be photographed, printed, written, or drawn can be transmitted by UPI Telephoto."

The Associated Press operates, in addition to Wirephoto and radiophoto, a transmission system called Photofax, which, like facsimile described above, needs no time-consuming development processing.

Picture Preferences of Readers

Polls, surveys, and statistics all go to show that the present-day emphasis on pictures falls well in line with popular reading preferences and tastes. Even the best-read stories are constantly outpolled by news photos and picture pages, according to a recent summary by the Advertising Research Foundation in its Continuing Study of Newspaper Reading. Although top-notch news stories rank next to pictures in male readership, they get strong competition from editorial page cartoons. Women rank pictures first, outstanding news stories second, humor panels third.

The record on picture sizes points to the three-column cut as the approximate optimum at which high readership and space economy meet. Male interest steps up sharply from one-column to three-column size with medians of 37 per cent, 49 per cent and 62 per cent. Among women the ratings for one- to four-column size are 45 per cent, 61 per cent, 67 per cent and 73 per cent.

Classified according to story appeal, three picture categories—human interest, crime, and national defense—won top attention among all readers.

Picture pages taken as units have a slight edge over the best-read news pictures outside such pages with readers of both sexes. The summary ranks median readership in the picture field as follows:

CATEGORIES	MEN	WOMEN
Picture page	89%	91%
News pictures	85	88
Sports pictures	63	25
Society pictures	31	79

We can see from all this that the days when newspapers regarded pictures merely as "something to break up the type" have long since passed. Present-day editors are fully alive to the new trend which Francis Henry Taylor, when director of the Metropolitan Museum of Art, characterized as "visual literacy." Here is how he put it in the New York *Times* Book Review:

An unprecedented visual literacy has come into being in which people read pictures as they have not done for hundreds of years, leaving to words the obligation of conveying abstract ideas not communicable in graphic forms. For just as the ear has been developed and refined by radio and phonograph to the point where classical music has become a commonplace in all walks of life, so will the eye be broadened and exercised in the years immediately ahead.

20
Journalism and the Law

Libel and Slander—"Visual Communication"—Privilege and Fair Comment—How to Avoid Libel—Penalties and Mitigation—Defamation on Radio and TV—The Protection of Copyright

Although freedom of the press exists under Constitutional guarantee, no paper is free to make false, malicious, or derogatory statements about any individual, any group, or any institution, either intentionally or through negligence or accident.

Man regards an unsullied reputation as a prized possession and resents any slur on it, either actual or implied, and seeks damages from any person or publication injuring his fair name. Shakespeare enshrined this attitude in memorable lines in *Othello*:

> Good name in man or woman, dear my lord,
> Is the immediate jewel of their souls;
> Who steals my purse steals trash; 'tis
>   something, nothing;
> 'Twas mine, 'tis his, and has been slave
>   to thousands;
> But he that filches from me my good name
> Robs me of that which not enriches him,
> And makes me poor indeed.

This filching away of a person's good name can be either a *slanderous* or a *libellous* action. Which is which?

Getting back to our quotation we can say that if Iago or anyone else called Othello a criminal, a thief, an adulterer, or a murderer in the hearing of one or more persons, then Iago would have slandered Othello, for *slander is defamation through oral communication.* If on the other hand, Iago had had his accusation printed in the Venice *Gazetta* of that day, he and the newspaper would have libelled Othello, for *libel is defamation by visible communication.*

As it is libel rather than slander which chiefly concerns the writer and the publication, let us give libel a more comprehensive definition. For the purpose of the newspaper writer, libel may be defined as any defamation either written or printed which falsely suggests that a person has committed a crime; or tends to injure him in his business or profession; or that holds him up to scorn, ridicule, hatred or contempt.

We can widen the scope of this defamation by quoting the actual language of the courts in specific instances.

Writing and printed matter has been held actionable per se when it

> *tends* to bring a party into public hatred or disgrace;
> *tends* to degrade him in society;
> detracts from his character as a man of good morals;
> imputes something disgraceful to him.

From all this we can make the generalization that a newspaper publication is libellous of any person if its obviously natural effect is to make those who read it think worse of that person. It doesn't matter what the publisher intended to say; the question is the effect on readers of what the story actually said.

From all this, three word categories emerge as ones likely to be libellous.

1. All words that imply crime, such as abductor, kidnapper, abortionist, bigamist, blackmailer, firebug, felon, horse thief, spy, traitor.
2. All words that convey the impression that a person is guilty of immoral or infamous conduct, such as adulterer, degenerate, dope fiend, drunkard, wifebeater, procurer.

3. All words that impute unchastity to a woman, such as bawd, mistress, prostitute, strumpet.

Just what constitutes libel in any given case may be a technical and complex question of law, but it is generally held that 75 per cent of all libel suits are based on stories which impute some form of criminality, and that the rest are inspired by stories which imply unchastity or some breach of the currently accepted moral code.

In general, it is not libellous to publish of a person that he has done something which he has a legal right to do even if that something may be unfavorably regarded by his community. A writer, for instance, could state that such and such a man was a "profiteer," but could not safely call him a "bookmaker" in any state in which bookmaking was listed as an illegal practice.

It is interesting to note that nine out of ten libel suits spring from trivial and unimportant news items that no one would have missed if the editor had "killed" them. As *Editor and Publisher* puts it: "Most libel suits result from two for a nickel stories that might better be thrown away."

Close on the heels of suits springing from imputations of criminality or moral shortcomings are those which arise from alleged injury to an individual in his professional or business capacity. In general, it is libellous per se to impute to a person in his official capacity, profession, business, or trade any kind of fraud, dishonesty, misconduct, incapacity, or unfitness which would tend to impair the income from his legitimate business which he would otherwise have received.

For instance, some years ago it looked as if the roof of a New York high school was about to cave in. One of the papers made the comment: "This does not speak very well for those who designed the school." The architect in question took the publisher into court and won a verdict on the grounds that such an accusation would injure him in his business. Similarly, a publication which charges a business concern, corporation, or firm with insolvency or with dishonesty is libellous.

Visual Communication

The phrase "visual communication" although applied chiefly to printed or written words includes, of course, all things that are actually seen, such as pictures, charts, statutes, puppets, and the like and photographic reproductions of these things. Here again, editors and publishers have to be on their guard. During the course of an anti-vice campaign, a metropolitan newspaper printed a map showing the location of certain disorderly houses. By mistake, a respectable house was included. The banker who lived in that house threatened suit. The paper settled promptly. A jury recently awarded $2,500 compensatory damages and $7,500 punitive damages to a plaintiff whose picture was recklessly used by a reporter who made no attempt to verify it. The Sunday supplement of a New York newspaper ran an article, "How Science Proves Its Theory of Evolution." As a pictorial embellishment, the paper printed a picture of a gorilla beside that of Zbyszko, a wrestler. Zbyszko's lawyer claimed that the gorilla comparison held his client up to contempt, derision, and reproach, and that as a result Zbyszko was being shunned by friends and neighbors. The court found in favor of the wrestler. It has even been found libellous to hang a person in effigy.

All the foregoing instances come under the head of *civil* libel which concerns damage done to a person, persons, or a firm. There is another category, seldom encountered, called *criminal libel* which refers to damage done to society or the state. The illustration frequently used in this connection is defamation of the dead which has on occasion led to riots and breaking of the peace.

The government itself may not claim the protection of the law of libel.

Some years ago, the city of Chicago sued the Chicago *Tribune* for libel. The city claimed that it had suffered $10 million damages because of *Tribune* editorial attacks and stories that were printed during a political campaign which charged mismanagement of the city government so serious as to threaten civic bankruptcy. The

Supreme Court of the state of Illinois held that a newspaper or a private citizen had an absolute right to criticize the government.

Privilege and Fair Comment

This brings us to a brighter side to all this. Although the libel laws work to protect the private individual's reputation and his legitimate vocation, they do not work to stifle or suppress criticism of mismanagement of public affairs, corruption and incompetence in office, or honest opinion on the quality of the work or the general abilities of individuals acting in a public or semipublic capacity.

1. The law protects the right of public criticism by setting aside certain types of material as immune against libel action. Certain kinds of publications are "privileged," which means that they cannot be held libellous. Among these are:
   a. All statements made by judges, lawyers, and witnesses in court proceedings *while the court is in actual session.*
   b. The debates in Congress and in the state legislatures.
   c. All material printed in public documents.

   What are not "privileged" in the foregoing categories are the statements made by judges, district attorneys, and other public officials that are not made during the actual conduct of a public, official, or judicial proceeding. Statements made by the judge, for instance, after he has left the bench are no more privileged than those of a private person. Also, testimony which has been ordered stricken from the record ceases to be privileged matter. In some states, documents filed in the County Clerk's office are only privileged when they have been used openly in court. In New York the contents of legal papers which have been served and filed in the course of judicial proceedings are now privileged except possibly in matrimonial actions upon which there has not yet been a ruling.

2. The law protects the right of public criticism by recognizing the right of the individual to make "fair comment" upon another when such comment is honest opinion, free from malice, and on a matter of general interest.

   This right of "fair comment" is one of the great foundation stones of the freedom of the press. It is the right the editorial writer exercises when he comments on public officials and candidates for public office; it is the right that upholds the reviewer and the critic in his comments on the arts—on books, plays, motion pictures, music, radio programs, paintings, sculpture and all such things that invite public attention. All this is libel-proof so long as it is an expression of honest opinion as distinguished from an assertion of fact. A critic can call an actor a "ham" in his acting or refer to his performance as an "outrage," but "fair comment" will not protect the critic if he refers to the same actor as a "wifebeater."

Heywood Broun, in the days when he covered the theatre, once called a man in one of his reviews, "the world's worst actor." The actor threatened suit, but nothing came of it, for Mr. Broun had the protection of "fair comment." When the man appeared in his next play, all Broadway wondered what Mr. Broun would say in reviewing him. The critic's comment was that the actor was "not up to his usual standard."

Most actors, musicians, painters, writers, and sculptors take newspaper criticism in good part. The one class of creative artists notably thin-skinned are the architects, and for some reason the courts have been surprisingly generous to architects.

This right to criticize is general and belongs quite as much to any other individual as to the newspaper writer, editor, or publisher. The *actions* of individuals are always legtimate subjects of discussion and criticism. But the privilege of criticism extends only to the *actions* or *works* of an individual; it does not extend to the *person*.

Judicial opinion in the United States and in the United Kingdom is outspoken in upholding this right of "fair comment."

"No one," said Judge Story, "can doubt the importance in a free government of the right to canvass the acts of public men and the tendency of public measures . . . to censure boldly the conduct of rulers and to scrutinize the policy and plans of government."

Here are echoes from the English courts.

Said Baron Alderson: "God forbid that you should not be allowed to comment on the *conduct* of all mankind, providing you do it justly and honorably."

Said Chief Justice Cockburn: "It is of vast importance that criticism, so long as it is fair, reasonable and just, should be allowed the utmost latitude, and that the most unsparing censure of works which are fairly subject to it should not be held libellous."

How to Avoid Libel

Most newspaper writers know in a general way what constitutes libel, but reporters run foul of the law on occasion through carelessness and negligence, through misapprehension as to what is definitely "privileged," and also because they feel they can take a chance.

Here are some ways to avoid libel:

1. Realize that a rumor is not necessarily a fact. The publication of a "rumor" that a person has been guilty of misconduct is as libellous as the direct charge.
2. Realize—although the general public doesn't—that phrases such as "it is alleged," "it is reported," "the police say" and the like do not in any way mitigate the effect of libellous matter and furnish no defense to the writer, editor, and newspaper.
3. Avoid the strong human temptation to make an accused person appear guilty before he has been proven guilty. The law regards him as innocent until then. A newspaper is always privileged, however, to publish a charge contained in a warrant for arrest.
4. When possible, tell both sides of the story. When charges are made against any individual, and when only one side of the story is given, the reporter should in fairness try to give the accused person an opportunity to answer at the same time as the original charges are printed.

   This course makes for a more complete and hence a better story; it appeals to the reader's sense of fair play; it may create the defense that the story was consented to or authorized.
5. Exercise care in copying names, addresses, and charges against persons arrested. A mistake in the spelling of a name or in an address can result in a libel suit. Criminals often give fictitious names and addresses, so names should be prefixed with "a man giving the name of" unless identification is positive.

Penalties for Libel

The theory of libel is to protect the private individual from unjustified defamatory statements in the press. To insure this protection the law provides four safeguards:

1. A civil suit for damages for libel.
    a. Nominal (six cents).
    b. Compensatory—to repay for damage done him. The sum fixed by jury after hearing arguments.
    c. Punitive (or exemplary)—Punishment for carelessness or negligence in handling story, awarded in addition to compensatory damages. This may run as high as a dollar for each copy of the libellous article published.
2. A criminal prosecution for libel—criminal action may be instituted against editor or publisher if it is shown that he has been unusually careless or negligent.
3. An action on the case for damages for a trade libel.
4. A suit for the invasion of the right of privacy—the individual instigating a libel suit is required to establish three elements in both civil and criminal libel.
    a. The words must be defamatory.
    b. The words must be published—the libellous statement must come to the attention of a third person, and not through the action of the aggrieved one. If a party is defamed in a letter addressed to him alone, he cannot collect for libel.
    c. The person or persons libelled must be identified—if the person defamed is not named in the article, it is not libellous if he cannot be identified from the context. Courts ordinarily hold in newspaper libel suits that the injured person must be known where the paper circulates, or there must be a chance that friends or acquaintances will see the libellous article.

Against whom are libel suits brought? Who is held responsible? The owner or owner corporation is always responsible, and in actual practice the owner is usually the target of suits. But the law also considers as responsible the editor-in-chief; the managing editor;

the department editor, if he knew of or authorized the story; the copyreader who passed the story; the reporter who wrote the story; and the news source or informer if he knew he was talking for publication. In addition to this wide segment of the newspaper's staff, the newsdealer can also be held responsible if he knows what the paper contains.

In the case of a libellous story going out over the wires of a news service, the area of responsibility grows wider still. Every newspaper publishing the libellous story can be sued everywhere it is published, and furthermore the service as well as the writer can be sued in every city or town where the service has a newspaper outlet.

Defenses Against Libel

The law provides three defenses against libel suits.

1. Truth. Truth is the best and a complete defense. A writer or publisher is exempt from all civil responsibility *if he can establish the truth* of his statement. The italics used in the last sentence point up the fact that it is not only important that an article containing matter which is libellous if untrue should be known to be true by the reporter, but it is also important that he should know that it is provably true. As the former International News Service used to point out to its correspondents, "a libellous story unprovably true is as dangerous as a story that is false."

2. Privilege. Privilege is an absolute defense to libel. Here the publisher or writer has to maintain his claim that the report was based on government proceedings, official hearings, and official records.

3. Fair comment. Where comment is restricted to a person's work and does not discuss his private life, such comment may be made freely so long as it is not made with malice.

"Every man who publishes a book commits himself to the judgment of the public," says an eminent English judge, "but this cannot be made the excuse for personal abuse of the author himself."

Malice is an important factor in all libel suits, and if the absence of malice can be proved, that absence usually works to mitigate any damages incurred. Where malice is shown to exist the penalties are often heavy. Some years back a popular author and playwright, Bronson Howard, felt that when he appeared in court before Magistrate Joseph Corrigan, the magistrate had been disrespectful and impertinent to him. He wrote a novel, *God's Man,* to square accounts. In this book the villain was a certain magistrate called Cornigan, but the author on one page spelled it "Corrigan" to make sure that no one would misunderstand. The magistrate, who was held in high esteem, sued the publishers for $200,000. The jury returned a verdict of $35,000 in favor of Corrigan. A higher court reversed this verdict, but it stands as an instance of a jury's reaction to malice.

Mitigation of Damages

If the writer or publisher as the defendant in a libel suit is unable to show that the defamatory publication is *true* or that it is *privileged,* then the insured plaintiff is entitled to a verdict in some amount. How small this sum may be will depend upon how good a case he can make out in mitigation of damages. The range here is wide. Underlying most defenses is the effort to prove the absence of malice. Here are some of the most important:

1. That as soon as the defendant saw that he was in error, he published a retraction, correction, or apology.

Immediate retraction if made in good faith has been effective in proving the absence of malice. This retraction should be full and frank and not grudgingly made. The character of the writer and of the paper is often shown by the way in which the imputations are withdrawn and regret expressed for having made them.

A half-hearted retraction will only injure the defendant's position.

In most jurisdictions, a retraction carried even after the suit is commenced may be introduced in mitigation of damages.

The failure to retract the defamatory statement is admissible to show actual malice, and in many jurisdictions will afford a basis for punitive damages in addition to compensatory damages.

2. That the general conduct of the plaintiff gave the defendant "probable cause" for believing the charges to be true.
3. That the libellous article was copied from another newspaper and believed to be true.
4. That the defamatory publication had reference not to the plaintiff but to another person of a similar name concerning whom the charges were true, and that readers understood this other individual to be meant.
5. That the allegation was made of a political antagonist in the hurly-burly of a political campaign.

Although, as Stanley Walker has pointed out, libel suits may be "the measure of a newspaper's alertness, the quality of its courage, and even of its devotion to public duty," they are also the evidence of the paper's decision to take a chance.

Many large papers retain legal advisers. These advisers will, in ticklish instances, point out the danger and leave the decision to publish up to the editor.

Copy usually has to pass four pairs of eyes before it gets into type, and these eyes are on the lookout to catch and blue pencil libellous material, yet many libels do slip through. Most are due to carelessness on the part of the reporter. He can avoid them if he verifies his statements and makes accuracy the keynote of his stuff. A true story seldom results in a libel suit.

Defamation on Radio and TV

Strictly speaking all defamatory remarks and implications made on radio and television are slanders, but the law is evolving to treat a false broadcast as libel.

Indicative of this trend is a bill passed unanimously by the Assembly at Albany, N. Y. in March 1960. This bill was designed to write into law various state court decisions that have held that a person is subject to charges of libel when he deliberately defames another person in a prepared text or script, or when a station releases to the press and public the script or stenographic text containing the defamatory statement.

Although broadcasters do not advocate for or against public questions to the same extent as writers in newspapers, magazines, and books, the rules of fair comment and criticism are of importance. For instance, some of the patter of a disc-jockey can only be justified under the theory of fair comment.

The Protection of Copyright

Another legal field with which the writer and the publication have concern is that of copyright. The United States Constitution protects this right of copyright. ARTICLE 1, SECTION VIII, Paragraph 8 of the Constitution reads:

To promote the progress of science and useful arts by securing for limited times to authors and inventors the exclusive right to their respective writings and discoveries.

In the case of writers, the law of copyright does not protect the idea itself, but the author's own expression of it. It protects his literary form, and it does this for a period of twenty-eight years. In addition, the law authorizes a renewal of copyright for another period of twenty-eight years.

The writer or publisher who wishes to secure a copyright files an application with the Register of Copyrights, Library of Congress, Washington, D. C. He pays the required fee, and he deposits the required number of copies of the published or unpublished work which he wishes protected. Usually two copies are required. He must also see that the work so protected carries on each copy the notice of copyright.

Although a title independent of a book, story, or article cannot be copyrighted, the distinctive and standing title of a newspaper column, cartoon, or feature may be protected by having it registered as a trademark. Trademarks receive statutory protection and are registered in the United States Patent Office.

21

Journalism on Radio and Television

Radio Writing's Distinctive Problems—Newscast Patterns—Radio and the First Amendment—Impact of TV on Radio Programming—News on Television—The "On-the-Spot" Telecast —TV Summary Broadcasts—The Advent of Video Tape—Editorials on the Air

As opportunities for careers in newspaper work tend to decrease with each successive newspaper merger, new opportunities open up in other phases of journalism and of writing, such as those in the fresh fields of radio and television.

Radio in its many services parallels in a way the bill of fare offered by the daily and Sunday newspaper.

It headlines "spot" news.

It has its Washington and foreign correspondents.

It gives wide sports coverage.

It gives editorial comment on the news through its commentators.

It presents many and varied news features.

It has its regular service-to-listener departments—fashion, cooking, child care, health advice, et cetera.

It has its columnists who cover Hollywood, the theatre, books, politics, et cetera.

It provides entertainment features, serials, stories, contests.

It carries advertising, and, as in the case of the newspaper, it is the advertiser who foots the bill.

And it gives all this in its own unique way, for its

appeal has to be to the ear and not, as in the case of the newspaper, to the eye. Accordingly, radio reaches a public even wider than the reading public, for many people find the ear their most useful channel to knowledge and information. Many have never read a book, and still more have never read anything but occasional papers. Children and uneducated adults get abstract knowledge through their ears more easily than through their eyes. It is the literate person's years of reading and study which have made him dependent on the visual approach.

Although radio news broadcasting began as recently as 1920 when Station KDKA in Pittsburgh put the presidential election returns of that year on the air, the oral announcement of events as well as the spinning of tales long antedate the earliest crude writing.

"What the radio is actually doing," as the *Saturday Review* has pointed out, " is to give back to the human voice the telling of stories and the narrating of events."

This emphasis on the ear rather than on the eye dictates the chief difference between copy written for the microphone and that set up for the presses. Words become sound symbols to the radio news writer rather than sight ones.

In 1935 the United Press began its news service to radio stations, and the practical suggestions which Phil Newsom made in his *United Press Style Book* are as valid today as when written. Their aim was to assist those already experienced in newspaper writing to adapt their skill to the requirements of radio. Here are some of them:

Radio news writing is more informal than newspaper writing, since people speak more informally than they write. . . .

Be careful about the use of personal pronouns. When you write "he," "she," or "they," be very sure there can be absolutely no doubt as to whom the pronoun refers. If there is any question, repeat the person's name.

Be very careful in the use of figures. Make them "round" whenever possible. For all practical purposes, 1,623 eggs becomes "16 hundred," etc. Don't say "a million." The "a" makes it come out "8 million" on the air. Say "one million."

Be sparing with words ending in "s" or the "th" sound. A series of "s's" on the air sounds like the start of the "skyrocket" cheer for old Siwash.

Remember that repetition is the backbone of radio. . . . the listener cannot refer back as he can in a newspaper.

The present tense ordinarily is the most desirable for radio.

Radio cannot, as the newspapers can, soften a startling statement by attaching a qualifier at the end of a sentence. The qualification must be clearly stated at the start.

Because of this close parallel between radio and newspaper, the training for radio news writing runs along lines similar to those for everyday journalism. It requires a good educational background, preferably a college background, with emphasis on one or more special subjects; practice in standard journalistic techniques acquired at a professional school or in a regular city room; and the facile pen of the ready writer. Many of the same standards and practices hold. Reporting should be fair, not as a matter of favor but of duty, and the main points of a news story should be made at its beginning. However, as the newcast enters the living room of so many homes, the standards of good taste in news coverage and presentation are if anything higher.

Accordingly, it is not surprising that the chief radio newscasters have behind them years of regular newspaper experience, and the pioneer commentators like H. V. Kaltenborn and Elmer Davis came to radio with years of distinguished editorial work.

The newsroom of a large broadcasting station duplicates in its main features the newsroom of a daily paper. There sit the news editor and his writers. The reporters and correspondents are covering an assigned event. There is the reference morgue. Amid the staccato of the typewriters sounds the constant rattle of the teletype machines as they bring in the news services of the Associated Press and United Press International.

We note a difference when we come to the newscaster. He may be a reporter and writer and again he may not. He has been chosen for the distinctness of his speech and his ability to convey orally the meaning of news bulletins. On small stations the news editor, the news researcher, the newswriter and the newscaster are all combined in one hard-working individual.

The basic content of all wire reports from all the wire services is "spot" news, and the basic principle in the writing is simplicity in construction. This enables the newscaster to move easily and smoothly through his script. The spot story organization is akin to all news writing: the more important facts are placed at the beginning to facilitate any last minute cutting.

Typical Newscast Patterns

The typical newscast is usually a five-minute period devoted to the latest headline news. It consists of from seven to ten swiftly moving summaries of front-page importance. Each item contains from 50 to 75 words—except the featured story. This may run from 150 to 200 words. The motivating idea behind the selection of items is variety. The newswriter, or the newscaster if he compiles his own script, selects local, national, international, economic, social, and religious items, if the day's grist provides them, in an effort to cater to a wide range of tastes, and he tries to end up with a human interest story, preferably one which will leave a laugh behind it.

This generally accepted form of the five-minute newscast stems from a compromise agreed upon by the radio industry and the press some years back at a time when newspapers questioned the right of radio to use its various news services. This compromise put the emphasis on the bulletin quality of radio news in the expectation that listeners who get but the swift announcement of an event would buy the newspaper to read the further details, just as a reader caught by a headline will readily dip into the news story.

Working with this format in mind, and guided by the need for variety, the radio news editor picks his items as they pour in over the teletype, and he frequently interlards them with local items of interest. Each item should have its date line, of course, and the current practice is to introduce the source of the news in the first sentence rather than merely to announce the name of a city or country before each item as in the case of a written news story. As news in itself compels immediate interest, its presentation in bulletin form requires no special attention-getting devices. In fact when color and dramatic phrasing enter into spot news programs, they do so merely to make the facts more vivid and not as ends in themselves. All this applies not only to the writing but to the actual newscasting as well. The listener feels that in a way he is having a paper's headlines read to him, and because of this the newscaster need feel no compunction to use the chatty style of other broadcasts.

The spot news broadcast is in a class by itself and must not be confused with supplemental news feature programs, with reports from radio correspondents around the nation and abroad, or with commentator programs.

The Radio News Reporter

The radio news reporter excels in what the British Broadcasting Corporation aptly describes as "actuality" reporting. He goes in for direct on-the-scene description and comment. He has to have words at his tongue-tip as readily, as aptly, and as speedily as his *confrères* in the newsroom have words at their finger tips. Perhaps he stands at the entry to a mine which has caved in, trapping seventy workers; perhaps he watches the launching of a great ship or the funeral procession of a potentate. In each and every case the radio news reporter conjures up for his listeners the actual picture of the event as he sees it, together with a hint of the emotional atmosphere, sorrow, tenseness, jubilation, gaiety which surround it. He may later follow this on-the-scene reporting with after-the-event commentary which may include public reaction to his first report.

The importance of the radio news reporter is on the increase as the importance of radio's use of news is on the increase with the better stations. This trend stresses the fifteen-minute news summary pattern which gives the news writer the opportunity to do some reporting in depth along with elucidating commentary. Across the land these summary broadcasts follow a time schedule which caters first to early risers, then follows with news around breakfast time, then at lunch time, at dinner time, and finally at bedtime. With stations increasing their local coverage, the radio reporter is entering on an expanding field.

Frequently radio's correspondents abroad use this actuality reporting, but more frequently they report on happenings in foreign countries after the event itself. As with newspaper correspondents, the radio man abroad has to interpret as well as report, and he becomes in fact quite as much a commentator as reporter.

The Radio Commentator

The radio commentator is the editorial writer of the air. Into his material go all the ingredients we expect in a good editorial—the news stimulation, the reaction to that stimulation, an analysis of the news when possible, and a reasoned explanation for the opinions set forth.

The best commentators give just that. Like the editorial writer, the radio commentator draws largely on his background, and his value to the listener depends on the richness and range of these personal resources. Commentators like Lowell Thomas, who have kept their public through the years, came to the microphone with a wide and colorful experience of foreign travel and correspondence and impressive records of authorship behind them. Some commentators, lacking everything but audacity, come—and go.

Featured commentators are the "prima donnas" of the newsroom, and they are usually assigned a fifteen-minute period, which, when the commercials are subtracted, leaves a speaking time of twelve or thirteen minutes.

Neither the networks nor the sponsors hold themselves responsible for the opinions expressed by the commentator, and usually a disclaimer to this effect precedes or succeeds the broadcast. This is just as well, for we could name commentators who give little news and less comment—merely a fifteen-minute outpouring of political propaganda and prejudice.

What the listener expects and feels he has a right to expect is an informed interpretation of events, along with an elaboration of association sufficient to place the event in its sequence and indicate its relative importance. With this guidance, the average listener can form his own opinions.

Newspapers and Radio

Newspaper publishers at first watched the growing popularity of radio with alarm. They felt that the vast sums which sponsors spent for radio shows would curtail the amount which the same advertisers would expend on newspaper advertising; they feared too that radio's broadcasting of the news would mean a drop in the circulation of their newspapers. Both fears proved groundless. Publishers found that their advertising revenue kept its status quo or improved, and that circulation figures did the same. In fact they began to see that radio newscasts actually benefited circulation. In many instances the listener, intrigued by the radio's bulletin announcement, made a point of getting the papers to read the details of the event. To make assurance doubly sure, many newspapers acquired radio stations of their own, and today approximately one-third of the nation's stations are controlled by newspapers.

Radio and the First Amendment

While the newspaper is the most privileged of American institutions, the radio is not. Radio air waves are controlled by the government, and radio stations can use them only if licensed by the Federal Communications Commission set up by the government. Potentially, at least, this means that radio is politically controlled.

The Communications Act of 1934, Section 301 reads: "It is the purpose of this Act among other things to maintain the control of the United States over all the channels of interstate and foreign radio transmission, and to provide for the use of such channels, but not the ownership thereof, by persons for limited periods of time, under licenses granted by federal authority, and no such license shall be construed to create any right, beyond the terms, conditions, and periods of the license."

In "Radio, Television and Society" Professor Charles A. Siepmann translates the foregoing involvement to mean that the wave lengths of the air have been deeded in perpetuity to the *people* of the United States. "They constitute a public domain to which the broadcaster is given conditional and temporary access, and once admitted into this domain, he may pursue profits for himself."

In 1949, the Federal Communications Commission permitted radio stations to present their personal views on current affairs, provided that such expression be "reasonably balanced" by the presentation of contrary opinion. This degree of "balance" is subject to appraisal, and the Federal Communications Commission has the right to revoke the license of any station. Minority "pressure groups," other propagandists, and the broadcaster's own presumption that he is peculiarly equipped to decide what the public wants to hear all add to the illusive curbs which affect what the listener hears and also what he does not hear. Ideally there should exist no artificial barrier, either economic or political, to the listener's freedom to listen.

"Facsimile" Transmission by Radio

The broadcasting of a newspaper over the air and the physical reproduction of it in a person's home open a new chapter in journalism. This seeming miracle has now well passed the experimental stage. Newspapers have actually been delivered by radio in Miami, in New York, in Chicago, and elsewhere. The process bears the name "Facsimile."

Facsimile is a method of transmitting written and illustrated material over the air waves. Just as radio sends impulses into the home which are converted into sound, facsimile transmits impulses which are converted into words and pictures printed on a sheet of paper.

Although transmitted by radio, facsimile does not emerge from the ordinary radio receiving set. A special attachment called a recorder is necessary for receiving facsimile broadcasts. Only a limited number of these recorders have as yet been manufactured. Their price so far is high, and the future of facsimile newspaper transmis-

sion rests on the extent of the public demand for it. So far, there
has been no public demand.

Evolution or Revolution?

Up to 1960, the two standard news broadcast patterns had established themselves—the five-minute and the fifteen-minute. The
first, minus the time out for commercials, gave three and a half
minutes of headline news, and the other about twelve minutes of
more detailed coverage. Both patterns kept in line with the standards of practice adopted by the National Association of Radio News
Directors in 1950 which declared that "the News Director, as a key
figure in the broadcasting industry, has the public interest as his
foremost responsibility. His principal purpose is to keep the public
well-informed."

Although some stations used these time patterns for broadcasting
local news, many stations relied on sponsored network news programs.

Toward the end of the 1950's, an evolution or revolution developed which affected the whole radio broadcasting program schedule
and made its chief impact on radio newscasts.

Dubbed either as "modern" or "formula" broadcasting, program
scheduling now consists entirely of popular music, commercials, and
"disc-jockey" newscasts. According to the *Hollywood Reporter* a
typical "formula" operation in Los Angeles breaks down thus:

Music	12 minutes,	41 seconds
News	1 minute	45 seconds
Commercials	15 minutes	34 seconds

Because of the huge income which the individual station gains
from the commercials in this style of setup, network affiliates are
replacing the network programs with this formula pattern. And if
this trend continues . . .?

"If the networks were to go under because of the sweep to
formula radio, radio sets would simply become coinless jukeboxes." *

* *Radio Is Worth Saving* by Wm. O'Hallaren, *Atlantic Monthly*, October
1959, pg. 70, Vol. 204, #4.

The wire services which supply the greater part of the news which comes over the airwaves are confronted by the increasingly diverse needs of two groups of broadcasters. The Associated Press Radio Committee sees one group as "the majority segment, apparently growing in number and voice," which seeks an abundance of short items "to supply a multiplicity of daily news programs," and the other group which wants "more than headlines, strong detail, some background and interpretation—in short, the whole story."

News on Television

Television gives us the picture paper of the air. Just as printed picture papers like the New York *Daily News* have rolled up colossal circulations, so television news has attained great popularity as an information source.

Commercial television got its start on July 1, 1941, but television news as a regular feature dates only from about 1947. At that time the country had only eight TV stations in eight cities, and about 60,000 TV sets in use. Since then the growth of TV has been phenomenal. *Broadcasting Yearbook* now lists the four competing networks with their number of affiliated stations as follows: ABC Radio, 200; ABC-TV, 205; CBS Radio, 210; CBS-TV, 205; NBC Radio, 205; NBC-TV, 195; MBS Radio 430 (daytime) 385 (night).

Early Techniques Develop

The first television newscasts hardly stood out as models of originality. Television merely trained its camera on radio broadcasters reading their daily stint from scripts. Soon visual aids to interpretation and understanding crept in. The camera began to show maps, charts, and "still shots" of places and personalities and to incorporate portions of newsreel film. Another practice merely pictured the typewritten news bulletins themselves and ran them across the television screen to the accompaniment of nondescript music. Soon sound motion pictures of the actual news events made their appearance; their newsworthiness depended on the speed of their reception and transmission. Large local stations discovered the potential popularity of local news films. Station WFIL-TV, Philadelphia, blazed the trail in 1947. Its local newsreel had a staff of five people who in an emergency could get a story on the air within an hour and a half from the time the film was taken. This speedy television of local news—speedy at that time—was made possible by close cooperation between the newsreel staff and the city desk of the Philadelphia *Inquirer*, the station's parent newspaper.

The On-The-Spot Telecast

Television has all the facilities to become one of journalism's ace reporters. It can bring a unique dimension of news to its audience—sound plus sight, authenticity plus immediacy, variety plus intimacy. Few newsmen deny that an on-the-spot telecast of a major news event encompasses the best techniques of reporting. And the completion of the coast-to-coast coaxial cable and radio relay hookup in 1951 offered television the advantage of blanket U.S. coverage in presenting outstanding news events.

Response to on-the-spot telecasts borders on the spectacular. Coverage of the U.S. Senate Crime Investigating Committee hearing in New York during March, 1951 marked a milestone date in the development of TV news. Television covered the hearings with skill and objectivity. Millions and millions of viewers followed each day's drama at first hand. Similarly expert coverage of successive political conventions gave the millions who watched and listened a sense of actual participation in their country's politics. As a New York *Times* correspondent pointed out, through TV the viewer could see for himself the chain of events through which a participant in a small country meeting can have a direct voice in the choice of a party's presidential candidate. What appeared on the television screen was a "vivid and unrivalled lesson in democracy at work."

Although at such an event newspapermen and electronic pressmen appear to get in each other's way, there is no real competition between TV and the printed word. They supplement each other. As *Time* magazine has pointed out when it comes to speed and fidelity to the news at the instant it is breaking, TV is in a class of its own. On the other hand for those who want a story rounded out and interpreted, and readable at their own pace, the printed page is worth "a thousand TV pictures."

Today this immense television audience continues to grow with every telecast of World's Series, State of the Union address, emergency U.N. Security Council meeting, or other front-ranking news stories.

The TV Summary Newscast

While such "you are there" type of visual reporting has won for television its widest acclaim, this spectacular covering of spot news constitutes only one assignment of TV news coverage. Daily news parades across the screen in five-, ten-, and fifteen-minute summaries.

Early television news programs seemed fascinated by moving pictures for their own sake. This obsession gradually gave place to the present-day concept where the idea takes precedence over the pictorial illustration. As Sig Mickelson, president of CBS News, puts it: "Both in our hard news and in our special reports, we decide first on what the story will be—and then see how best we can illustrate it. If there are no pictures that will help out, we go without pictures."

This practice in television news puts the emphasis on the reporters, the writers, the analysts, and the creators and brings to the fore the essential in TV news presentation—coordinated team work.

CBS's top news show "Douglas Edwards with the News" can stand as a good example of this teamwork concept. First put on the air in 1948 as a pioneer in television newscasting this program can utilize the services of some 600 collaborators. In addition to CBS's own news team, numbering some of the top men in electronic journalism, the Edwards show has the facilities of the regular wire services, the Associated Press, United Press International, and Reuters, whose correspondents are stationed in strategic spots around the globe. From these newsmen, correspondents, and cameramen flow a constant stream of cable reports and news film to the show's midtown Manhattan headquarters. To select, integrate, and present all this collaboration in the tightly packed fifteen minutes on the air, Edwards has a battery of people working behind him—two full-time writers, a producer-director, a news editor, film news reporters, and others.

News comes first too on NBC's successful evening television newscast, the "Huntley-Brinkley Report." This show has a distinctive formula—two newscasters of equal rank working from different cities as a team. Both men, Chester Robert Huntley (New York) and David McClure Brinkley (Washington), have sound professional backgrounds and pride themselves on being newsmen, not showmen. This duet presents the news with restraint, authority, and a pleasant informality, and also with valuable "interpretation." As members of a team, each compliments the other. Each broadcast deals with five or six main themes, the top place going to the day's lead story. Each member of the team knows in a general way what the other will cover.

The basic idea of a competent newscast is to vary the different visual aid techniques and at the same time to present the news in an informative manner. It represents the combined efforts of the news director, writers, artists, cameramen, film editors, sound effects man, audio man for records, control room men, stagehands, electricians, and other technicians.

Preparation for an evening newscast gets under way in the morning when the news director calls a preliminary conference with his writers to discuss the day's budget. This first conference does not produce a complete line-up since the day's news breaks cannot yet be predicted. Often though, the director and his staff agree on at least one or two stories scheduled to break during the day which lend themselves to some visual aid treatment. The artists then get to work preparing a graph, map, or diagram.

By early afternoon the director has a fairly good idea of the news items which will appear on the evening newscast. With his staff he then decides the order of each item and the amount of time to be allotted for reporting it. He also decides which film stories will go into the newscast. But the director's line-up is always subject to change up to the time the newscaster opens the program. For although it may be too late at that time to include a visual aid, important late news can still be presented by voice with the camera on the newscaster.

Most of the writing for the newscast is done in late afternoon and early evening. TV news writing is patterned after radio news writing and demands the same clarity and conciseness of expression. Most TV newsrooms are staffed with men trained in radio news writing or newspaper reporting. A necessary requirement for TV news writers is that they be familiar with the graphic arts so that they can present the news in terms of visual aids. Their goal is to make each newscast a one-page newspaper.

Television's Effect on Radio

With the advent of television, the sudden popularity of this new medium with viewers and consequently with advertisers made a serious impact upon radio, which it eventually managed to withstand.

From 1949 on, advertisers turned increasingly from audio to video, which meant a tremendous loss in income to the radio networks. Oddly enough, however, local broadcasting continued to do well. In this period the nation's listening habits changed radically. While television took its place in the living room, radio moved to the bedroom, the kitchen, and the family automobile.

To meet the new situation, specialists searched for a formula which would incorporate flexibility and immediacy and fall in line with average listeners' habits and wishes. They came up with "saturation" radio. This new idea did away with the old rigid program timing into hour, half-hour, or quarter-hour shows. Instead the broadcasting hour could divide into segments of any length from a twenty-minute interview to a six-second commercial. This permitted great flexibility to an advertiser who could purchase air spots through the entire day and "saturate" the air waves with his message.

The National Broadcasting Company pioneered in 1955 with its program "Monitor," a forty-hour melange of music, interviews, features, news, and commercials, devised, as an official spokesman put it, "to bring listeners into touch with everything important, interesting, or entertaining anywhere in the world." Originating in NBC's Radio Central in New York City, it can do just that, for it has at its disposal every important world news center and newsroom connections with affiliated stations in more than 200 cities across the land. The other networks quickly followed, presenting programs such as ABC's "New Sounds for You," and Mutual's "Stand By Round the World."

Standard news programs such as the "World News Round Up" continue to bring first class summary coverage from the home base and from correspondents abroad.

Radio remains a superb vehicle for news tranmission and reception. It boasts instant news coverage, ubiquity, and great flexibility. From here to there and from there to here radio brings "news with the speed of sound," news as it happens. With easily handled field equipment which nowadays includes miniature tape recorders that can slip into one's pocket, and with car-size mobile units, an independent station can with economy bring its listeners a front page in sound—the sound of the news itself and the actual voices of the individuals concerned.

The Disappearing Time Lag

While television news at the beginning found itself hampered by the time lag between the actual news event and the arrival of news film or "stills" to illustrate the happening, that time lag is fast disappearing. The early shows had to rely on film clips from old newsreels. Today the time lag is being conquered by inspired gadgetry and in a few years time may even cease to exist. High quality telephone and radio circuits link most of the world for immediate communication. Less cumbersome equipment, such as the "knapsack" camera, facilitate the reporter's work. Mobile units, which yearly gain in compactness and maneuverability, can now initiate broadcasts from wherever they choose to park.

The newest and most spectacular technological development in television is videotape. Use of videotape can ease the load on telephone circuits, but its chief asset is that it plays back as recorded without the necessity of processing, giving it a substantial time-saving advantage over film. A royal wedding may take place in

London at eleven in the morning. Its sounds and sights are recorded on videotape. Thanks to the difference in time, thanks to the speed of jet aircraft, the tape can reach the headquarters of the Canadian Broadcasting Corporation in time to be put on the air for Canadian viewers and through the National Broadcasting Company for American viewers at two in the afternoon the same day.

This videotape link with European news may soon be replaced by a live transatlantic relay. Experts claim that such a link is already technically feasible.

The Television Documentary

Allied to television's coverage of the news is the television documentary. The documentary, a feature of growing importance on all networks, frequently stands out as an excellent example of visual reporting in depth. Usually, in an hour long format, the documentary has sufficient time to develop its subject effectively. Probably the public's growing acceptance of the concept of education through entertainment had its beginnings in the popularity of "See It Now," a type of television journalism devised by the noted correspondent Edward R. Murrow and his co-producer Fred Friendly. *Cue* magazine described this innovation when first introduced as a "living magazine . . . with the accent on 'insight' rather than on 'news beats.' " "See It Now" has passed into history but the partnership behind it has carried on its virtues into the production of outstanding documentaries. The growing interest in science opens up a vast field for documentary subject matter, and commercial sponsors have from time to time entered it. The Bell Telephone System's hour-long film on the role of the sun in providing the energy without which there cannot be life illustrated how the worlds of science and show business can join to bring general enlightenment.

Newspaper Headlines from TV

Newspaper editors who not so long ago regarded television as anathema must nowadays regard with some wry amusement their dependence on Sunday television for arresting Monday morning headlines. Television interviews and participation by international figures on such widely watched panel shows as "Face the Nation," "College News Conference," "Searchlight," and "Meet the Press" receive, because of their newsworthiness, marked attention in the nation's press. It would almost seem as if the said international figures had formed the habit of reserving their most potent pronouncements for such high-spot telecasts.

In a way the watching public can do its own reporting. It watches the sudden reaction of the interviewee to an unexpected and perhaps unwelcome question. It notes the involuntary change in facial expression—more difficult to control than the tone of the voice—and the public draws its own conclusions. It was from these subtle accompaniments to the spoken word that the old-time reporter obtained his story—in the old days before the public relations expert came between the interviewee and the press with a prepared statement.

Editorials on the Air

Although many radio and some television independent stations have regularly aired their views on important public questions national or local, the major networks have not to any great extent taken advantage of their opportunity to express opinion. The rule which the Federal Communications Commission lays down for individual stations applies equally to the networks. It states that while a licensee is entitled to air his point of view, he must permit others the chance to disagree.

Radio's commentators and "reporting in depth" programs have long had considerable editorial content, and television for some time has been moving toward greater expression of opinion. For years NBC's nightly news report consisted chiefly of bulletins. Since Chet Huntley and David Brinkley took the assignment in 1957, they have given much of their time to "interpretation." CBS's initial editorial was in its own interest—the right of TV to have access to public hearings. Later its New York outlet WCBS gave the company's views against off-track betting—a local issue. But many of Howard K. Smith's able commentaries could well be considered as expository editorials. ABC expresses its opinion with considerable frequency and aims at achieving the desired over-all balance.

It is up to affiliated stations to decide for themslves whether or not to carry the network's editorial opinions. Under the Federal Communications Commission's rules, the individual station licensee is responsible for what goes out over his station, no matter where the program happens to originate.

As the editorial function is increasingly expanded, television's role for the future may be the important one of mobilizing opinion.

22
Advertising in the Mass Media

History and Development—Curbs on Advertising in Print and on
TV—Its Relation to Circulation—The Audit Bureau of
Circulation—Advertising's Many Skills—The Appeal of Color—
The Claims of Rival Media

Advertising pays the bills for daily, weekly, and monthly journalism as well as for the information and entertainment of radio and television. Newspapers as a rule receive two-thirds of their revenue from this source. The economics of this situation have led some people to believe that because advertising forms the chief support of a newspaper it also dominates its policy and influences its editorial point of view.

Like other popular beliefs, this generalization is too sweeping and wholesale. Undoubtedly advertising exerts a strong influence on the chief journalistic media, but that it "dominates" them or any one of them is open to question. Critics who talk of the newspaper's "alliance with big business" seem to forget how natural such an alliance is, for the newspaper itself is often big business. And even in small towns, as the late editor of *The Emporia Gazette*, William Allen White, once pointed out, the association of the editor and the local big business man is inevitable:

I know of no editor so high that his mind is not affected by his industrial environment. The fact that he lives in daily contact with the rich people of his community, whether the community be large or small, that he gangs with them at the country club, eats with them at the leading hotels, and indeed prays with what might be called a pluto-cratic congregation, colors his views, and he sees things as his friends and associates see them.

Probably many instances have passed into history where papers have done their best to please their advertisers and have even kow-towed to them. Or, at most, they have avoided biting the hand that fed them. With well-established journals such subservience is as unthinkable as it is unnecessary. The New York *Times* put the situation clearly in an editorial, "Free Press and Advertising."

A strong newspaper's advertisers do not "support" it in the same sense that a subsidizer supports an enterprise. They pay for a service. As advertising is a business transaction, this service is worth as much to them as the money they pay. If an individual advertiser withdraws advertising out of pique or disagreement with some editorial policy, he hurts his own business interest by doing so. The newspaper loses advertising, but he loses public good-will and sales. . . .

A responsible newspaper's primary duty, from a business as well as an ethical standpoint, is to the community. When it gives its readers the news, when it enlists their continued support, advertising follows, for the advertisers need readers just as much as the newspapers do. If an honest newspaper is "dominated" by anybody, it is not by its advertisers but by its reading public. It owes that public full and im-partial news and its candid and unbiased editorial comment.

Few, if any, journals survive without advertising. The newspaper *PM* made a notable attempt to get along without it, but to meet its deficits it had to fall back upon the fortune of its sponsor. Eventually it decided to accept paid advertising, and its sponsor, Marshall Field, gave the reason for so doing:

"I cannot but help feeling," Mr. Field wrote, "that there is more potential danger to *PM's* independence in the fact that its existence so largely depends on whether one man desires to support it than could possibly arise from accepting support from the advertisers of the community." The *Times'* editorial, just quoted, appeared as that paper's comment on the Marshall Field statement.

Enlightened publishers have come to regard advertising not only as a service to journalism, but one of journalism's services to its readers. They claim that advertising's competitive price offers safeguard the public from profiteering, and that advertising keeps the public informed on the latest products and labor-saving devices.

Advertising and Its Development

Basically, we can consider advertising as any device—printed, oral, pictorial—which aims to sell anything that the seller wants sold—merchandise, services, ideas. Its development in journalism through all existing media of information has been spectacular. Because of the interest-compulsion of its contents, its wide circulation coverage, and its daily or weekly publication, the newspaper ranks as the top medium for advertising's commercial message.

America's first continuing newspaper, the Boston *News Letter*, led off with the country's first paid advertisement in its second issue on May 8, 1704. This fell into what today we would call the classified ad category under "Lost and Found" as it had to do with two lost anvils.

In fact all early advertising had this classified ad appearance. It was set in single-column width, in the ordinary body type of the paper, and with little or no attempt at display. By the middle of the eighteenth century these announcements, which is really all they were, filled three to five pages of the chief papers. They took note of runaways, offered Negroes and Indians for sale, listed general merchandise without prices, sought recruits for the army, and proclaimed quack practitioners and cure-all remedies. The rates for these announcements ran from three to five shillings for the first insertion and one to three shillings for subsequent ones. After the Revolutionary War, the rates rose to ten shillings and stayed at that figure for the next twenty years.

Up to then nothing resembling display advertising had come to the fore beyond a blocked initial letter or stock woodcuts showing a runaway or a sailing ship which the papers used over and over again. In 1875 advertising began to appear in double-column spreads with cuts and with larger type, and it took over page one in many of the papers, leaving only one column, if any, for news.

During the first half of the nineteenth century, advertising took up about one-half of the typical newspaper, which was then a four-page sheet. It still resembled our modern classified advertising in appearance, as the increase in the amount of it limited the space for display. A common practice with newspapers at this time was to charge $32 to $40 for an advertisement to run the whole year with a subscription thrown in.

The year 1850 saw the advent of the eight-page paper, and with that advent advertising left the front page. James Gordon Bennett's New York *Herald* led the field in the amount of advertising during this period, but he reduced all advertisements to agate type in single-column measure without stock-cuts or two-line initials. In 1858, the *Herald* printed the largest advertisement which had ever appeared, when Robert Bonner took seven solid pages to announce his weekly, the New York *Ledger*.

By the end of the Civil War, advertising had grown into an annual business from $12 million to $15 million, and advertising agencies began to spring up. By 1890, the annual amount spent for advertising was about $70 million, with patent medicine advertising leading the national field. But the advent of the automobile in 1899 brought a change in this picture.

During the present century advertising has developed with spectacular rapidity. The amounts spent on it have swelled; the taste and artistry contributed to it have reached high peaks of excellence; and the skill brought to its planning and projection has been of such high quality that advertising at its best these days almost ranks as a science.

By 1914 the amount spent annually for advertising had reached the half billion mark. By 1929, the year of the financial crash, it had climbed to $800 million. In 1945 the total outlay for advertising in the United States came to over $2.8 billion. By 1960 the total reached $11 billion. Advertisers predict that the total will top $15 billion before long.

Curbs on Advertising

Fraudulent claims by patent medicine concerns and misrepresentations made by other advertisers awakened public conscience to the whole question of advertising ethics. As a result the Federal Food and Drug Act went on the statute books in 1906, primarily as a curb against patent medicines, and in 1912 the Federal Post Office Act included the regulation that reading notices and such announcements must be clearly marked as advertisements. All this alerted advertisers themselves to the need for regulations in the craft, and in 1911 *Printers' Ink*, a trade publication which had become a force for clean and honest advertising, devised a statute which was adopted by twenty-two states and, in a modified form, by fifteen more states. This regulation made any advertiser's "untruthful, deceptive, or misleading statements" a misdemeanor.

The 1930's brought about more regulations and legislation governing advertising. In 1932 the Association of National Advertising Managers acting in conjunction with the American Association of Advertising Agencies drew up an ethical code to cover advertising and established a Review Committee to enforce it. Then, in 1938, the Wheeler-Lea Bill gave the Federal Trade Commission jurisdiction over misleading advertising.

A heyday of the patent medicine ad coincided with the era of the Civil War. This period saw the first tax levied on advertising. During the conflict between the states, the Federal Government put a three per cent tax on newspaper advertising, but repealed it in 1867.

Public criticism levelled against unwarranted claims and similar practices in advertising's history has spurred the advertising business itself to establish ethical codes for the craft. For years now, such codes have held to the slogan "Truth in Advertising" as a fundamental principle. Recent additions to existing codes hold interest as they tend to extend the basic conceptions of advertising's social responsibility. As, for instance, the following drawn up by the National Better Business Bureau:

1. Advertising should not be used to undermine the child-parent relationship.
2. Advertising should not be used to coerce parents into buying by falsely implying that failure to buy constitutes neglect of family responsibility and duty, and contributes to maladjustments.
3. Advertising should not make use of inaccurate assumptions regarding psychological problems to instill guilt and inadequacy in the minds of readers.
4. Advertising should not make use of themes tending to subvert the stability and unity of American family life by sowing seeds of dissension, disunity or distrust.
5. Advertising should not be used irresponsibly as a law unto itself in disregard to the public interest.

Following on the heels of the "rigged" quiz shows and "payola" scandals which shook the public's faith in television's integrity, the American Association of Advertising Agencies tightened up its code on television advertising.

The new interpretation pointed out that television commercials are often seen by mixed family groups, including children, and that listening to them was not always voluntary as was the reading of print advertising.

"For these and for other reasons," the interpretative statement said, "they magnify any faults of taste and manners of advertising misrepresentation." The association advised sponsors of commercials and the agencies representing them that they had a "severe obligation" to act with good manners as guests in the viewer's home.

"Any commercial that offends the sensibilities of any large number of people should be seriously questioned. Judgments should be stricter than those applied to print advertising, because of the guest relationship between the viewer and the advertiser, and because commercials are often seen by mixed family groups."

Directing attention to commercials that by use of costume, props, or settings, imply that certain persons are connected with the medical, dental, or nursing professions, the association called such use deceptive unless accredited members of these professions are the persons seen in the commercial.

Advertising and Circulation: The A.B.C.

The value of any journalistic medium to the advertiser depends on the size and quality of its circulation. Newspapers and magazines accordingly base the rates they charge on the size and type of the readership they reach. Research and audit surveys establish these factors with precision to the satisfaction of both parties.

This is a fairly recent development. The post Civil War years saw advertising grow as a business but in haphazard ways. The better papers of the time realizing the growing importance of news to the American public pushed all their advertising to the inside pages. Advertising agencies would buy space from them at low rates and sell it to their clients at high rates, making commissions thereby of from 25 per cent to 75 per cent. Small wonder that these agencies cropped up all over the country. The rates charged by the newspapers varied all the way from the ten cents a line paid to prosperous weeklies to the dollar a line of the New York *Herald*. No longer is there confusion of rates. Modern advertising rates are quoted in terms of agate lines with set rates and no discounts.

The relationship between advertiser and medium rests today on the solid basis of fact. The cornerstone of this mutually satisfactory foundation is the Audit Bureau of Circulation, known in the business as the A.B.C. This bureau, founded in 1914, operates for the benefit of advertiser and publisher alike, and its directorate consists of representatives from both the buying and the selling groups. Article IV of the Bureau's *By-Laws and Rules* provides for a board of directors to consist of twelve from the advertiser group; three from the advertising agencies; six newspaper publishers; two magazine publishers; two farm-paper publishers; and two business-paper publishers. And Article V limits the presidency of the Bureau to a member of either the advertiser or agency groups.

The Bureau's chief function is to verify circulation. It regards its work as self-regulation in the advertising and publishing industry and describes its threefold services as standardizing the publishers' circulation statements, verifying the same by establishing a uniform method for auditing paid circulation, and furnishing accurate reports to its membership. It has done all this so well that the journals now belonging to it command over 90 per cent of the country's circulation. The A.B.C., in fact, provides the only standard measurement in absolute terms of circulation of any advertising medium.

A parallel service performs a similar function for the publications of business organizations and other groups. These publications are usually distributed free of charge to individuals with an interest in the work or ideas of such organizations. This agency, known as the Controlled Circulation Audit Bureau, Inc., is usually referred to professionally as the C.C.A. Trade and business journals which have paid circulations can become members of the A.B.C., and about 350 trade journals have joined that organization.

Advertising's Many Skills

Modern advertising utilizes many highly developed skills. It expends vast sums, but no longer haphazardly. Today, the basis for making advertising scientifically profitable for the advertiser rests on accurate market and reader analysis. Once these have been secured and studied, artistic skill comes with the preparation of layouts and the drawing of point-making illustrations. When it comes to the text or copy for the ad, the skill of the psychologist as well as that of the writer comes into play, for it is keyed to one of the several appeals to which human nature habitually responds, or the ad hints at some fear against which human nature habitually strives to protect itself.

As Paul B. West, President of the Association of National Advertisers sees it, "Advertising is a serious, sober business—the business of applying talent, time, and money to the job of keeping sales moving and the economy alive."

In his article, "Should You Go Into Advertising?" for the career guidance series of the New York Life Insurance Company, he outlines the steps leading up to the launching of a product through advertising:

Let's suppose that a great new product has been developed and it is your job to introduce it to the American people.

You don't just dream up a slogan. It takes skill, creativity, teamwork and long, patient effort on the part of dozens, perhaps hundreds, of specialists to produce effective advertising.

First, the product is pre-tested among consumers to make sure it fills a real need and is acceptable to them. Then various advertising campaigns are prepared and examined in an effort to find the single, most dramatic and convincing selling theme. Meanwhile, media specialists deliberate on how best to deliver the message. Should it appear in national magazines or local newspapers? Star-studded TV shows or radio "spots"? Should you combine these media and others to boot—outdoor posters, car cards and the like?

Month after month, you and your associates work to develop and test the campaign. Finally it is launched from coast to coast and you await the results anxiously. If the product moves according to expectations, fine. If not, it may mean going "back to the drawing board" and starting the grueling process all over again.

Writing Effective Advertising

The writer of an advertisement for any medium aims at clearness. His message must be readily apparent and unmistakable. The late Arthur Brisbane, an astute business man as well as a famous editor, made these points clear in an address to students:

The fundamental idea in advertising is to get a thought from your mind into the mind of another person. Before you can write successful advertising you must first know what you want to say, and second, put it in such words that it can be readily understood.

You have to do five things in advertising. You must make people see it; read it; understand it; believe it; and want it.

How does one write a good advertisement? To answer that query let us call in the experts. Schwab, Beatty & Porter, Inc., of New York City, members of the American Association of Advertising Agencies, have not only been highly successful in their own field, but in addition have shown themselves successful interpreters of their calling. Here is the recipe for effectiveness in advertising suggested by this firm:

To Write a Good Advertisement

Base it on these 5 fundamentals:

1. GET ATTENTION with a layout so striking that it stands apart from competition—or so uncommonly simple that its very restraint attracts—and with a headline holding out your product's promise to do something that people want done for them.
2. SHOW PEOPLE AN ADVANTAGE. What can they have, gain, accomplish with your product? What can they lose or risk if they don't buy it?
3. PROVE IT. With facts, specifications, consumer commendations, awards of recognition, guarantee.
4. PERSUADE PEOPLE TO GRASP THIS ADVANTAGE. Sum up your copy appeal. Re-draw a quick word-picture of the advantage of your product in use, and how easy it is to get it.
5. ASK FOR ACTION. If you want immediate action, give people something specific to do—and, if possible, put in an extra "hook" inducement, or reason for doing it *at once.*

How effectively these five basic fundamentals are used determines the difference between the writer who fills white space with words and the writer whose words fill stores with customers.

How long should an advertisement be? Probably this question has as many answers as there are products and advertisers to proclaim them. Messrs. Schwab, Beatty & Porter, Inc., believe that the briefer-the-better idea has been overworked. They point out:

Some advertising men continue to berate copy which to them "seems" too long. But the trend, based on successful experience belies them. . . .

It's a rare copy idea that can be presented with great brevity and still get immediate action. . . .

The longer your copy can hold the interest of the greatest number of readers, the likelier you are to induce more of them to act.

Reader Interest in Advertising

That reader interest in advertising ranks high is borne out by all surveys which have been made. Here we have median figures on the readership of newspaper departments based on the report of 140 Continuing Studies of Newspaper Reading by the Advertising Research Foundation.

EDITORIAL DEPARTMENTS	MEN	WOMEN
Per Cent of Those Interviewed		
Who Read Any	*Median All Studies to Date*	
Editorials	43%	27%
Editorial Page Items	83	79
Comics	81	78
Financial News	28	10
Radio Programs or News	40	50
Society News or Pictures	37	83
Sports News or Pictures	76	34

ADVERTISING DEPARTMENTS		
Per Cent of Those Interviewed		
Who Read Any		
Display Advertising	80%	95%
National Advertising	53	60
Local Advertising	74	94
Department Store Advertising	39	85
Classified Advertising	39	45
Amusement Advertising	43	59

Journalism's Belief in Advertising

A proof of the effectiveness of daily journalism as an advertising medium would appear to be the newspaper's own fervent belief in it and constant use of it. Hardly a day passes when the metropolitan reader does not find a full-page ad in his own paper which calls attention to the virtues of some other newspaper, a rival or an out-of-towner. These ads stress the paper's readability, its news coverage, and its effectiveness as an advertising show window.

The *Wall Street Journal* made one of the neatest and most dramatic demonstrations of this type of thing to date and one which also showed the flexibility of the newspaper medium.

In four cities startled readers of daily newspapers saw the front page of *that same day's Journal* looking out at them from a full-page ad. Life size, and on top of the day's business news, the reproduced page was cropped of its lower third to make way for this message:

Imagine seeing this morning's *Wall Street Journal* here! This advertisement is just as timely as the *Wall Street Journal* itself. You see the same first page that greeted regular *Wall Street Journal* readers this morning.

Its almost simultaneous republication here is probably the most dramatic example you'll ever see of how closely an advertiser can time his message in a daily newspaper. No other medium can give you this valuable flexibility. The only national business daily is the *Wall Street Journal.*

If you want to finish reading the vital articles on this front page, . . . ask your newsdealer for today's *Wall Street Journal.*

The ad was seen on the same day by readers of newspapers in New York, Chicago, Detroit and, on the day before, in Cleveland. To add to the pulling power of its advertisement, the *Journal* scattered several teasers in each of the four papers—all one column by four inches. They said such things as: Secretaries: save the boss's time—see page—and Executives: don't miss page—.

The Appeal of Color

Advertisers spend increasing billions of dollars each year on multicolor advertisements. And the reason? Experiments have clearly shown that the addition of color increases the advertisement's attention value.

The magazine *Advertising & Selling,* describing a research project conducted by Daniel Starch, reported:

In an analysis of 5 million enquiries involving 2,349 ads run by 163 firms, color brought an average of 53% more returns per 100,000 circulation than black and white.

In the same survey, Mr. Starch reported these figures on two identical advertisements which ran both in black and white and in color:

AVERAGE VISIBILITY OF AD FOR	BLACK AND WHITE	FOUR COLOR AD
Men only	30.9%	46.4%
Women only	31.1%	52.1%
Men and Women	30.7%	50.5%

Artists preparing color advertisements naturally fall back on the findings of researchers and psychologists in the field of color preferences and the effect of color on individuals. Much remains still to be explored. To date experiments show that the favorite colors of the adult population tested were blue, with red a close second; then green, followed by violet, orange, and yellow.

Delving deeper the psychologists contend that color preferences are closely related to personality and emotional makeup: the outgoing extrovert preferring red; the reserved introvert preferring blue and green.

Another factor can well stand out in considering the effectiveness of color in advertising. This is the marked development of color printing processes—first in the European publications and then here. This technical excellence so enhances the subject depicted that the eye is often caught by the beauty of the picture before the advertiser's message registers.

Color printing in the daily press naturally suffers when compared to color work in the glamourous "slicks" because of the rough quality of newsprint paper. Nevertheless the increase in newspaper color advertisements has been swift since World War II. For instance, the Milwaukee Journal which ran only 346,867 lines of ROP (run-of-press) color ads in 1946, carried 2,400,344 in 1958.

This growing use of color in advertisements ties in with a present-day trend. Popular magazines go in more and more for color illustrations, and the daily press, particularly in the West and Far West, yearly increases the use of ROP color in news photographs.

Naturally the advertiser who uses color is convinced of its drawing power or he would not authorize the marked increase in price over black and white. For instance, he pays $6,324.72 for a color page in the Chicago Tribune, while the bill for black and white if he preferred that would be $4,374.72.

Claims of Rival Media

While the advertiser or his agency selects the channel of communication which is felt the best to serve his needs, each mass communication medium puts forth claims for his attention and his patronage.

The newspaper, first in the field, makes its claim for pre-eminence. Jenkin Lloyd Jones, editor of the Tulsa *World,* pointed out to the Newspaper Advertising Executives Association that although the number of newspapers has shrunk since the beginning of this century, the circulation of newspapers has increased spectacularly—from 15 million in 1900 to 58 million today. While the population of the United States has increased 100 per cent, daily newspaper circulation has gone up 415 per cent. And the reason? According to Mr. Jones: "Some of this was due to more general prosperity. Some of it came about because city newspapers circulate over wider territories. Some of it was due to the almost complete washout of illiteracy. But at least part of it was due *to an increase of public confidence in the product.*"

Whatever the cause, newspapers still lead the field and have been claiming that advertisers annually invest more money in newspaper space than in television, radio, magazines, and billboards combined. Newspaper publishers point in passing to the record amounts which television networks are now spending to advertise their programs in the daily press.

Magazines, another front contender among the print media, have, as their executives point out, a longer life than newspapers—a week in the case of weekly magazines, a month in the case of monthlies. This means that the magazine reader may encounter the advertiser's message as often as he turns to the magazine. Alfred Politz, a researcher in this field, has developed through detailed study this "repeat exposure" factor. Magazine advertising, he maintains, lives longer. "It has the marked advantage of *repeat* exposures. These can have the same effect as *repeated advertisements* without the additional cost." The advertiser bears all this in mind as he mulls over statistics which place the annual circulation of magazines in the United States at 183 million, or four copies to every household.

Radio's claim to the advertiser is that radio listening, and daily radio listening at that, is part of the American way of life. Despite dire predictions to the contrary, radio managed to adjust to the impact of television and today finds its popularity growing. As a medium of communication it is relatively ubiquitous. Statistics place radio in 95 per cent of the nation's homes, and in over 50 per cent of the nation's automobiles. Many of the 150 million sets in use can travel from room to room at home and accompany their owners to many outdoor pastimes. This element of flexibility ranks high in radio's interest to advertisers. Another element, the intimacy of the medium, ranks high too. The listener frequently feels that the message over the air comes personally to him. Although little homogeneity exists in the national population which consists of a variety of publics, the radio advertiser can, through the type of program he sponsors, select the particular segment of the public he wishes to reach.

Television's rapid growth in popularity marks it as the communication phenomenon of the century. Its antennae sprout from the roofs of rich and poor alike. By 1957 three quarters of all the nation's homes owned TV sets; today 88 per cent have them. Despite the high cost of TV sponsoring, advertisers who use this medium point to the proved impact on public attention and to the variety of appeals it can make. It can reach the viewer through the printed word, through the spoken word, through pictures (still or in action), through color, animation, and through sound effects.

Which medium shall the advertiser choose? He chooses the one or the ones best suited to his purpose. He knows that by the print media, by sound, and by sight and sound, he has the choice today of methods of communication unmatched in their range and in their potency in the long history of mankind.

How TV Programs Are "Rated"

Advertising agencies and sponsors of network programs put great faith in the findings of those research organizations which endeavor to gauge the amount of popular approval won by the various shows on the air.

Although there are a number of organizations which do research and various analysis jobs in broadcasting, three stand out as leaders in the field and are the ones whose "ratings" are of chief concern to the networks and the advertisers. They are Trendex, Nielsen, and "ARB"—the American Research Bureau.

Each produces a rating which is an estimate of the percentage of TV sets tuned to a given show. A rating of 20 means that a fifth of all sets are tuned in to the show in question; the other 80 per cent are either tuned in to other shows or are dark.

Trendex. This service telephones individuals whose names are picked at random from phone books while a particular program is in progress. It phones a total of 800 people in 15 cities—about one-third of the calls are made in New York—for each half hour the program is on. Each of the cities chosen has at least three stations competing simultaneously with network programs.

Actually this organization attempts to compare the popularity of television programs only during the first seven calendar days of each month. Programs on the air during the balance of the month—about three-quarters of all shows—are not taken into account. Trendex does not conceal the limitation of its method. It labels its report for what it is—the most popular shows in one week. But because its report is issued once a month, there is a tendency to interpret it as a barometer of success over the longer period. The findings are published one week after the analysis has been made.

Nielsen. The A. C. Nielsen Company, another major service that rates the popularity of TV shows, does check all programs. But its handicap is that the results are not announced until three weeks after a given show has left the air.

Nielsen attaches mechanical gadgets to TV sets in 850 homes, about 150 of them in New York. This sample is supposed to be a cross-section of the whole TV population. A film in the device records minute by minute the stations to which the set is tuned. After the films have been collected and analyzed, Nielsen is able to supply information as to when people tuned in and tuned out.

The American Research Bureau. ARB uses a nationwide sample of 2,800 people, some 375 of them in New York. These people keep diaries for a week out of each month, reporting various details about their viewing. ARB's strongest point is that it tells how many people watch and who they are—men, women, or children.

The New Public

Alert advertisers have become increasingly conscious that a sophisticated public actually exists. Whatever might have been true in the era of Phineas T. Barnum, a "sucker" is no longer being born every minute; the rate today is now much slower.

Straws in the wind all indicating the large army of sophisticated consumers serve to remind advertisers that it is in their self-interest to avoid the mistake of not giving the consumer credit for being an intelligent, thinking human being.

As Robert Alden has pointed out in the New York *Times* (February 21, 1960), "Advertisers should be reminded that in society they play a key role. They can shirk this role and bcome a static force, doing what is safe, hanging on to the coattails of an imaginary man-in-the-street or the apron strings of an imaginary woman-in-the-kitchen. Or they can play a leadership role, winning the loyalty of the intelligent people of the community and in the process of raising the tastes of society as a whole, stimulating the interests of the people and thus creating new markets in a culturally alert community."

23
The Field of Public Relations

Public Relations Develops—Public Relations at Work—Influencing
Public Opinion—Public Relations and Society—Something about
Propaganda

Many people frankly have difficulty in distinguishing
publicity from advertising and press agentry from public
relations. This difficulty is hardly the public's fault, for
the practitioners in these several fields have a way of
using terms in referring to their work which tend to
blur the lines of demarcation. Let us take each of
these words and phrases in turn and attempt to clear
up the general befuddlement.

Publicity we can define as the process of making
something known. It is as old as the first gesture of
announcement. It utilizes all existing media of communication—oral, written, pictorial. It makes known
what it wants through advertising, through press
agentry, and by means of pamphlets and billboards.
Publicity succeeds when it brings its information to its
desired public.

Advertising is the commercial phase of publicity.
Through paid announcements in the press, over the
radio, on television, on painted signs, or on the lowly
handbill, the advertiser endeavors to sell the articles or
beliefs which he wants sold.

Press agentry as a phrase covers the diversified and
sometimes frankly devious methods used by press
agents to secure publicity for their clients in one or all
of the mass media free, gratis, and for nothing. Press

agents are most familiarly associated with a Broadway or Holly-wood clientele, but their clients may be corporations, government departments, resorts, plays, books, theories, institutions, or individ-uals. Their resourcefulness and unorthodoxy, no doubt, led the New York *Times* to make the editorial comment that "press agentry is a profession whose subtle methods of approach are viewed by newspaper editors with a cold eye." When, however, the professional drum beaters for Broadway organized themselves as "New York Theatrical Press Agents" the same *Times* congratulated the group for the "frank and disarming fashion" in which they announced themselves.

Nothing could be more straightforward than the description of themselves put forth by the new organization. A [theatrical] press agent is defined as a person who handles legitimate attractions for theatrical producers, and who is responsible for "the publicizing and exploitation of such attractions."

No attempt is made here to describe the press agent as a person engaged in using the American drama to educate the American people to new social horizons. People nowadays who are not afraid to describe themselves as engaged in publicizing and exploiting deserve a Carnegie hero medal.

Public relations, the newest term of the four, describes an or-ganized system devised for the influencing of opinion. It utilizes when necessary all the skills and techniques of publicity, advertising, and press agentry toward this end, and it does this after careful investi-gation, thus giving rise to the "two-way communication" concept (see p. 334). Averill Houghton, public relations counsel, claims that opinion is formed by outside impressions.

The multiplicity and speed of these impressions through modern communications make it possible to achieve social changes in a few years which in the past would have taken generations or centuries.

Today the publicity man, the press agent, and the public rela-tions counsel control the news which newspapers get from very many important sources—whole fields of news. Much of the local and Washington news we read emanates from them, as does a sizeable percentage of what comes over the wire services. Papers and news syndicates alike have become more and more dependent on them. They constitute what a critic has called "the new journalism."

Public Relations Develops

Abraham Lincoln foreshadowed the inevitable development of public relations when he pointed out: "With public sentiment nothing can fail; without it, nothing can succeed. He who molds public opinion goes deeper than he who enacts statutes or pronouncements."

The advent of public relations as we construe that work today began after the turn of the twentieth century, when some of the railroads and other large corporations started to realize that unpopularity did not pay, and that something must be done to counteract the growing hostility of the public. Writers, chiefly newspapermen, were found to put the aims and the methods of these corporations in a favorable light before the public. A classic example is the work which the late Ivy Lee did in behalf of Standard Oil and the Rockefeller family. During World War I, the late George Creel used existing techniques and invented new ones to demonstrate through his Committee on Public Information the power of mass publicity when used to mold opinion.

Public relations has been called by its advocates "the control tower of modern society" and by its critics, "a menace to journalism." At this point, less biased definitions are in order.

Let the one fashioned by *Public Relations News* stand as authoritative:

Public Relations is the management function which evaluates public attitudes, identifies the policies and procedures of an individual or an organization with the public interest, and creates a program of action to earn public understanding and acceptance.

This definition facilitates our understanding as it highlights the three main functions of the professional counselor:
1. To study, analyze and evaluate public opinion.
2. To advise his client on the best ways of dealing with this ascertained climate of opinion.
3. To utilize his skill in the use of the communications media to

educate and influence the individuals who comprise the particular "public" he has studied and analysed.

Scott M. Cutlip and Allen H. Center in the second edition of their comprehensive textbook *Effective Public Relations* * feel that "the one term 'public relations' cannot be used to label both the *means* and *ends* without creating confusion." They claim that this confusion can be clarified in part if the term is restricted to describing "the planned effort to influence opinion through acceptable performance and two-way communication."

Edward I. Bernays, a long-time successful practitioner and an articulate commentator, calls the process of public relationships "the engineering of consent." His metaphor has real significance as it implies that bridges must be built between the public relations counselor and his various publics for that "two-way communication" which Messrs. Cutlip and Center emphasize.

The calling which puts these precepts into practice has been called by *Harper's* magazine "the fastest growing industry." It showed substantial development between the two great wars. But since World War II both the number of public relations firms and the number of men and women employed by them have increased rapidly enough to substantiate *Harper's* comment. At the outset of the 1960's upwards of 100,000 individuals worked in this calling. By 1970, according to reputable prophets, that figure will reach the 200,000 mark.

Public Relations at Work

Whether the size of a public relations outfit numbers one or one hundred individuals, it falls into one of two main categories:

1. It works as a department within an employing organization—an industry like General Motors, a social agency like The American Foundation for the Blind, Inc., a hospital, a university, a religious denomination.

2. It operates as an independent counseling firm.

---

* Scott M. Cutlip and Allen H. Center, *Effective Public Relations, second edition*, copyright 1958. Prentice-Hall, Inc.

Each of these two categories boasts its own unique advantages. The department works from within its organization and develops that inside information inevitable in such a relationship. It can pool and unite its various talents as a team, a team moreover that is always on the spot.

The independent counselor can claim objectivity. He can work for his client completely divorced from whatever office politics and prejudices which a department's close connection might well develop. In addition, the independent counselor has the possible advantage of greater mobility. He can operate for his client on a continent-wide or even a worldwide stage.

Whatever the type, the procedures of the public relations units follow parallel paths. Each assignment necessitates initial fact-finding and intensive research, for "public opinion" as a phrase covers many publics and many opinions. On the basis of valid information thus secured, the unit can plan its campaign, as military headquarters in wartime sets a timetable and marshals its resources to attack. In the case of the public relations unit, the "attack" puts the communications media to intelligent use. And just as headquarters, the smoke of battle past, calculates its gains and losses, so, in the final phase, public relations men evaluate the result of their efforts.

Influencing Public Opinion

It would be hard to find any comment on public relations which failed to announce the aim as the influencing of public opinion. Probably we can assume that the technique of influencing dates from prehistoric days when man began to communicate by gestures and uncouth sounds. It then as now had to do with the attempt to convince and with the attempt to persuade.

Theoretically, the process of convincing appeals to the mind with the object of getting its chain of reasoning accepted, while the process of persuading aims directly at the will, with the hope of getting action. If man were completely rational and governed by his mental processes, we should endeavor to convince him in order to win assent. But man follows his feelings and his prejudices quite as often and sometimes oftener than he follows the light of reason. Therefore in actual practice the arts of both conviction and persuasion blend to achieve the same purpose.

Earl Newson, an expert in both the theories and practices of influencing public opinion, has in two of his published addresses enunciated basic principles. Messrs. Cutlip and Center in their revised text, *Effectve Public Relations*, from which we have already quoted, have compiled these principles and to each have added their own effective paraphrase:

1. *Identification Principle.* People will ignore an idea, an opinion, a point of view unless they see clearly that it affects their personal fears or desires, hopes or aspirations.

Your message must be stated in terms of the interest of your audience.

2. *Action Principle.* People do not buy ideas separated from action—either action taken or about to be taken by the sponsor of the idea, or action which people themselves can conveniently take to prove the merit of the idea.

Unless a means of action is provided people, they tend to shrug off appeals to do things.

3. *Principle of Familiarity and Trust.* We the people buy ideas only from those we trust; we are influenced by, or adopt only those opinions or points of view put forward by individuals or corporations or institutions in whom we have confidence.

Unless the listener has confidence in the speaker he is not likely to listen or to believe.

4. *Clarity Principle.* The situation must be clear to us, not confusing. The thing we observe, read, see, or hear, the thing which produces our impressions, must be *clear*, not subject to several interpretations.

To communicate you must employ words, symbols, stereotypes that the receiver understands and comprehends.

This *clarity principle* stands out as of supreme importance for the journalistic writer. The most effective example of public relations that history records—the "selling" of Christianity to an antagonistic world—made striking use of it by putting across ideas in simple narratives "that the receiver understands and comprehends":

A sower went forth to sow . . . some seed fell by the wayside . . . some fell upon stony places . . . but others fell into good ground and brought forth fruit. The seed is the Word.

Success in public relations rests in no small measure on the skill with which the practitioner uses the methods and media of communication.

As he seeks to gain understanding rather than merely to attract attention, he as a rule tends more and more to leave *press agentry* to the showman.

As part of his job is to report his client's newsworthy activities, he makes constant use of *publicity*. Here is how public relations publicity worked in a given instance:

When a big hotel was wrongly rumored to be closing, the patronage naturally fell off. The management saw that denials would be useless; they would only spread and strengthen the rumor. A public relations counsel got the management to renew a long term contract with their internationally famous maître d'hôtel. The huge salary itself made news. The implication was obvious and it worked.

Because of the expense involved, *advertising* as a method of communication is used chiefly by the public relations departments or counselors of industrial and business concerns. The advantage of this method of communication is that the sponsor can choose his audience and present his message in his own words.

There is small need in this day and age to labor the effectiveness of the mass communications media—the press, the radio, television, motion pictures, *et al.* But it is interesting to note that despite the clamor of the newcomers, the newspaper, one of the first communicators in the field, maintains its old position of preeminence. The majority of American adults read a newspaper each day, and while the actual number of papers tends to shrink, the circulation of newspapers tends to grow. The skilled public relations expert understands

newspaper practice and newspaper reader habits, and strives to culti-
vate and extend his journalistic contacts.

Public Relations and Society

Even greater than the impact of public relations on journalism is
the impact of public relations on society at large. This has always
been so but never so apparent as now. When Bolingbroke employed
Nicholas Amherst as his press agent for warfare on Walpole, a small
edition of a tiny sheet was sufficient for it reached the handful of
men who made the public opinion of England at the time. When
Alexander Hamilton put the *Federalist* in the mind of America, he
did it through a little paper of possibly 1,500 circulation. Today
modern communications have shrunk the world to its present and
manageable size, and as Averill Houghton puts it "have given to
public relations something far swifter than the wings of the morning."

Even a short-memoried public can hardly forget what the art of
public relations allied with propaganda as skillfully practiced by
Hitler and Goebbels achieved in record time. It was only sixteen
years that lay between the Beer Hall Putsch in Munich and the
beginning of World War II in 1939. And it can be argued that
public relations organized against them brought about their downfall
and that of their Third Reich. It is in this play and counterplay
of public relations that both the social significance of the system
and our safety would seem to lie.

Something About Propaganda

From all of this we can clearly see the close relationship which
exists between public relations and propaganda. Although the word
propaganda has gathered unpleasant connotations around it, it is a
perfectly good word and stands for a process neither good nor bad
in itself but one that must be judged by its source, its purposes, and
its results.

There are as many definitions of propaganda as there are social scientists extant to concoct them. To one it is "the effort to spread a pattern of behavior"; to another it appears "a concerted scheme for the promotion of a doctrine or practice"; to yet another it is "the technique of influencing human action by the manipulation of representations"—all contributing in one form or another to "the art of making up the other man's mind for him."

In a more general way, we can call propaganda "any attempt to persuade anyone to a belief or to a form of action. Limiting it to a journalistic concept, propaganda could well become "language aimed at large masses to influence mass attitudes on controversial issues."

Of course these educational processes to influence opinion are as old as civilization and older. It is in the adroit use of the communications media toward that end that stands as a fairly recent development.

Before the Christian Era, Julius Caesar used the existing journalism of his time to develop a favorable attitude toward himself in the public mind. He made sure that the *Acta Diurna*, posted each day in the Forum, would give him a fine spread when he refused the crown which Marc Anthony thrice offered to him. He is even reported to have fired an editor who failed to keep the name Julius Caesar sufficiently before the public's eye.

His successor, Augustus, used the same publication to further his crusade against race suicide. In it he publicized and praised those Romans blessed with large families.

Today propaganda confronts the individual at every turn. He gets it in his newspapers, in his magazines, and in his books. He hears it in speeches and sermons, and over the air in commentaries and interviews. He sees and hears it on television, on the motion picture screen, and from the stage.

In an article, "The Analysis of Propaganda: A Clinical Study," in the *American Journal of Sociology* (September 1945), Alfred Mc-Clung Lee analyzed and classified many of the important propaganda appeals.

In addition to Adolf Hitler's successful concept—the bigger the lie and the more frequently it is repeated, the greater the likelihood of its being believed—there exist a number of well-established propaganda devices and practices. Here are a few of the main ones, the effectiveness of which have been amply proved.

Bandwagon. Everyone likes to be on the winning side. Propaganda uses the "get-on-the-bandwagon" appeal to stampede individual judgment.

Transfer. The speaker with a framed picture of a national hero behind him or the national flag on a staff by his side tries to channel the emotion aroused by these symbols toward the acceptance of his ideas.

Card stacking. This device shuffles lies, half-truths, evasions, innuendoes, overemphasis, understatement all together like cards in a pack. If the truth is on any of the cards dealt, it would take more than human powers to discover it.

Testimonial. Here the pet device of the advertiser is used to sell ideas. The suggestion that because someone of note uses or endorses a particular product gives place to the appeal: "So and So holds this idea, why don't you?"

"Plain folks." In homespun style the propagandist makes it clear that he is just "one of the folks"—oh so honest and free from guile.

Glittering generalities. This technique attaches broad ideals to particular situations in a high-sounding but hazy way which gains its effect even though it won't stand up to critical examination.

Name-calling. This device is probably the oldest of the lot. It attaches a bad name to the adversary and, of course, a good name to the cause or person championed.

24
The "Morgue" and Reference Library

The Newspaper Morgue—Its Function and Value—The Working Journalist's Shelf of Reference Books

Some writers have what we can call card-index minds. That is, they have a great deal of accurate information filed away in the vast deeps of their retentive memories. But even they, along with the many writers not so blessed, have frequent occasion to seek out an exact fact, a definition, a date, a quotation and to endeavor to find what they are after in the shortest possible time.

It has long been said that a large part of the mastery of knowledge in modern times is acquaintance with the sources of information. It is knowing where to look. More and more, as the interests of the modern world expand and take on complexity, scholarship and information are bound to assume the character of index-scholarship and index-information.

The writer attached to a modern newspaper has at his disposal the immense resources of his paper's "morgue" and his paper's reference library, and on the larger papers, he has a trained corps of librarians to help him. All newspaper morgues look much alike. They boast row after row of steel cabinets in which are filed away hundreds of thousands and sometimes a million or more newspaper and magazine clippings. Each morgue has three basic subdivisions: the "clips" filed under PERSONS; those filed under SUBJECT;

341

and the photographs and prints under PICTURES. Each day the morgue workers clip and file, combing not only their own paper but the leading papers of the country and of the world. The result of their work is a repository of invaluable up-to-the-minute as well as background information, much of it not yet between the covers of books and in its comprehensiveness unattainable in any other way.

In most newspaper offices the reference library proper adjoins the morgue and forms part of it. Its shelves have the standard books of reference and, in addition, works of biography, history, science and invention, and frequently a special section allotted to maps. More shelves house the thousands of bound reports from the various governmental agencies (federal, state and municipal), from colleges, and from charitable and business organizations. In the old days bound volumes of the newspaper itself from its earliest date of publication took up considerable space. Today, these newspaper files photographed on microfilm are far less bulky and far more readily accessible.

The free-lance writer who works at home must depend on his own bookshelves and his own miniature morgue and when they are found wanting, on the public library. The newspaper, the home, and the library have many of the same books. They are the standard reference works to which the general public and the journalist alike turn for information.

Broadly classified, the usual subjects inquired about in the public libraries of our great cities fall into five categories: current events, contests, household problems, people and places, curiosities. And the chief books or classes of reference books which the librarians consult to satisfy these questioners include (1) dictionaries, with *Webster's New International* most frequently turned to; (2) encyclopedias, with the *Britannica* most in demand; (3) almanacs, with the *World Almanac* in the lead; (4) indexes such as the H. W. Wilson Company's *Readers' Guide to Periodical Literature,* and the *New York Times Index*; (5) biographical sources, with *Who's Who in America* and *Current Biography* leading.

For years the librarian's own best friend has been "Mudge," alias *Guide to Reference Books* by Isadore Gilbert Mudge. Now the new editions of the same opus are edited by Constance M. Winchell. The free-lancer and the layman can find it in all libraries and will discover that it points the way to the sources of information sought.

Let us take up some of the leading reference books in the order of the categories just mentioned for the sound reason that what interests the general public must interest the writer who seeks to attract and serve that public. Many of these books may well find a place on any working writer's personal shelf.

1. **Dictionaries.** A good dictionary stands out as a "must" when it comes to reference books. What are its uses? First, to check spelling. That is the chief use which both specialist and layman make of their dictionaries. Second, they turn to it as a guide to the meaning of words. To define the exact meaning of a word, without using that word itself or some compound of it, is one of the hardest things we can be called upon to do. Here the dictionary comes to our aid. Third, all good dictionaries gives etymologies which break up the word into its component parts and indicate the original meaning. A knowledge of the original elements gives the word a tangible and an imaginative quality which enables us to use the word with a new definiteness of application. Fourth, grammatical information. Transitive or intransitive? The dictionary will tell us. Fifth, usage. If our word appears in the dictionary without annotation we know it satisfies the requirements of formal composition. If we find it followed in parenthesis by the term "obsolete," we know the word's a dead one. Similarly such comments as archaic, dialectic, poetic, or scientific give us a clue to the word's status. Sixth, idiom. Every language has its little ways, its peculiar habits of associating words. These often have no basis in logic and cannot be reasoned about. We just have to know. Does one, for instance, inveigh upon or inveigh against? If in doubt, the dictionary will tell you that you inveigh against. Finally, we can note that the wealth of quotation which the larger dictionaries give to show the word in its various literary settings will help us to appreciate the word's connotations— the remoter intellectual and emotional associations which it has gathered around itself in the course of the years.

Dictionaries are usually classed by the size of their vocabularies, by the number of actual words they list. The largest of the "un-abridged" run to over 400,000 entries. Into this category fall *Webster's New International* and Funk and Wagnalls' *New Standard.* Next come the large "abridged" dictionaries which boast some 200,000 entries or more, such as the American *New Century* and the British *Shorter Oxford.*

For the writer's table, the so-called college or adult dictionaries serve most purposes. Here we can list *Webster's Collegiate,* the Random House *American College Dictionary,* the *Macmillan Modern,* the Funk and Wagnalls' *Practical Standard* and the Thorndike-Barnhart *Comprehensive Desk Dictionary.* In the bargain department, the Random House *American Everyday Dictionary* based on the *American College Dictionary* is considered the best on the market at its low price.

2. Encyclopedias. The value of these huge compendiums of information is so obvious that it needs no stressing. Their object and their practice is to summarize in a systematic way all knowledge that is considered significant to mankind. All libraries have one or other of the leading encyclopedias available, and many writers find the one volume abridgements readily helpful. The majority arrange their material alphabetically from A to Z with authoritative articles on each subject. Encyclopedias are classed not so much by size as by price. The comprehensive *Americana* and *Britannica* range from $150 up; in the $50 to $100 group, come the *American Peoples'* and the *National,* while in the one-volume class (priced around $25) we have the *Columbia* and the *Lincoln Library.*

3. Almanacs. Although one may not be able to afford an encyclopedia for home use, everyone will find that the latest edition of the almanac is within economic range. If the almanac he chooses happens to be the *World Almanac,* he knows that he has the reference book most widely used in newspaper offices. A legend persists that the book most frequently turned to is the Holy Bible, but fact insists that the *World Almanac* has the edge on Holy Writ. Started in 1885 by the old New York *World,* the almanac is now continued by the *World-Telegram and The Sun,* and it stands out as the foremost source book in the country where facts and figures about the world and its inhabitants are brought up to date every year. No other reference book offers so handy a coverage of so many diverse items. Where else, it has been asked, could you find in a single volume:

The latest election returns.

The weight of the human liver.

The area and populations of all the countries on earth.

The birthplaces of top-ranking movie stars.

The Preakness winners.

The number of acres of public lands in the U.S.A.

How many cups make a quart?

Some features, still retained, link this volume with the farmers' almanacs of earlier days. Some of these features are the weather and astronomical data, which are so precise that pilots have been known to chart their courses by them; the listings of holidays and festivals; the perpetual calendar; the Ten Commandments and the Apostles' Creed. Of outstanding importance is the detail given on the federal government and its departments; on the states and the leading municipalities; on the neighboring countries, Canada and Mexico; on the year's scientific developments; on religious denominations and charitable benefactions; on the United Nations; atomic research and sports, trade, and education.

As a recent runner-up in the same category comes the *Information Please Almanac*. This book mixes fun with its facts and makes a point of having its leading surveys written and signed by specialists. Thus the theatre record of the year bears the by-line of a noted drama critic, and the sports roundup that of a famous commentator in that field. Its editorial policy is also to include each year what amounts to a book-length section on some leading current problem. Both almanacs have good indexes and sell at approximately the same price.

4. Indexes. It is well to stress the value of a good index. In a newspaper office where every second is often precious, the worth of an index which points with precision to the fact sought is beyond rubies. Of paramount importance in this field is the *New York Times Index*, which was first started by that paper in 1913. It came out

first as a quarterly; later in 1930, it appeared in monthly issues. Today the nine-pound volume issued annually represents the accumulated harvest of the entire year. Its fullest usefulness is, of course, in connection with the files of the New York *Times* whose contents it summarizes, classifies and cross-indexes every day of the year. But the volume because of its wealth of dates and succinct but sufficient identification of topics can serve just as well as a guide to the files of any newspaper. As a matter of fact, this index's information is so complete that a researcher will frequently find sufficient data to satisfy him without recourse to the files.

5. **Biographical reference.** The greatest study and certainly the greatest interest of mankind is man. Men had not been six generations on the earth, according to the Scriptures, before they were divided vocationally. From that source we learn that Lamech's three sons—Jabel, Jubel and Tubal—were respectively the fathers of cattlemen, musicians and artificers in brass and iron. This remote record becomes the prototype of the modern *Who's Who.* Today this identification by occupation continues with certain incidental qualifications.

Naturally the most frequently referred to biographical source on this continent is *Who's Who in America.* James M. Cain, the author, calls it "one of the most valuable books published," and states, "I use it ten times more than any book except possibly the big Webster Dictionary." Why? Well, this comprehensive work, which the A. N. Marquis Company of Chicago first started in 1899, contains not only the condensed biographies of some 50,000 varieties of Americans, but general information as to the antecedents and educational advantages of those named in it. The standards of admission to the book divide the eligibles into two classes: first, those selected because of special prominence and second, those included by reason of their official position, civil, military, naval, etc.

Beyond the specific utility of such a book in supplying names and addresses and essential facts, it furnishes material for generalization regarding the different kinds of education and the influence of environment, heredity, and occupation. Not only the novelist but the feature writer can strike a paying vein in its pages, and the hurried reporter may sometimes glean at a glance the help he needs for a sudden interview.

The parent to this whole group is the British *Who's Who*. Published in this country as well as in London, this book takes not just the United Kingdom but the whole world as its parish, and accordingly its great value lies in its comprehensiveness. The really prominent in any country on the map crop up for biographical treatment in this mine of interesting, curious and entertaining information.

The popularity and usefulness of this type of book have led to the publication of any number of specialized volumes such as *Who's Who in Canada, Who's Who in New York* and who's who in the various professions and occupations, such as the *Who's Who of Commerce and Industry*.

"Who's Who" in Society comes out in New York and in some other cities as *The Social Register*. These volumes give little biographical data but keep the society editors of the various papers up to date on the matrimonial alliances of those included.

More authentic in their social importance and far more interesting by reason of the careful and accurate information recorded are *Burke's Peerage* and *Debrett's Peerage*. These listings of titled Britons were used in former years in connection with international marriages. Today, they add color and background to the many articles with which the press strives to meet the insatiable interest of Americans in the British Royal Family. For instance, the new edition of *Burke's Peerage* traces the family tree of the present monarch back in detail to Egbert, Ruler of Britain in 825. These genealogical annuals also give picturesque detail to the occasional human interest stories surrounding American claimants to ancient stately honors. The larger libraries will have on their shelves *The Complete Peerage*. When the compilers of this bulky book, in combing old documents, came upon family superstitions and legends, a meaty quote in an old letter, a good anecdote or bit of folklore, they had the generosity to include their discoveries as elaborations of their factual material or as footnotes. The feature writer and the fiction writer should not pass this human treasury by. *The Complete Peerage*, for instance, gives the only fairly complete list of the illegitimate children of Charles II. It names fourteen.

In former years the supreme blue book of all was the *Almanach de Gotha*, the hereditary Bible of European aristocracy. Its last edition came out between the two world wars and because of the marked decline in numbers, fortune, and prestige of its clientele, it is doubtful if this blue book will survive the modern age. But in its day it led the field and was to the other peerages, as a wit put it, "as the New York Social Register is to the more comprehensive democracy of the phone book."

Back again on the broad plain of democracy, we can round out this biographical category by listing two useful yearbooks, the *Congressional Directory*, which gives us the names, addresses and committee assignments of the members of both houses of Congress, and the *Statesman's Yearbook*, which is a standard reference book on the nations of the world.

6. Quotations. From "Who's Who" it's a logical step to "Who said what and when and how?" Newspapermen and writers generally have long found the answers to these questions—from 1855 to be exact—in *Bartlett's Familiar Quotations*. The latest edition of this famous reference book has been edited by Christopher Morley and Louella D. Everett, and they have endowed it with greater bulk and inclusiveness. There are nearly twice as many quotations here as in the volume which came out in 1914. Following John Bartlett's original practice, the new editors arrange the quotations chronologically by authors. The cross-indexing is richer than in the earlier editions, and the preface by Christopher Morley forms a little essay in itself and suggests the use of *Bartlett's Familiar Quotations* for reading as well as reference.

Although akin in type, Burton Stevenson's *Home Book of Quotations* is unlike in format. Mr. Stevenson has arranged the quotations for his book by subjects, with the utmost care and exhaustiveness. The latest edition of this *Home Book of Quotations* not only contains about a thousand additional selections but has a greatly enlarged concordance index. It offers a new richness of interest in the volume's appendix where political quotations are traced to their sources, and the refrains of popular songs fill sixteen pages of reminiscent rhythm. The editor also gives brief biographical notes in his author's index.

7. **Atlases.** The first lesson war teaches is the geography lesson, with the result that the first job of atlas and gazetteer publishers is to scrap the old maps which war makes obsolete and catch up with history and the subsequent changes. The new name for the Rand-McNally Atlas indicates an altered conception in line with the times. It is now called the *Rand-McNally Cosmopolitan World Atlas.* It is "cosmopolitan" where it used to be "commercial." Its maps are all newly drawn and represent a great advance in American map making. Specifically the reporter or free-lancer finds here 117 pages of maps, 27 pages of "comparative" or "distribution" maps (world climate, vegetation, trade routes, population, and so on) and other varied information of varying utility. The all-in-one index which includes all names on all maps goes far to make this atlas a real work of reference. In addition, the atlas boasts some 57 pages of supplementary material which includes information on the earth and the solar system; steamship and air distances; climatic and economic tables for the United States and the world; and an historical gazetteer of geographical names. Of similar scope and size in the same field we have the *American Oxford Atlas* which supplies 72 pages of maps (with greater emphasis than before on North America, since this is specifically an "American" edition), 24 pages of distribution maps and 96 pages of gazetteer.

There can be few reference libraries of any account that fail to find room on their shelves for at least some of the famous little red books turned out by the house of Baedeker. Karl Baedeker, the practical traveller, keeping little notebooks, started it all in 1827 with his travel book on the Rhine. Since then the Baedeker guides, still compiled by the same family, have enlightened the tourist on all sections of the European continent. Although printed originally in German, there have been English editions of these guides since 1864. They all boast excellent maps, accurate information, and succinct description. They are used constantly in newspaper offices to augment when necessary scanty details cabled in by correspondents.

8. Directories. From the many entries which could go under this heading, we select but one, Ayer's *Directory of Newspapers and Periodicals*. Here the reporter or author will find complete lists of all daily and weekly journals in the United States and in Canada, together with the names of their chief personnel. In addition, the directory lists the thousands of trade journals, many of which make excellent markets for free-lance manuscripts.

9. Holy Bible. Last on this list and yet first in intrinsic importance comes the Book of Books. Among the versions of the Bible kept constantly for reference in newspaper offices and on writers' desks throughout the country, that known as the King James Version holds the foremost place. Translated from its original sources at the end of the great Elizabethan period when the English tongue itself had reached a peak which it has not since equalled, the language of this version—with its sonorousness and simplicity—has commended itself for generations to mankind. Its pithy prose has become part of the fabric of our everyday speech. Constantly we quote from the Bible and often without realizing the source:

> Highway and hedges.
> Bite the dust.
> The root of all evil.
> The sweat of his brow.

The list is long and meaty. For hundreds of years writers have shaped their written and spoken style on the Holy Bible.

In addition to using the Bible as a source of quotation, we also find in it a constant field of allusion. Although our average reader no longer reads the epics of Greece and Rome and knows little of classic myths, he still has a certain familiarity with the histories, dramas, poetry, and parables of the Old and New Testaments. Adam and Eve, Samson and Delilah, David and Bathsheba, Solomon and his wisdom and wives, the Prodigal Son, the Good Samaritan still kindle gleams of recognition in his mind.

It is because speakers, writers, and commentators so frequently quote from the Bible or base their allusions on it, that copyreaders and editors have constantly to keep the Bible near at hand to check the accuracy of these borrowings. Another version kept for reference is the Douay, which is used by Roman Catholic speakers and writers.

It is conceivable that in a generation's time the writer and speaker may be quoting the phraseology of the Revised Standard Version of the Bible, published in 1952, instead of that of the King James Version. This is the sixth authorized version of the Bible in English, and the authorization comes this time from the National Council of the Churches of Christ in the United States of America, which represents thirty Protestant and Eastern Orthodox denominations.

The differences in the two versions are primarily those of time. The men who gave the world the King James Bible in 1611 were doing what the twentieth century revisers have done. They were translating the Bible in the terms of their own seventeenth century idiom so that the people of that age would be able to read and understand the Scriptures.

It is because 341 years can make a great difference in a living language that a committee of Protestant scholars, after fifteen years of effort, have achieved this monumental revision, spurred on by the conviction that its modern language and more accurate translation would lead to a greater understanding of the Bible.

Whether or not the contemporary cadences will commend themselves as forcefully or as universally as have those of the King James Version, "the noblest monument of English prose," remains a question for the future to answer.

We can well couple with the Bible as a reference source, the Book of Common Prayer. In it we find that the old prayers and services of the early church were translated into English in the reign of Edward VI who was the young half-brother of the great Queen Elizabeth. Although in use here by one denomination, the Protestant Episcopal Church, the prayer book contains the traditional Marriage Service and that for the Burial of the Dead on which most denominations base their rituals. Newsmen and fiction writers alike have occasion to turn to the prayer book when the characters with whom they deal choose to say—"to have and to hold—for better or for worse—for richer for poorer—in sickness and in health—to love and to cherish—till death do us part."

Index